SEEING THE BIGGER PICTURE

Politics
Media &
Popular Culture

David A. Schultz, *General Editor*

Vol. 9

PETER LANG
New York • Washington, D.C./Baltimore • Bern
Frankfurt am Main • Berlin • Brussels • Vienna • Oxford

Mark Sachleben
& Kevan M. Yenerall

SEEING THE BIGGER PICTURE

Understanding Politics Through Film & Television

PETER LANG

New York • Washington, D.C./Baltimore • Bern
Frankfurt am Main • Berlin • Brussels • Vienna • Oxford

Library of Congress Cataloging-in-Publication Data

Sachleben, Mark.
Seeing the bigger picture: understanding politics through film and
television / Mark Sachleben, Kevan M. Yenerall.
p. cm. — (Politics, media, and popular culture; vol. 9)
Includes bibliographical references.
Filmography: p.
1. Politics in motion pictures. 2. Motion pictures—Political aspects—United
States. 3. Television and politics—United States. I. Yenerall, Kevan M. II. Title.
III. Politics, media & popular culture ; v. 9.
PN1995.9.P6S14   791.43'658—dc21   2003006621
ISBN 0-8204-6248-9 (paperback)
ISBN 0-8204- 7144-5 (hardcover)
ISSN 1094-6225

Bibliographic information published by **Die Deutsche Bibliothek.**
Die Deutsche Bibliothek lists this publication in the "Deutsche
Nationalbibliografie"; detailed bibliographic data is available
on the Internet at http://dnb.ddb.de/.

Cover design by Joni Holst

The paper in this book meets the guidelines for permanence and durability
of the Committee on Production Guidelines for Book Longevity
of the Council of Library Resources.

Acknowledgments

It has been often said that any book is a collective effort: there are many people behind the scenes who do not have their names affixed in the author's space. This could not be truer with *Seeing the Bigger Picture*. We wish to express our collective gratitude to the following individuals for their support, cooperation, and encouragement during the completion of this project. Given our passion for politics and film, it has been a labor of love.

We have been assisted along the way by several people and we wish to formally thank them now: Christopher S. Kelley, for being a good friend, helping to get this project launched, and for allowing both Kevan and Mark to bounce ideas off him; Ernest Giglio, who offered sage advice and inspiration; David Schultz, Phyllis Korper, and everyone at Peter Lang, for their patient help and insight; Christina Baumgartel, Kristen Hallagan, Estella Wilkinson, and Lana McClune for their generosity and assistance with the filmography; Brent Heminger, who selflessly offered research assistance and insight; Andrew Dudas, for his technical assistance and for allowing us to briefly use his wedding reception to hash out a few ideas; Dotti Pierson, Oliver Funk, Mark Morris, Kris Pence, Ryan Barilleaux, and everyone at the Department of Political Science at Miami University and the PSSP Department at Clarion University who have offered their input, support, comments and encouragement; and to all those unnamed who have helped us through this project, we thank you from the bottom of our heart.

Mark Sachleben wishes to thank . . .

Clearly there are many people to thank: First and foremost, my wife Angela, who has been a constant source of support and help. I would especially like to thank my parents as well, who have been very supportive in all my endeavors. My gratitude also goes to my students at Miami University and Antioch College for watching some of these movies and providing comments; their help was invaluable. Also, to the departments of Political Science at Miami University and of Government and History at Western New England College for their support. My thanks also to several people who have offered support and encouragement throughout this process, have encouraged my interest in both film and politics, and have been a source of inspiration as well: Richard and Patricia Smith, Allen Mills, Louise Gibson, and several (unnamed) people at the Great Lakes Cinephiles Society for their input. Finally thanks should go to Cubby and Jelly, who have provided me with companionship, and who have reminded me what is really important: paying attention to them.

Kevan Yenerall wishes to thank . . .

My friends, family, students, and colleagues who have of-
fered encouragement, understanding, feedback, and old-
fashioned camaraderie along the way, especially: my father,
Joseph D. Yenerall; Sylvia Stalker; my PS 302 "Politics and
Film" students; Bob Girvan, Phil Terman, Patrick McGreevy,
Herb Luthin, Julia Aaron, Brian Dunn, Todd Pfannestiel,
Chris McCarrick, Bill Miller, Clyde Brown, Stan Green, Steve
Johnson, Pat Dunham, Ed Carroll, Tim Colbert, Maryrose
Bendel, John E. Lane, Jr., assorted members of the Red Mas-
quer Nation, and any other kind souls and kindred spirits
roaming in and out of my life, or Founders Hall, who have
voiced their support and helped ease, or at least *understand,*
this glorious burden. This is also an appropriate occasion to
sing the praises of Professor Richard Benzinger's film
classes at Duquesne University. "American Film of the
1950s" on Wednesday nights, an intellectual rite of passage
not to be missed.

Finally, an immeasurable debt is owed to my grandparents, Joseph and Mary Ellen Yenerall, who were the first to
seriously spark my interest in citizenship, politics, and public service. Their decency, spirit, and permanence are sorely
missed. When I was six, grandma would give me a silver
dollar for repeating, in order, the 39 presidents (thank you
1976 World Book Encyclopedias). Sometimes Chester A. Arthur or Rutherford B. Hayes would trip me up, but I usually
managed to get by just fine. At age eight, I went with my
grandparents to deliver political literature to neighborhood
houses, the first of many quixotic crusades in the realm of
politics (some things never change).

Through the years I spent an enormous amount of time
at their home at 609 Warden Street, in Irwin, Pennsylvania,
and much of that time was spent talking about public affairs. Thanks to the many party dinners, benefits, and pic-
nics we attended together, I was able to see, hear, and

sometimes meet some of the major national political leaders of the day. My grandfather, a laborer at the East Pittsburgh Westinghouse plant, was not suited for a life of retirement—he loved interaction, conversation, and service far too much. Therefore, nearly immediately after retiring from Westinghouse, he was rewarded for his many years of local party committee work and took a job as tipstaff at the county courthouse in his hometown of Greensburg. When my grandfather suffered a debilitating stroke in October 1995, it was in an elevator at the Westmoreland County Courthouse, where he went to work, day in and day out, until he was 80 years of age. My grandma, also involved with local party politics with my grandfather, would often tell me that "one day you'll grow up to be president." Their enthusiasm and belief in the nobility of service and citizenship—and the profound example of their basic goodness and decency—are not lost on me. I miss them dearly, and hope that, in some small manner, this book, my work, and my life stand as a testament and tribute to their lives and love. But they are never far away: I see them, as Bob Dylan sings, "in the sky above/ in the tall grass/ in the ones I love."

Image Sources

Absolute Power
  Source: poster (authors' collection)
  Copyright 1997 Columbia Pictures Corporation

Air Force One
  Source: poster (authors' collection)
  Copyright 1997 Columbia Pictures Corporation

"All in the Family"
  Source: photographs (authors' copy)
  "All in the Family 20th Anniversary" publicity shot,
  copyright 1991, Columbia TriStar Home Video, Act III
  Television and Columbia Pictures.

All the President's Men
   Source: lobby card (authors' collection)
   Copyright 1976 Warner Bros., Inc.

Bob Roberts
   Source: poster (authors' collection)
   Bob Roberts copyright 1992 Miramax Films and
   Polygram/Working Title

Canadian Bacon
   Source: poster (authors' collection)
   Copyright 1995 Dog Eat Dog Films

Fall of the Romanoffs
   Source: advertisement in the *New York Times,* September
   16, 1917

Great Dictator
   Source: image from authors' collection
   Copyright 1958 United Artists Corporation

In the Line of Fire
   Source: poster (authors' collection)
   Copyright 1992 Columbia Pictures and Castle Rock
   Entertainment

Invasion of the Body Snatchers
   Source: photographs (authors' copy)
   Copyright 1956 Republic Pictures

The Kaiser, Beast of Berlin
   Advertisement from the *Chicago Tribune,* March 1918

Network
   Source: lobby card (authors' collection)
   Copyright 1976 MGM and National Screen Service
   Corporation

On the Beach
   Source: image from authors' collection
   Copyright 1959 United Artists Corporation

Primary Colors
   Source: poster (authors' collection)
   Copyright 1998 MCA/Universal Pictures

Seven Days in May
   Source: lobby card (authors' collection)
   Copyright 1963 Joel Productions, Inc., and Paramount
   Pictures

 "The Simpsons"
   Source: Still photograph (authors' collection)
   The Simpsons, copyright 1989–2003 Twentieth Century
   Fox

Photograph of Alfred Hitchcock
   Image from authors' collection

CHAPTER 1

Introduction

We love movies. Not only the authors (of course we do), but people in general. Film is the most popular art form and television is one of the most popular forms of entertainment in the world. Film and television provide millions with common frames of reference—whether it involves life, death, sex, work, religion, or politics. In a culture such as ours, communication among people often relies on quotes, scenes, and anecdotes from popular films and television shows to foster ideas and meanings. Consider Homer Simpson in the United States and many societies around the world. The bumbling, kindhearted patriarch has become synonymous with his famous "d'oh!" Using the utterance "d'oh!" for many in our society now refers to a boneheaded mistake or misstep that reflects a general lack of common sense or intelligence.

Our hope in writing this book is to tap into the appeal of movies and television to raise some interest in the world of politics and to provide some examples of contemporary political debates. One of the troubling aspects of our society over the past fifty years or so is the citizenry's declining interest in politics. In a political system where citizens are supposed to be informed and engaged in politics in order to participate in democratic governance, there is an apparent apathy among people to the ideas, institutions, and debates in politics. Many scholars have written extensively about waning civic involvement and the disintegration of institutions necessary to revitalize our communities, discourse, and politics. Moreover, voter turnout in the United States, which is the lowest among industrialized democracies, is on a 40-year decline. There are many reasons why these dynamics have occurred—but our aim is to make politics more accessible and hopefully to make it more interesting.

The plan of this book is to survey some significant issues in politics across a spectrum of fields in political science. What this means is that there are a number of political issues that are not covered by this book, but we hopefully raise a diverse array of concerns and questions so that you will be able to make links to other political issues that you may be interested in. In calling this book *Seeing the Bigger Picture,* we are asking the audience to see beyond the story, film, and television clip. We encourage the readers to become a critical audience and ask the following questions: *What are the messages behind these films? How might they help us understand and explain the governing institutions, political dynamics, and critical debates that shape the complex world in which we live?*

The book discusses and describes a diverse array of films and television shows. By diverse, we mean that the book is not limited to the discussion of films from a particular genre, country, or time. We see this as important for a number of reasons, but two are worth mentioning here. First, moving images have the ability to transport the audience to a number of different times and places. By examining films and television shows that are not limited to a single place and time, it allows us to examine issues from a number of different standpoints. Second, films from different time periods allow the audience to see how contemporary thinking on certain subjects has evolved. We should not make the mistake in thinking that all films and television shows have represented mainstream public opinion; but knowing that a certain film was popular at a certain time allows us to assume that the message of the film perhaps resonated with audiences.

Using a diversity of films does present some problems, however. Popular culture seems to crave what is new and what is current. It is not very often that films that are more than a couple of years old hang around on the video store shelf. In the United States particularly, since most Americans do not deal with languages other than English on a regular basis there is a great reluctance to engage in films that are shot in languages other than English. Hence access to foreign language films, particularly outside major metropolitan areas, is often difficult. Nevertheless, the movies in this book are generally available if you are willing to look.[1]

Politics and Film?

Logic would seem to dictate that, in order to begin a cogent discussion of how film and television can potentially educate, provide context, and spur debate in the political arena, we must first determine what makes a film "political." However, the object of *Seeing the Bigger Picture* is not to define political film. Others—notably Michael Genovese and Ernest Giglio—have already traveled this intellectual terrain and have provided an enlightened, solid foundation for students and scholars alike.[2] Genovese's framework, for example, suggests that a political film must meet one or more of the following requirements in order to be included in the political film genre:

- the film serves as a vehicle for international propaganda
- the film's major intention is to bring about political change
- the film is designed to support the existing economic, political, and social system[3]

Giglio builds on this foundation by offering additional—and alternative—qualifications (i.e., intent and effect), but ultimately suggests that, despite our best intentions to be systematic in our study of politics and film, the audience's diverse interpretations may make any exact, unambiguous definition unattainable. Indeed, the following chapters will consider a number of films, television clips and animated shorts that have heretofore not been deemed explicitly (or perhaps even implicitly) political.

Therefore the aim of this book is to not necessarily to examine strictly political films *per se,* but to use *all* kinds of films to demonstrate concepts and topics in politics. For example, it is difficult to classify the classic Bugs Bunny–Elmer Fudd cartoons of the 1950s as political films. But we will examine one of these films because it helps to reveal some important concepts. In that sense, the book omits or scarcely discusses some of the most famous political films ever made in favor of using a wide variety of films to access key topics and debates.

Different Films–Different Messages?

A common complaint for many people is that films sometimes look old and antique. In an age of DVDs, stadium seating theatres, and digital surround sound this grievance is understandable. Many of us are unaccustomed to viewing other types of films. We, the authors, ask you to make an effort at seeing some of these films. Once you have become familiar with different mediums and styles from various eras we think that you will appreciate the differences. It is also worth mentioning some of the history behind these different types of films.

Many, particularly younger people, have complained that they do not like black and white films. It is true that prior to 1950 or so most films were black and white, and afterwards most films were filmed in color. Television programs sometimes continued in black and white into the later 1960s. Yet, color techniques were widely available to filmmakers from almost the very inception of the medium in the 1890s. (Color television was slow in coming because of the cost of color television sets for the public.) Films like *Nothing Sacred* (1937) and *Gone with the Wind* (1939) were shot in color. However, the technology remained expensive and World War II necessitated that cost be minimized wherever possible in order to support the war effort.

Yet after the war, there continued to be a number of black and white films. Often this was the choice of the director, the person in charge of actually completing the film, rather than an economic choice. A particularly popular genre of the late 1940s was *film noir*. Literally French for "black film," film noir was designed to capture the darkness of life, portraying the darker sides, hidden temptations, and appetites among people. Therefore, it seemed a logical choice for many directors to use black and white photography to help accentuate the darkness of their subject. Black and white photography is still used in film on various occasions. Directors who are usually considered artistically inspired have used black and white films to create dramatic effects. Woody Allen used black and white photography in *Manhattan* (1979) and *Stardust Memories* (1980); Martin Scorsese depicted the world of boxer Jake La Motta in black and white in the film *Raging Bull* (1980); and, director Gary Ross used black and white photography mixed with color techniques as part of the narrative in the film *Pleasantville* (1998). Joel and Ethan Coen even revisited the classic *film noir* genre with their stylish black and white epic *The Man Who Wasn't There* (2001).

Going even farther back in time, there was a period when films had no spoken words. Now commonly known as "silent films," most of the time "silent films" were neither silent nor usually black and white. Silent films were almost always accompanied by music in some form or another. Small-town and second-run theaters would employ at least a piano player to accompany the picture, while some of the larger theaters would use full orchestration. Full color was somewhat of a rarity during the silent period, but not unknown. However, most films were dyed different colors to enhance the story line. For example, a blue tint usually meant that the scene was taking place at night.

With the 1927 exhibition of *The Jazz Singer,* movie studios clamored to make full-talking pictures. By 1930, although there were a few exceptions, most films were made as talking pictures. Clearly, many people do not see silent films today. However, this book argues that for an understanding of the politics prior to 1930, silent films provide an indispensable resource. Since a number of issues such as race relations in the United States as seen from a perspective of 1915 are no longer acceptable politically to be depicted without commentary, films of that era provide a critical background and understanding. Outside of the United States, after the 1917 Russian Revolution, film in the Soviet Union became an important medium for explaining the themes of the revolution. The films made during this period provide us with an excellent record of how the leaders, and frankly many people, saw the problems of the early twentieth century.

This raises an interesting question—why not just show documentary footage from the time period or subject in question? Documentaries, films that use actual footage of events or attempt to reconstruct events, are an important resource for understanding politics, and the book uses some documentaries to discuss some topics, especially civil rights and social justice. However, narrative films, films that tell a story, offer the audience an engaging way to look at the topic in question. Using a narrative structure, the director can build suspense, allow for introspection among characters, and engage an audience that might otherwise be uninterested in a subject.

Consider a simple example of how a narrative story might offer more insight: a documentary feature about Rick Blaine (a fictitious character) might discuss his fighting on the side of the Loyalists in the Spanish Civil War, his time in Paris, his move to Casablanca during the Nazi invasion of France, and his subsequent opening of a nightclub there and joining of the Free French. Yet the same story in the context of *Casablanca,* allows the audience to see the personal struggle the Rick as he decides what should be done. His personal interaction with corrupt French officials, Nazi officers, and the underground that he tries to ignore at first, but is eventually won over by, gives context and meaning to the larger struggle of World War II. The intention of the filmmakers was to suggest that Rick's life and policies mirrored that of the United States.

There is a problem with an overreliance on narrative films. Because they are designed to tell a story, the filmmakers have an artistic license to change pieces of the story for dramatic effect. Many very entertaining films offer false premises in their assertions because they are trying to lead audiences down a certain path. The key for us is to understand this and to dissect the ways in which this may happen and the reasons why.

Documentary films help us understand problems inherent in narrative films, but they have a problem as well. We should remember that documentaries are not unbiased. Documentary filmmakers make films about subjects they care about; thus they are portraying a point of view that they probably have. This is not to say that a great portion of people who make documentaries do not try to be objective, but simply by choosing their subjects documentary filmmakers are making a choice. The presumption here is that in a free society all voices should have a chance to be heard.

Sometimes it is difficult to distinguish between a film with a point of view and propaganda. Generally propaganda is considered a relatively deliberate attempt to manipulate a debate.[4] This manipulation can include, but is not limited to, a distortion of facts, a disregard for alternative arguments,

and general oversimplification of ideas, symbols, and policies. Thus, some films of the Nazi regime in Germany, such as
Triumph of the Will and even *Kolberg,* are offered as examples
of propaganda.[5] Whether or not some American, British, Soviet, or other films of the period are propaganda is the subject
of some debate. This book leaves it for the reader to decide.

Whether propaganda, documentary, or narrative, films
from other countries give the audience an opportunity to
experience a completely different existence. If film has the
ability to transport the viewer to another time and place,
then foreign films can make that trip much more realistic.
American films about Africa, for example, are filtered
through a perception of how Americans think about Africa.
However, an African film about Africa is apt to reflect how
Africans see their lives, rather than another's preconceived
notions.

It is common for people to say that film transports audiences, but that transportation can be even more realistic
with foreign-language films. When one travels abroad people in other countries often do not speak English. The tem-
perament and tone of actors in foreign-language films are
reflected in their own tongues. With many DVDs foreign-
language films can be dubbed so that a movie can be seen
with an English-language soundtrack. Our preference is to
see a subtitled film, but to watch such a film takes some
practice. Whichever way you choose to see a film, we want
to encourage you to consider these films, because they give
a unique insight into how people from other countries and
cultures see the world around us: a world similar to ours,
but often with different interpretations.

Troubling Images

One aspect of concern in a book such as this is to give the
reader ample warning of upsetting images sometimes contained in films. Whether it is killing, skinning, and gutting
rabbits for furs or meat (1990's *Roger & Me*), Senator Jay
Billington Bulworth's obscenity-laced raps about corporate

malfeasance and political corruption (1998's *Bulworth*), or bloody fight scenes and ample sex (1999's *Fight Club*), films have the potential to trouble, disturb, and offend. Yet they may also be vanguards in the movement to use film to connect us to politics.

One of the most effective films in discussing ethnic conflict is the film *Before the Rain* (1994). Unfortunately, some may consider the film to be too overwhelming, the violence and tension too great, to be able to sit through it. The film is graphic and the violence, at times, is unsettling.[6] There is also a brief scene of nudity during the part of the film that is filmed in London, which some may find objectionable. While mindful that certain subjects may be difficult for some viewers to watch, it is difficult to discuss the real tragedy of some situations, such as the former Yugoslavia, without some realization that violence was a part of the problem. Violence and the use of sexual attacks were one of the hallmarks of a conflict that captured the headlines of the world press over and over again in the 1990s. In the discussion, we used the film *Cabaret Balkan* (1998) to back up the complexity and the brutal nature of ethnic conflict in the former Yugoslavia. However, using *Cabaret Balkan* as a film to depict the effects of ethnic conflict to a wide variety of people may be even more difficult at best. It is a film that is very disturbing, including sexual attacks, murders, and offensive language. While this may accurately capture mid-1990s Serbia, it may be too intense for many students, young people, and many adults. Our sense is that neither the nudity nor the violence in *Before the Rain* is any worse (and maybe better) than most R-rated movies that hit American screens. However, we want to insure that the viewer is cognizant of scenes that might be especially troubling. We have created a list of sensitivities for each film that is included in our filmography.

Outline of the Book

In order to tackle a broad spectrum of topics, the book organizes chapters by topics. The following chapter of the book examines the liberal ideology—that is, philosophic ideas that form the basis of democracy and market economies. One should not confuse liberalism in the classic sense with the liberal or "left-wing" politics today. There is a distinction between the two. Both Democrats and Republicans in the United States are considered classic liberals, because both embrace the ideas of democracy and market economics. The domestic debate between left-of-center parties and right-of-center parties in democratic governments often focuses on how to implement democracy and the proper use of government to deal with the failures of the market.

The films examined in the next chapter on liberal ideology take a look at what kind of benefits and drawbacks are offered by a democratic and market-oriented society. In doing so, the chapter examines what assumptions we make in our political lives. One should also consider how film and television has reinforced these assumptions. As a counter-position, the chapter also examines some films that question the assumptions of democracy and capitalism.

The third chapter is an examination of alternative ideologies to liberalism. Perhaps the two greatest challenges to liberalism in the twentieth century were fascism and communism (or Marxism).[7] In examining fascism and communism the chapter focuses primarily on films from the Nazi periods of Germany and the Soviet period of Russia. Yet, it also considers American feature films and documentary films as well. In considering arguments against the two ideologies the chapter primarily examines the anti-fascist American films of the early 1940s, and the Czech New Wave films of the 1960s.

The fourth chapter examines the institution of the American presidency. We should be mindful that this is not the only institution in politics—the U.S. Congress, the courts, the parliament, the presidency of France, the British monarchy, for example, are all vital institutions that film has examined over the years. However, the book chooses to examine the presidency because of the widespread availability of films and the number of films that have been made on the subject. Moreover, the 1990s witnessed an explosion in the number of presidency films: more than 40 U.S. films in that decade dealt with some aspect of the American presidency.

Chapter five deals with civil rights and the search for social justice. Here, we consider how commercial films and documentaries have reflected, deflected, explained, and debated racism, the legacy of the Ku Klux Klan, the civil rights movement, anti-semitism, and racial profiling. In addition, Hollywood's treatment of homosexuality and hate crimes are examined. Lastly, this chapter uses films and documentaries to examine labor struggles in the United States—from Matewan, West Virginia to Flint, Michigan, to Austin, Minnesota.

What are the key dynamics and realities that underlie and define American elections in the media age? Chapter six considers this vital question by exploring the depiction of campaigns and elections on theater and television screens over the past several decades. From the reel *(fictional candidates and elections)* to the real *(actual campaigns and elections covered in documentaries),* these works address many of the crucial dynamics that influence campaigns and elections and, in process, the civic and electoral health of our republic. From the *Simpsons* to *Bulworth* to *Journeys with George,* the film and television reviewed in this chapter offers wide-ranging, prescient, and at times, controversial commentary on the influence, roles and consequences of— and challenges faced by—party machines, pollsters and image-makers, the media, third parties, and the American voter.

Chapter seven examines the issue of war. While theories of war are briefly considered, the thrust of the chapter is a debate on whether war can be averted or if it is sometimes necessary. The chapter then considers the impact of nuclear war, and the new faces of conflict: ethnic conflict and terrorism.

Chapter eight reviews film's powerful ability to provoke, challenge, and influence the politics of a number of ongoing and emerging issues at home and abroad. Contemporary controversies in the domestic and international arena, including the media, the environment, the death penalty, human rights, and colonialism will be presented. The problems considered are only a short-list of issues in the world today.

Getting Started

We should keep in mind that we live in a media-saturated society. We hope that seeing and discussing these films and programs will give us a starting point to discuss topics and themes that are important to a participatory society. However, we should remember that just because a subject or fact makes it onto a movie or television screen does not mean that it is necessarily a fact. As Oliver Stone's provocative and controversial films, such as *JFK* (1991) and *Nixon* (1997) illustrate, there is a great tendency to partially fictionalize political stories and situations in order to heighten drama and pose tough questions. At first glance this appears to be a huge problem—it takes some knowledge to differentiate between historical fact and artistic license. There is a significant danger in asserting, for example, that the czar and his family were really good and misunderstood during the Russian Revolution as in Twentieth Century Fox's *Anastasia* (1997). Without understanding the actual context of history, the real reasons for the revolution are completely missed. This is why the book attempts to establish a context for understanding films and provides additional readings, in the form of endnotes, to help the viewers to gain a background as to what is reality. In a media-saturated society, being able to distinguish between fact and fiction in the media is a skill critical to media literacy and critical thinking.

The popcorn and politics are ready for us to consume. Without further ado, let's start the show . . .

CHAPTER 2

Liberal Ideologies: Democracy and Capitalism

Introduction

One of the early scenes of the classic comedy *Monty Python and the Holy Grail* (1975) finds King Arthur searching the length and breadth of Britain for knights who are willing to join him at his court in Camelot. Set in 932 A.D., the film is a parody of the tales of the knights of the roundtable, using modern references and outrageous situations to poke fun at the tales that are so often told with such reverence. As Arthur approaches one castle he asks a peasant, "Who lives in the castle?" He is told that no one does. The peasant, Dennis, goes on to tell the king that they have no lord, but instead live in a communal cooperative based on democratic socialist ideas. Another peasant, an old woman, asks who Arthur is. He tells her that he is king of the Britons. She remarks that she had never voted for any king. Arthur replies that kings are not elected—that he was chosen king when the lady of the lake held aloft Excalibur, signifying by divine providence that he was to be king. Dennis argues that strange ladies hanging around in ponds, distributing swords, is no way to form a government. Instead, Dennis says, supreme authority comes from a mandate from the masses.

Traditionally what we in the modern era think of as democracy stems from a rational philosophy of good governance and a liberal philosophy about the rights of humans. Rational thinking in bringing order to a chaotic world depends on accessing the wants and needs of the governed. At the same time, liberal writers insist that individuals have an inalienable right to participate in matters that affect them. Since each person is deemed capable and rational, each should have some say about the rules affecting their lives.

Throughout North America, many people typically think of the development of liberal democracy as a particularly American phenomenon. However, democratic thought and practices developed in several parts of the world, each taking on nuances relevant to local situations. The most recognizable examples of the development of democracy outside North America are clearly France and Britain. The eighteenth century saw the rise of rational and liberal thought among the French elite, culminating in the French Revolution in 1789. In Britain, the progression of parliamentary sovereignty, and in particular the dominance of the House of Commons—the body that represents the general population—signaled the dominance of participatory government. As students of politics, we should be mindful of other democratic experiences as well. Iceland, for example, has had a parliament, the *Althing,* that has met for well over a thousand years.

In the twentieth century, many scholars began to assume that liberal politics (democracy) matched or even fostered liberal economics (capitalism). Others suggested that the opposite was true, that capitalism fostered democracy. Certainly by the end of the century there appeared to be a high correlation between the two. But scholars remain divided on the exact nature of the relationship between capitalism and democracy. Some scholars have argued that capitalism, which has a tendency to accumulate wealth in the hands of a few, tends to undermine democratic societies because those with more money have a disproportionate amount of political power. On the other hand, Milton Friedman, economic advisor to the Reagan administration, has argued that democracy corrupts capitalism by allowing people to elect politicians who might interfere with the market. Friedman argues that politicians will be tempted to interfere with the market in order to satisfy the desires of the electorate, and thus stay in power.

The relationship between democracy and capitalism is an intriguing problem for scholars and policymakers. Evidence suggests that the relationship is complicated, and varies depending upon many factors. Certainly there is no logical reason why one could not exist without the other. Regardless of the relationship, both capitalism and democracy point to a theoretical tradition that emphasizes the role of the individual.

In this chapter, we will explore how democracy (i.e., mass participation and majority rule) and capitalism (i.e., the free market economy) have been portrayed on film. While the chapter considers films that are supportive of democracy and capitalism and films that are critical of each, it should be noted that some of the films' political positions are rather ambiguous. Consider the diverse films we have included in this chapter and the significant political messages they convey. Do you agree or disagree with their perspectives? Do they reinforce or challenge your political beliefs and values? Then consider what other messages about democracy and capitalism, admittedly sometimes implicit or ambiguous, are present in films and television programs you may be familiar with but are not considered in this chapter.

Democracy

The Films of Frank Capra

Over the course of his career, Frank Capra (1891–1962) made a number of films that praised the democratic impulses and institutions of his adopted country, even as he used his artistic vision to criticize the excesses, imperfections, and corruption that occasionally threatened its future. Born in Sicily, Capra embraced the individual freedom and participatory processes present in the United States, and, in several films, used a stock character—the everyman—to promote democracy and fight for the good of the masses. Capra's "everyman" protagonists—whether named Jefferson Smith (a boyish U.S. Senator in *Mr. Smith Goes to Washington*), George Bailey (a small-town, populist savings and loan operator in *It's a Wonderful Life*), or even Grant Matthews (an independent-minded industrialist and presidential candidate in *State of the Union*)—were idealistic and honest, often to a fault, and used politics, or their livelihood, to battle entrenched selfish interests. In Capra's films, which were frequently sentimental and patriotic, these antagonists were media moguls, conniving businessmen, greedy financiers, or wayward politicians. The everyman that battled these undemocratic forces, even if naïve or without riches, worked feverishly to defeat the manipulation of the masses and make life better for everyday Americans. In short, in most of Capra's body of political films, activism, idealism, political participation, and trust in the common sense of the American people were the weapons wielded to slay the corrupt giants.

Mr. Smith Goes to Washington

Clearly Frank Capra and Twentieth Century Fox understood the message they were trying to convey in the classic political drama *Mr. Smith Goes to Washington* (1939). The trailer to the film used the famous radio commentator, H. V. Kaltenborn, to promote the film. Mr. Kaltenborn proclaimed

Mr. Smith a significant film because it emphasized "democracy in action." The film follows the journey and political awakening of Jefferson Smith (James Stewart), a Midwestern everyman and hero of "Boys Nation" appointed to fill a vacancy in the U.S. Senate. Smith, a popular patriot who can recite Lincoln and Jefferson by heart, arrives in the nation's capital starry-eyed and in awe of Washington's sacred monuments. However, a cynical, hard-drinking media and Jim Taylor's vile, graft-hungry political machine quickly shake the spirit of the fledgling senator. The media has fun smearing Smith as a lightweight cornball, and it doesn't take long before the jaded politicos stop the junior senator's initiatives. When Smith proposes legislation to build a national Boys Nation camp in his home state, the Taylor machine, along with their chief political crony Senator Paine (Claude Rains), use their power and persuasion to try to kill the legislation. The new boys camp would be built on Willet Creek, a lucrative location where a pending dam project engineered by Taylor (Edward Arnold) and Paine would bring huge profits to Taylor and his denizens. When the Taylor machine fails to dissuade Smith from pursuing his boys camp, they manufacture allegations to ruin his reputation and, later, manipulate the media to brand the idealistic senator an enemy of the common man who delays anti-poverty legislation.

Distressed and depressed, Smith returns to the hallowed ground of the Lincoln Monument for solace and inspiration. He is reborn and revitalized after his meeting with Abe, and returns to the Senate to fight the corrupt Taylor machine. With the support of his assistant and love-interest, Saunders (Jean Arthur), Smith embarks on his Herculean task. In the famous climax of the film, an exhausted yet determined Smith uses the filibuster—the process of "talking a bill to death"—to maintain the Senate floor and keep the nasty Taylor machine at bay. Capra, through radio commentator Kaltenborn, uses the occasion of Smith's filibuster to praise U.S. political institutions, criticize undemocratic regimes, and promote the idea of "democracy in action":

This is H.V. Kaltenborn speaking. Half of official Washington is here to see democracy's finest show, the filibuster: the right to talk your head off; the American privilege of free speech in its most dramatic form. The last man in that chamber—once he gets and holds that floor, by the rules—can hold it and talk as long as he can stand on his feet, providing always, first, that he does not sit down; second, that he does not leave the chamber or stop talking. The galleries are packed. In the diplomatic gallery are the envoys of two dictator powers. They have come here to see what they can't see at home: democracy in action.[1]

It is the most famous filibuster in Hollywood history, and Smith's honesty, tenacity, and use of U.S. political institutions ultimately rule the day, as Senator Paine cracks under the weight of guilt and corruption. It is perhaps a tad ironic that the filibuster—a minority-driven process of "talking a bill to death"—is used to celebrate the American experiment in representative government (what Kaltenborn calls "democracy in action"). The filibuster has been used, for example, to thwart federal civil rights legislation—and other policies—for decades. Thus, it is not always the friend of the "little guy" or the majority. The only way to stop a senator from holding the floor indefinitely is to invoke cloture. To do this is no small task: senators must first submit a petition—which requires the signature of at least 16 senators—for a cloture vote. Then, at least 60 senators must vote for cloture.

The debate over the democratic nature of the filibuster aside, *Mr. Smith* clearly stands as an explicit example of promoting widespread political participation and celebrating democracy. The monuments and participatory institutions housed in Washington, D.C. are revered. And, in the end, the ruthless Taylor machine is not defeated by bullets or a coup d'etat, but by embracing the opportunity to speak your mind, without fear of repression, in the sacred chambers of American representative government.[2]

Revisiting *Mr. Smith:* The Satire of *The Simpsons*

The 1991 *Simpsons* episode "Mr. Lisa Goes to Washington" is an example of a humorous retelling of the heroic, romantic *Mr. Smith* story. In doing so, Matt Groening's landmark long-running animated series offers its trademark subversion and biting sociopolitical commentary. It both embraces *and* lampoons the romantic patriotism of the 1939 Capra classic. In this installment of the hit series, Lisa Simpson, second grader—and resident over-achieving intellectual in the Simpson clan—writes a patriotic essay for a contest advertised in the journal *Reading Digest* (needless to say, a delightful spoof of *Reader's Digest*). Lisa ultimately wins the local Springfield competition of the "fiercely patriotic" essay contest and earns an all-expenses-paid trip to Washington, D.C. for herself and her family. There, she will compete with young Americans for the national essay contest championship. During the essay competition sequence, we see flashes of several speeches, and most of the essay excerpts poke fun at the "fiercely patriotic" genre of such contests. On one infamous speech, notorious Springfield elementary bully Nelson Muntz offers this zealous stream of jingoistic-flavored thought:

> So burn the flag if you must, but before you do, you better burn a few other things! You better burn your shirt and your pants! Be sure to burn your TV and car! Oh, yes, and don't forget to burn your house because none of these things could exist without six white stripes, seven red stripes, and a hell of a lot of stars![4]

During the Simpsons' time in the nation's capital, there is a playful updating—and lampooning—of Jefferson Smith's unwavering reverence for the nation's monuments and government buildings. There is also heavy criticism of the American populace, which is often portrayed as disinterested. Times have clearly changed. Here the sheer awe present in *Mr. Smith* has turned to angst, contempt, and sexual imagery: Homer loudly boos the IRS building (the stuffy IRS bureaucrat opens the window and retorts, "oh, boo yourself"); Marge giggles at the Washington Monument, finding it to be quite phallic in nature; and the Simpsons stay at the Watergate, the hotel-condominium complex which serves as the enduring symbol of political corruption that brought down the Nixon presidency. The American voter is also portrayed as apathetic and pathetic. When the Simpsons get a special V.I.P. tour of White House (Homer asks the tour guide what V.I.P. stands for), the family doesn't find activism or vigorous dissent alongside Pennsylvania Avenue. Instead, as the Simpsons enter the White House, we see several lollygagging, lethargic "protesters" sitting on the curb—or lazily walking and whistling along— with signs that read "Things are fine," "No Complaints Here," and "No Opinion."[5]

And in the most direct send-up of *Mr. Smith*'s veneration of political institutions and leaders, Lisa visits the Lincoln Monument to seek inspiration and solace after witnessing her congressman, Rep. Bob Arnold, take a bribe. But instead of being able to conduct a solemn conversation with the 16th president, Lisa finds every manner of citizen crowded at the monument, hurling petty, picayune questions at Honest Abe. Her serious concerns cannot be heard over the cacophony of selfish Americans, who treat the hallowed grounds as a crude self-help line. Lisa then takes her shattered faith in American democracy to the Jefferson Memorial, seeking advice and inspiration. When she arrives and tells Thomas Jefferson that she has a problem, the Jefferson statue replies: "I know, the Lincoln Monument was too crowded!"

Lisa's witnessing of raw corruption in Congress forces her to rip up her old, fiercely patriotic essay and craft a new speech to reflect her disgust with Rep. Arnold's bribery. Her new entry is called "Cesspool on the Potomac." (According to her father, Homer, this essay was not as "crowd-pleasin'" as her first *Reading Digest*–winning essay.) In her new speech, Lisa offers this assessment of the state of the union:

> The city of Washington was built on a swamp some 200 years ago and very little has changed; it stank then and it stinks now. Only today it is the fetid stench of corruption that hangs in the air."[6]

In the end, however, Rep, Arnold is arrested in a sting oper-ation, and young Lisa Simpson's faith is apparently re-stored—at least for the time being.

State of the Union

Frank Capra returned to the theme of noble public servant in 1948's *State of the Union*. This time, however, the honest "everyman" does not come from the same humble begin-nings as the patriot Jefferson Smith. Here, Grant Matthews (Spencer Tracy) is a wealthy industrialist and political out-sider who seeks the presidency in order to battle corruption and work like the dickens for the majority, not the special interests. His democratic crusade is seriously compromised, however, by his chief campaign sponsor: the cold, wealthy, and conniving newspaper magnate Kay Thorndyke (Angela Lansbury), with whom he has had an affair. This is never ex-plicitly stated, but there is ample innuendo throughout to sug-gest that this the case. This reality makes this Capra protago-nist more flawed than previous incarnations of the honest everyman or outsider, à la Jefferson Smith or George Bailey.

As the ebullient Matthews loses his way, becoming more and more controlled by the advisers and image-makers pro-vided by Thorndyke, and caving in to the narrow special interests in order to win their support at the nominating convention, he begins to lose his moral and political com-pass, as well as faith in himself. The conclusion of the film is a paid radio program, broadcast live from Matthews home. It is a carefully orchestrated, slick production and is meant to show family unity in the face of rumors concerning Thorndyke and Matthews. Grant's wife, the dutiful Mary (Katharine Hepburn) is painfully forced to grin and bear the phony arrangement, tolerating the presence of the schem-ing Thondyke in her own home. Witnessing the pain and anguish of his wife, Matthews regains his sense of crusad-ing, democratic spirit, throws off the shackles of the image-makers and advisers, and blows the whistle on this absurd and staged media circus masquerading as an authentic po-litical event:

I had the right idea when I started to talk to you people of America. The idea that you voters, you farmers, you businessmen, you working men, you ordinary citizens of whatever party, are not the selfish ones that venal politicians make you out to be. I thought I could speak my peace straight-out and forward. I thought I could tell you that this country of ours is young, it's not old, that we've just begun to grow. That all we need is courage, and from out of that courage could come a greatness greater than we ever dreamed. I wanted to tell you that we Americans are the hope of the world, and the secret of our great plenty is freedom, and we've got to share that secret and all that plenty with the other nations of the world.

I wanted to tell you that we face a great problem because when people are cold and hungry and scared they gather together in panicky herds, ready to be led by communists and fascists, who promise them bread for freedom and deliver neither. These are the things I wanted to say to you, but I lost faith in you. I lost faith in myself. I was afraid I wouldn't become president. I forgot that the one thing you've got to do is speak your piece, no matter what. So with the help of this gang of parasites, I convinced myself that the way to be elected was to play down to your lowest common denominator, instead of up to your highest. To cater to the hatred of every class and race, to appeal to the worst in you, and not the best in you. I used my wife, my kids, and my friends. My whole campaign was a fraud. This is no simple fireside broadcast paid for by your dollars and dimes. This is an elaborately staged professional affair. I've spent $200,000 in exploitation and publicity on matches for present campaigns. I thought I could hijack the Republican nomination. I become an Al Capone of politics, but I forgot one thing: I forgot about how quickly the Americans smell out the double deals and the crooks. . . . And so, here and now, I withdraw as a candidate for any office, not because I'm honest, but because I'm dishonest. I want to apologize to all the good, sincere people who put their faith in me and I want to apologize to my wife.[7]

Matthews' final speech presents several recurring Capra themes: the transcendence, if occasional imperfection, of America's governing institutions; the power of freedom and individual liberties in a democratic system; and, perhaps most of all, a belief in the wisdom and governing ability of the everyday people. And, as in H.V. Kaltenborn's criticism of "dictator powers" in the filibuster scene in *Mr. Smith,* in Matthews' climactic soap box address and confessional we see a direct attack on communism and fascism—two ideologies in competition with liberalism.

Why We Fight

Such faith in people, democracy, and a diverse pluralistic society (note Matthews' belief that there should not be exploitation of divisions by race and class) is also exemplified in Capra's famous *Why We Fight* films. *Why We Fight,* a seven-part series, was produced from 1943–45 and sponsored by the federal government. The movies were explicitly used as a recruitment and propaganda tool during World War II. The seven films in the *Why We Fight* series—*Prelude to War* (1943), *The Nazis Strike* (1943), *Divide and Conquer* (1943), *The Battle of Britain* (1943), *The Battle of Russia* (1943), *The Battle of China* (1944), and *War Comes to America* (1945)— discuss the necessity of U.S. involvement in the war, and, to varying degrees, celebrate the "melting pot" theory of the United States. This perspective, present in several of the films, suggests that whether you are a farmer, immigrant factory laborer, rich or poor, black or white, Catholic or Protestant, cosmopolitan East Coaster or rural resident, you could—and *must*—unite and work together to win the war.

Capra's *Why We Fight* was a seminal tool used by the U.S. government to maintain unity, promote the war effort, celebrate our social and political fabric, and promote the notion that the liberal ideologies of democracy and capitalism were superior to communism, fascism, or any other system of government. How better to achieve this mission than to bring notable Hollywood directors on board to use the most popular art and entertainment form to make their case? This direct Hollywood-Washington political connection also included the likes of Walt Disney, who used federal largesse to keep his studio afloat in the 1940s. During World War II, Disney—"despite a passionate opposition to socialism and to any government meddling in free enterprise"—used money from the federal government to produce a plethora

of propaganda and military training films.[8] In this short period of time, government contracts for these pro-American
films constituted 90 percent of Disney's studio's output.
Disney's propaganda and military training films included
such titles as *Food Will Win the War, High-Level Precision
Bombing,* and a *Few Quick Facts About Venereal Disease.*[9]

Looking back at the romantic, often idealistic, films of Frank
Capra, one might ponder how far modern films are from
the unabashedly pro-democratic sentiments espoused by the
native Sicilian. While *Mr. Smith* glorifies and sanctifies the
symbols of U.S. government and mass participation—such
as the Washington Monument, Lincoln Memorial, and
White House—some modern films have offered rather luke-
warm or ambivalent messages about such things. Indeed,
some have even taken a more confrontational tone. The
summer 1996 sci-fi-action smash *Independence Day,* for example, features a scene where alien intruders blow up the
White House. As was widely reported in American press at
the time, thrilled audiences cheered at the sight of "The
People's House" being smashed to smithereens. The sci-fi
blockbuster is but one example of how Hollywood has
treated monuments in recent times—but it is perhaps a prescient one. For better or worse, Capra it is not.

The West Wing: An Updated, Sophisticated Capra Comes to Television

Like a modern day Frank Capra, NBC's popular
Wednesday-night political drama *The West Wing* has presented the viewing public with plot lines that routinely celebrate diversity, pluralism, and the finest aspects of democratic governance. The show promotes the paramount
importance of political participation on a regular basis—
and often does so in a very explicit manner. Consider this
rallying cry from White House Press Secretary C.J. Craig
(Allison Janney) at a jam-packed "Rock the Vote" rally in
Cambridge, Massachusetts:

Twenty-five years ago, half of all eighteen to twenty-four year olds voted. Today it's 25 percent. Eighteen to twenty-four year olds represent 33 percent of the population but only account for seven percent of the voters. Think government isn't about you? How many of you have student loans to pay? How many of you have credit card debt? How many want clean air and clean water and civil liberties? How many want jobs? How many want kids? How many want kids to go to good schools and walk on safe streets? Decisions are made by those who show up. You gotta rock the vote![10]

Sandwiched in between sets by Aimee Mann and the Barenaked Ladies (it *was* a Rock the Vote benefit concert, after all), Craig's message from the fourth season episode "College Kids" reflects one of the show's persistent themes: if you do not roll up your sleeves and play the noble and necessary game of politics, politicians *and* public policy will leave you behind. Rock the vote, indeed.

The Noble, Democratic Everyman Returns: "Mr. Willis of Ohio" and "The Short List"

In the episode "Mr. Willis of Ohio" from *The West Wing*'s inaugural season (1999), the Wednesday-night drama, à la Frank Capra, celebrates the profound impact and positive difference one person can make within the democratic institutions of government. Here the "Mr. Willis" is a new congressman from Ohio, an African-American social studies teacher who has replaced his late wife, Janice Willis, in the House of Representatives. He is one of three swing votes on the Commerce Committee who can help, or prevent, the Bartlet Administration from getting a sampling provision for the census approved and, in the process, pass the latest appropriations bill. Initially, Willis is not sold on the Bartlet administration's rationale behind census sampling. He believes it may be too slanted by partisan considerations. In the end, however, after extensive negotiations with White House Communications Director Toby Ziegler (Richard Schiff) and personal reflection, the Ohio teacher sides with the president and votes for the appropriations bill. Rep. Willis' decisive

THE WEST WING

Pure Entertainment or Politically Charged Celebration of Democracy?
The Creator, the President (Bartlet), and a Producer Weigh In

What kind of administration is the Bartlet administration? We like to think we project the ideal way to serve. Naturally, we can't always solve every problem, but we'll always identify them. There's a lot of politicking, of course, that's what we do for a living—the characters, that is. But there's no proselytizing. It may be that we have given bureaucracy, or at least bureaucrats, a good name! We've certainly given them a face, and a heart, and a breath. And we've given recognition to their humanity and their public service. . . .

We're not the real deal, of course. We're only fantasy. And yet, within this fantasy we have to be credible. We committed to a certain course in the very beginning, long before the show was popular. We had a goal. You can call it liberal. You can call it Democratic. You can call it Humanist. However it is perceived, we were pointing the direction where this ideal administration would lead the nation, and we stay the course, trusting that people will find some measure of their own ideals and, perhaps, experience some degree of expansion to their own imaginations.

—Martin Sheen, President Josiah "Jed" Bartlet[11]

I think we're all very flattered when we hear that the show illuminates certain things. We hear it from high school history and social studies teachers. We hear it from the politicians themselves. We hear it from people who lead certain causes. Whether it's on drug policy, or the census, or AIDS in Africa, or the death penalty, or what have you.

We're delighted when we hear that, but that's not our goal. Our goal is the same as David Kelley's goal on *The Practice* and *Ally McBeal* and John [Wells's] on *ER*, and Steven Bochco and David Milch's on *NYPD Blue*. It's simply to captivate you for an hour and when the hour's over make you feel like, That was worth it. I had a good time and I want to watch again next week. We are storytellers first and last. If we do something else, well then, that just speaks to the power of storytelling.

—Aaron Sorkin, creator, writer, and producer[12]

An aspiration of the show is the idea that people who choose government service, or public service, are not suspect. They are, in fact, sacrificing their chance to make more money and have better career opportunities to try and make a difference. The people we've met in Washington are genuinely committed to trying to make the world a better place.

—John Wells, executive producer[13]

vote in the Commerce Committee—and his very ascension to the position of congressman—simultaneously celebrates two potential attributes of participatory democracy. First, the notion of inclusion—that teachers and minorities can serve in the highest levels of governance—is promoted. Second, Rep. Willis uses his power not for personal gain or petty politics but for public service in the grandest sense: putting country and what is right above all tactical, political considerations. He votes for the bill because he believes it is best for the country. His decision to follow conscience and the public good over crass partisan politics is reflected in the following exchange between Toby Ziegler and Rep. Willis:

TOBY
    I was wondering, what changed your mind?

MR. WILLIS
    You did. I thought you made a very strong argument.

TOBY
    Thank you . . . I'm smiling because . . . well, around here the merits of a particular argument generally take a backseat to political tactics.[14]

This simple, kindhearted teacher, much like the benevolent everyman Jefferson Smith from years past, represents the machinery of representative government being used for the most noble purposes.

Also from the first season, "The Short List" celebrates the ability of everyday folks—in this case, minorities with the socio-economic deck heavily stacked against them—to rise to greatness and serve the public in a democratic system. This hour in the life of a fictional television presidency follows President Bartlet's (Martin Sheen) attempts to nominate a new Supreme Court Justice. Initially, the president and his advisers zero in on Peyton Cabot Harrison II (Ken Howard), who is seen as a safe, moderate, credentialed and confirmable—if rather uninspiring—choice for the highest bench in the land. But it soon becomes apparent that the rich, stuffy elitist judge does not share the administration's view on a constitutional right to privacy. In fact, he doesn't believe that such a fundamental right exists. Rather than take the safe road with the wealthy, white Harrison—"of Philips Exeter and Princeton, a Rhodes Scholar, editor of the *Harvard Law Review* and dean of Harvard law School"— Bartlet and his team decide to take a huge political risk by choosing a Hispanic from New York City, Justice Mendoza (Edward James Olmos), to serve as an associate justice of the U.S. Supreme Court.[15] Mendoza—a graduate of "P.S. 138 in Brooklyn, CUNY, and the New York Police Academy," and who worked his way through law school by serving in the NYPD and as assistant DA—is a liberal judge far more in sync with Bartlet's views on privacy.[16] Mendoza, unlike Harrison, believes that mandatory drug tests would constitute an illegal search, and as such, would be unconstitutional. With the choice of Mendoza, we once again see *The West Wing* celebrate a system where folks from humble beginnings have the chance to make a difference; where they can serve honorably in the most powerful political institutions in the world.

Current Events: Keeping the Masses Informed

Another aspect of *The West Wing* that smacks of unrepentant pro-democracy sentiment is its ongoing attempt to further public dialog and debate on a wide array of public policies.[17] One of the chief tenets of majoritarianism is the belief that the masses, not just the elites, should be engaged and informed. Press Secretary C.J. Craig's comments at the Rock the Vote rally, cited at the outset of this section, clearly reflect this view. Moreover, in addition to the plot lines from over four seasons work of work, *The West Wing* has used its online presence to rock the vote and promote an engaged citizenry. Starting in the fall of 2002 with the two-hour premiere "20 Hours in America," NBC's official *West Wing* web page featured links to political issues raised in each episode of the new season. Visiting the program's home page in the fall of 2002, for example, you would come across this message: *"Find out more about each week's political, economic, social, and 'hot' topics. Click here for information and links to related online sites"*[18] A mere two episodes into the 2002–2003 season, "The West Wing Hot Topics" web page featured substantive links to web pages dealing with the economic, social, and political issues and institutions raised in the episodes "20 Hours in America" and "College Kids"— among them: Title IX (equality for women in collegiate athletics), NASDAQ, the Department of Labor, the New York Stock Exchange, Farm Aid, U.S. Department of Agriculture, the Commission on Presidential Debates, and Rock the Vote.

But informative web sites aside, in the final analysis there remains no better place to receive the egalitarian message that one person can make a profound difference in the engines of democracy than the show itself. "Two Cathedrals" (2001), season two's dramatic cliffhanger, finds the recently deceased Mrs. Delores Landingham (Kathryn Joosten), the president's secretary, discussing the challenges faced by Bartlet and the nation. Because he was not forthright with the American people about his affliction with multiple sclerosis, the president's popularity has plummeted; a media feeding frenzy has descended on the White House, and his own party hints that they no longer want him as their standard bearer. Bartlet laments his situation and ponders his political future. Should he seek another term? Is he finished? What about the problems of the country? Can he still make a difference? After his conversation with Mrs. Landingham, the answer is clear:

> BARTLET
>   Give me the numbers.
>
> MRS. LANDINGHAM
>   I don't know the numbers, you give them to me.
>
> BARTLET
>   How 'bout a child born in this minute has a one in five chance of being born into poverty.
>
> MRS. LANDINGHAM
>   How many Americans don't have health insurance?
>
> BARTLET
>   44 million.

MRS. LANDINGHAM
What's the number one cause of death for black men under 35?

BARTLET
Homicide.

MRS. LANDINGHAM
How many Americans are behind bars?

BARTLET
3 million.

MRS. LANDINGHAM
How many Americans are drug addicts?

BARTLET
Five million.

MRS. LANDINGHAM
And one in five kids live in poverty?

BARTLET
It's 13 million American children. Three and a half million kids go to schools that are literally falling apart, we need 127 billion in school construction, and we need it today.

MRS. LANDINGHAM
To say nothing of 53 people trapped in an embassy.

BARTLET
Yes.

MRS. LANDINGHAM
You know if you don't want to run again, I respect that. But if you don't run because you think it's gonna be too hard . . . or you think you're gonna lose . . . well, God, Jed, I don't even want to know you.[19]

Capitalism

The United States emerged from the Second World War as a country that was unrivaled in its position in the international arena. Although the U.S. lost around three hundred thousand persons during the military conflict, this was negligible compared to what other major combatants had lost. Since European and Asian countries had the war fought on their territories, Britain had received substantial bombing of its infrastructure during the war, and six or more years of war had worn down the other major powers. Secured by two oceans, sustained by stable political institutions, and fueled by an expansive free-market economy anchored by a massive industrial base, the United States entered the post-war era with its infrastructure in place, a dominant military deployed, and preparing a world order for the post-war era. During the war, the United States had already taken steps to devise a post-war world in which key economic and political issues would be addressed.

During the war the United States caucused its major allies to hammer out an economic plan for recovery and maintenance. The lessons learned from the pre-war years was that an unstable economic environment led to political instability and war. In Germany, the fall of the democratic Weimar Republic was attributed to the massive hyperinflation and severe economic depression. In Japan, the military was allowed to seize control of the government in an effort to modernize and develop the country to make it a major economic power. In both cases, the lessons learned was that the economic instability and lack of development in relative comparison to other powers led Germany and Japan to pursue a belligerent policy in order to achieve their goals. The Conference at Dumbarton Oaks sought to establish institutions[20] that would help regulate the world economy and promote economic growth and development.

As the emerging economic giant of the post-war era, the United States and its film industry were only too ready to promote the economic values espoused by American society. Generally, American political and corporate leaders sought to make the values of economic liberalism and free trade the primary driving force of international economic policy following the war. Time and time again during the war, films and popular culture touted the benefits of free markets and democracy. Films such as *Lifeboat* (1944) and *Mr. Smith Goes to Washington* (1939) latently and blatantly give the audience an explanation as to why democracy and the workings of government are so important. Other films, such as *It's a Wonderful Life* (1946) celebrated the idea that working hard and being honest leads one to economic security (if not wealth) and happiness.

The primary tenets of economic liberalism are found in the writings of some eighteenth- and nineteenth-century economists, particularly David Ricardo and Adam Smith. Both of these economists theorized that if states would allow markets to develop autonomously, without undue interference and without as many barriers as possible, they would maximize their own efficiencies. Doing so would create more wealth, which in the end would benefit all. Hence, liberals base their analysis on three assumptions: first, individuals are the principal actors in the economy; second, individuals are capable of making rational decisions, meaning individuals are capable of making a cost-benefit analysis and choosing between economic decisions; and third, individuals will choose decisions that will maximize the benefits and minimize their costs.[21]

Hollywood was only too ready to help educate the public about the benefits of free trade and capitalism. Using film shorts, which were commonly shown before feature films prior to the advent of television, major studios offered their interpretation of capitalism. In *Stuff for Stuff* (1949), filmmakers argued that there was a need to rebuild the economic and political infrastructure of Europe following the Second World War in order to secure the prosperity of the entire world. *Stuff for Stuff* argues the logic behind this theory by reviewing economic history. In ancient Egypt, according to the film, people began to conquer the elements. With the invention of the plow, one person could begin to feed many people. With surplus commodities, people were free to engage in other types of commerce. Trade allowed for the development of wealth. The film traces the development of trade and prosperity through the Greeks, Spanish, Portuguese, and English.

The film portrays history very specifically. In 1914, the Germans made a bid for world domination and countries began to become aware of how interdependent they were as each was drawn into the First World War. After the First World War, the United States replaced Britain as the leading economic power. During the Great Depression, the cessation of two-way trade took its toll on the economic prosperity of the world. By not trading with one another, orders and trade between countries were cancelled. By canceling orders jobs were lost, and out-of-work citizens became a pool of people susceptible to radical ideologies. *Stuff for Stuff* calls on the people of the world to accept the ideology of free markets, if not, "Civilization will be destroyed . . . unless undeveloped areas are developed . . . unless destroyed areas are rebuilt . . . and developed areas are allowed to engage in two-way trade."

Another form of the short subject is the ever-popular cartoon. *When My Ship Comes In* (1934) is a Betty Boop cartoon set during the depression of the 1930s. In the cartoon Betty fantasizes about what she could do to help people during the economic tough times. With a snappy little song of the same title, Betty daydreams that she wins a million dollars. Rather than saving the money for herself, she elects to to spend it all on materials. By purchasing items she stimulates the economy. Each item she buys requires people to make the item and people to sell it. When she buys the goods, the merchant and the manufacturer make money, which they in turn purchase items with, which helps out other merchants and manufacturers. At the end of the cartoon Betty imagines the map of the United States as a machine—as more money is fed into it, the more the machines revs up, until it runs at full-steam.

In the mid-1950s famed cartoon director Friz Freleng directed a trilogy of cartoons that were designed to be lessons on economics and capitalism. Freleng was the head of the Warner Brothers' cartoon department from 1933 to 1963, when the department was closed down. A long-time friend of the more famous animator, Walt Disney, the two had worked together in Kansas City, and Freleng briefly worked for Disney when he first arrived in Hollywood. Although overshadowed in name recognition, Freleng would direct and/or animate over 260 cartoons for Warner Brothers, produce the Pink Panther television series in the 1960s, and win several Academy Awards.

In 1954 Freleng directed *By Word of Mouse,* which had an American mouse lecturing his European counterparts on the fundamentals of American economics. The next year, Freleng directed *Heir Conditioned* (1955), which stars Sylvester the Cat and Elmer Fudd. Sylvester is the beneficiary of an inheritance and Elmer is the financial advisor who explains the benefits of investing rather then spending the inheritance. Elmer convinces Sylvester that by investing his money he can increase his standard of living. To close out the trilogy, Freleng directed *Yankee Dood It* (1956), which is a film on the methods of capitalism.

While most of us assume that cartoons are purely entertainment, there has been a long history of education and propaganda as well. Warner Brothers cartoons are especially known for their biting satire and social commentary. A casual glance at a program of Warner Brothers cartoons (such as Bugs Bunny, Daffy Duck, Foghorn Leghorn, Sylvester and Tweety, etcetera) reveals references to popular culture and social commentary about the 1930s, 1940s, and 1950s. Warner Brothers cartoons would use catch phrases from radio programs like the "Fibber McGee and Molly Show" and television programs such as "This Is Your Life." The social commentary of the studio was particularly vociferous during the war. However, during the depression several cartoons addressed the issue of poverty.[22] Given the time period of their popularity, roughly 1935–1960, the cartoons were instrumental in advocating free market economics to the American movie-going public.

Raising Concerns about Democracy

It is a well-worn commentary that the framers of the American constitution were wary of an unmitigated public, a tyranny of the masses, running the affairs of state. The Constitution, in its original form, established some institutions, such as the Senate and the presidency, as being indirectly elected to assuage these fears. It was not until 1913 that the Senate was directly elected. Concerns about the full participation of the electorate can be demonstrated in the films of the silent period. The question of women's suffrage was addressed in films such as *When the Men Left Town* (1914?).[23] Seen from today's perspective, these films might seem silly and ineffectual. But the concept of women gaining the vote, kicking the men out of town, and then society falling apart, as the plot of *When the Men Left Town* suggests, was a serious comment on the state of suffrage in the early part of the twentieth century.

Likewise, a similar scenario, painted in less comedic terms, was presented to the country in *Birth of A Nation* (1915). Directed by the famous and important director D. W. Griffith, *Birth of a Nation* was the first large-scale American blockbuster and took filmmaking to new heights. There is no doubt as to the importance of *Birth of a Nation* in film history; however its message is certainly more controversial than those dealing with suffrage of women. The story takes place before, during, and after the American Civil War, and focuses on two families, the Stoneman family from the north, and the Cameron family from the south. In the film, during the reconstruction following the war, all males of the Southern society, including the African Americans, are enfranchised to vote. In what is purported to be a historical reconstruction of the events, African Americans take control of the Senate in South Carolina. The film focuses on some fairly shocking stereotypes of how African American politicians behave in the Senate. Politicians, with no shoes on, are seen with their feet propped up on their desk, several senators are eating fried chicken in the chambers, and others resort to drink before engaging in important votes. Griffith's message is seemingly very clear: there are some segments of society that are clearly not ready or able to be entrusted with the power of voting. Instead of suggesting that all people are capable of knowing what is in their best interest, Griffith is arguing that some—most notably African Americans—are not capable of that knowledge.

Thus, democracy and placing in the hands of the masses the decisions of state can lead to undesirable consequences.

Robert Rossen's film, *All the King's Men* (1949), based on the novel by former U.S. Poet Laureate Robert Penn Warren, explores the rise and ultimate fall of Willie Stark. Stark, a thinly disguised portrayal of real life Louisiana governor Huey Long, is a backwoods man who begins his career fighting for the common people of his state. The film is told from the point of view of a newspaper reporter, Jack Burden, who, as the films opens, is sent to cover Stark in his attempt to win the seat of county treasurer in rural Kanoma County. The political machinery in Kanoma County is clearly lined up against Stark, nevertheless he carries on a campaign against corruption and cronyism. As Jack arrives to cover Stark's campaign, he witnesses Willie being harassed by the police and arrested for speaking to a group of more than five. For disturbing the peace, Jack has his camera seized, and although it is returned later, the film has disappeared. The central issue of the campaign is the funding of the new school building and why the county commissioners did not take the lowest bid, and what safeguards have been taken for the building. The owner of the local brick factory is the brother-in-law of one of the commissioners and it uses convict labor, according to Stark.

Willie ends up losing the election and spends his time afterwards privately pursuing a law degree with the help of his wife Lucy. Willie is vindicated when a stairwell in the new school collapses killing and injuring several children. His crusading message now resonates with the populace and Willie Stark is a threat to the political machine in the state. The machinery recognizes the challenge and attempts to co-opt the effect of a Stark run for the governorship. At first, in the hands of the political machine, Stark is lackluster as a candidate, repeating boring statistics and dry solutions. It is only after he realizes that he is being played by the machinery—and a night of heavy drinking—that Stark comes out as an orator who will fight for the rights of the common people. He tells his audience that they are all "hicks," and that the only person who is going to look after the "hicks" is another hick, Willie Stark. Despite a miraculous turn around, Stark falls just short of winning the election. Jack is crushed, but Willie tells him not to worry because of what he has learned. What Willie has learned is how to win.

Four years later finds roles somewhat reversed. Jack has quit his job on the newspaper because of his support for Willie and the newspaper's support for a rival four years earlier. Since that time, Willie has positioned himself to become governor of the state. Willie rescues Jack and makes him part of his staff. Willie rolls to an overwhelming win, and seeks to fill out his staff.

Democracy as Ineffective and Inefficient: *Gabriel Over the White House*

Gregory La Cava's *Gabriel Over the White House* (1933)—produced by none other than the persistently political newspaper magnate, William Randolph Hearst (the primary target of Orson Welles' 1941 classic *Citizen Kane),* and distributed by Republican Louis B. Mayer's studio MGM[24]—provides moviegoers with another cautionary critique of democracy. In *Gabriel,* the message is clear: democracy and a separated system of checks and balances is ineffective and impractical in times of economic crises and national emergency.[25] Presidential candidate Judson C. 'Judd'/'Major' Hammond (Walter Huston) is an opportunistic playboy, telling the masses whatever it takes to get elected. Once in office, he takes a hands-off, laissez-faire approach to a deepening depression, and has no intention of addressing unemployment and racketeering by implementing massive government programs. But things change: while driving recklessly, President Hammond is in a near-fatal car crash and descends into a coma. Unbeknownst to the public, he is visited and resuscitated by the angel Gabriel, who transforms a selfish, weak chief executive into an assertive, determined leader.

Blessed by this new spirit, the president dismisses his cabinet, institutes martial law, defies and overwhelms

Congress at every turn, and demands that allies repay their World War I debts immediately (he brazenly threatens them with war if they do not repay their debts). In addition, he tramples on civil liberties and decisively sends the full might of the U.S. military after mobsters and bootleggers, court-martials them and then sentences them to death, and in one of the more outlandish scenes in political films has the mobsters executed, gunned down just outside the Statue of Liberty. The message here is unambiguous: public consent and the machinations of representative government may be alright when things are fine, but to fight bootleggers, keep our allies and enemies in line, and defeat depressions, we should empower a benevolent dictator to take the reins of power and act according to his own vision. Democratic institutions, civil liberties, and checks and balances are ineffective in the face of such threats.

Minority Report (2002): Be Careful What You Wish (and Vote) For!

It is the year 2054, and the Justice Department's new "pre-cog" anti-crime program is wildly popular with the American people. This is the setting for the summer 2002 blockbuster *Minority Report,* a futuristic political thriller directed by Steven Spielberg. In the film Detective John Anderton (Tom Cruise) is the chief of the Justice Department's new "Pre-Crime Unit," and serves alongside the program's director, Lamar Burgess (Max von Sydow). Together, they help execute a new anti-crime program that uses three genetically altered humans that to see into the future to prevent murders. How does the elite anti-crime unit function? Armed with the expert cognitive ability of the genetically-altered "pre-cogs" and modern computerized technology, the crime unit uses the pre-cogs' reports to see what crimes *will be* committed in the future, and then uses these reports to arrest the suspects *before* they commit a crime.

The American public, scared of violent crime and impressed by the seemingly flawless work of the Pre-Crime Unit, votes to dramatically extend the scope and power of the anti-crime program. Through the completely democratic process of the plebiscite, the people give Director Burgess more authority to expand and execute the program. Yet several troubling questions arise: What happens if the system is not full-proof? What if the pre-cogs and their reports can somehow be manipulated by humans so that innocents can be arrested for crimes they have no intention of committing? At its very core "the movie presents us with a classic totalitarian trade-off, upgraded by technology and the paranormal: Would you surrender a slew of civil liberties for a world without crime?[26]

Dubbed "a fabulous, witty totalitarian nightmare" by *Salon.com, Minority Report* offers an ominous glimmer into what horrors can arise when vast, unchecked police power—explicitly backed by popular will—is given to a select few under the guise of security.[27] Indeed, as it turns out, the pre-crime unit *is* manipulated and abused by forces within the program, and soon Detective Anderton finds himself the target of someone's high-tech scheming. He is on the run, fighting for his life, while trying to determine how such an advanced system could be used for evil purposes. The horrific abuse of the popular futuristic pre-cog pre-crime unit provides us with a potentially sober lesson about democracy: what the majority wants—and indeed votes for—is not always what is best or sound. Democratic decisions can prove to be the most insidious if they empower opportunistic individuals with their own agenda or sinister intent. In post-9/11 America, with the passage of legislation designed to fight terrorism and ensure security—such the popular Patriot Act—many found the release of the fantasy sci-fi political thriller to be especially timely.[28]

Critiquing Capitalism:
Battling Wal-Mart

Store Wars (2001) raises questions about the desirability of unchecked capitalism—in this case, the further expansion of the world's largest retailer, Wal-Mart. The film is a documentary set in the small town of Ashland, Virginia, just outside

Richmond. The film chronicles a year in the political life of the city as the world's largest retail chain, Wal-Mart, petitions for a store to be built in Ashland. Two sides quickly coalesce as to whether or not Wal-Mart should be allowed to build. One side favors the development because it is seen as a way to bring jobs to the area, increase the visibility of Ashland, and to give citizens access to products at a lower cost. Those opposed to Wal-Mart coming to town, represented by pink flamingoes, fear that the increase of traffic will destroy the small town atmosphere of Ashland, and that the jobs created will come at the expense of higher-paying jobs lost in the town's smaller businesses that Wal-Mart would force out of business.

Ashland's political leaders are at a loss for what to do. Initially their primary concern is the traffic problems a new Wal-Mart would create for the town. The proposed development is huge compared to the town's ability to supply infrastructure. As citizens become organized, they voice concerns about the economic and political impact on Ashland. Wal-Mart provides an information video on the positive impact it has had on Tappahannock, Virginia. A delegation from Ashland makes the trip to Tappahannock to discuss the issue with local political and business leaders. Business leaders tell them that the effect Wal-Mart has had on the community leaders is that all the small, locally owned enterprises have gone out of business. The argument used by those who opposed Wal-Mart is that profits make by local businesses are recirculated within the community, while profits made by Wal-Mart are taken back to Arkansas, the corporate headquarters of Wal-Mart.

Wal-Mart's first proposal to build in Ashland is turned down by the planning commission. The Commission felt that the proposed development did not address the traffic concerns nor would it fit into the quaint, small-town charm that Ashland was supposed to invoke. The celebration among the pink flamingoes is muted. They understand that the rejection is really an invitation to re-state the proposal. A few months later Wal-Mart submits another proposal that incorporates some of the city's concerns and scales down some of the plans. Additionally, the proposal calls for the store to be decorated in (yellow and green) rather than Wal-Mart's more commonly used red and blue in order to fit in better with Ashland's quaintness.

The new proposal solves many of the concerns the city council, mayor, and planning commission had with the original proposal. The pink flamingoes become even more active and begin lobbying city council persons directly. One commissioner tells representatives of the pink flamingoes that even if all the residents of Ashland signed a petition against Wal-Mart, he would still vote for the proposal because he thought it was in the best economic interest of Ashland. Wal-Mart intensifies its efforts as well. Many town residents remained skeptical and hostile. At a town meeting, a lawyer representing Wal-Mart insisted on Wal-Mart's right to buy property and build where it wanted. A member of the audience, quoting Sam Walton's (the founder of Wal-Mart) autobiography, asked about his pledge not to locate a Wal-Mart in any town that did not want one. A full-page advertisement, taken out in the local newspaper by Wal-Mart, touted the benefits of a new Wal-Mart. Included in the advertisement was a reference to the positive economic impact that new Wal-Marts bring to an area. The 1995 report co-authored by Professor Barnes was cited as evidence. A supporter of the pink flamingoes called the professor at Massachusetts "Dartmouth," who said that among the conclusions of her study was employment levels did not increase and at best new Wal-Marts had no economic impact on an area.

One of the significant points of the film is how divided Ashland becomes over the issues. Elections for mayor and the town council are held shortly before the final decision on whether or not to approve the proposal. The election, which is bitterly contested, yields a slate of candidates opposed to the development. However, the city council, as a lame-duck council, votes to approve the proposal. By 2002, Wal-Mart had not only become the largest employer in several U.S. states, but was the largest private employer in the entire country. In Pennsylvania, for example, where Wal-Mart possessed 94 discount "supercenters"—and 20 Sam's Clubs warehouses—the retail chain now employed over 39,000 people.[29] Ashland's store, therefore, stands as a link in an ever-expanding chain of unrivaled retail power.

Fight Club: Battling Mindless Materialism and Corporate Power

David Fincher's controversial $63 million sex- and violence-dominated sociopolitical statement *Fight Club* (1999), starring Gen-X box office draws Brad Pitt, Edward Norton, and Helena Bonham Carter, draws serious attention to the darker, more extreme impulses of capitalism: materialism and corporate manipulation run amok.[30] Driven to spend inordinate and irrational amounts of money on cars, clothes, furniture, and household minutiae, American males Tyler Durden (Brad Pitt) and "the Narrator" Cornelius (Edward Norton) realize that they, like other men of their generation, have become slaves to corporate manipulation and mindless materialism, buying "shit that they don't need" from catalog after catalog and trendy store after trendy store.[31] They have become part of the ever-expanding consumer class, wedded to Starbucks, Viagra, Calvin Klein, Tommy Hilfiger, DKNY, IKEA, and endless amounts of the "right" fashion, food, furniture, beverages, perfume, and household amenities that we are told we need.

For the iconoclast Tyler Durden, the crisis of modern American manhood is not caused by Great Depressions or foreign wars but by "a spiritual war" brought on by consumerism and the false belief—broadcast ad nauseam on television and everywhere in American capitalist society—that everyone will become rich if they work hard enough. This is a hyperactive capitalism gone crazy. Americans work all day so that they can buy at night and the weekend, trying to move ever closer to the unattainable nirvana of purchasing power and possessions. We have become, in Durden's words, pathetic slaves with "white collars." To combat this predicament, the radical Durden, along with his "protégé"—the narrator, Cornelius—channel their aggression about the state of affairs and their programmed minds into secret male societies known as "Fight Clubs": gatherings of men where folks batter each other senseless. Later, the two men and their minions engage in smart-ass shenanigans, pranks, and small-time terrorism designed to disrupt the ongoing capitalist, consumerist slavery. Eventually the group's activities—dubbed "Project Mayhem"—turn darker, ultraviolent, and illegal, and include the planned destruction of the major credit card companies. Why credit card companies? So we can, in Durden's words, "erase the debt and start at zero"

"Project Mayhem" is financed in a variety of ways, but soap is the essential component of the Fight Club economic engine. Stealing cellulite left over from liposuction, the members of "Fight Club" use the fat to make expensive, trendy, soap ($20 a bar) that quickly becomes extremely fashionable at department stores. Thus, the renegades literally sell fat back to the weight- and image-conscious consumers of America. As the narrator states, they were "selling rich women their own fat asses back to them." The angst of Durden and the narrator is also driven by the injustice that they see. For example, the narrator's work is basically concealing routine—and severe—corporate malfeasance. His company produces faulty car parts but, regardless of the numerous fatalities and injuries caused by their faulty products, they fail to correct them because their cost-benefit analysis reveals that it is cheaper to keep making the shoddy, life-threatening parts and pay (mostly) paltry settlements than to correct the mistakes. The narrator uses damning information he has culled from years as an insurance adjuster for the company to blackmail his corporate bosses, his silence shrewdly traded for money to finance the anti-corporate "Project Mayhem" of Fight Club.

Released in the fall of 1999, *Fight Club* raised eyebrows, provoked a great deal of criticism, and, ultimately underperformed at the box office in its U.S. release. Opening to U.S.

audiences on October 15th—just a few short months after the shooting rampage at Columbine high school in Littleton, Colorado—one prominent film critic asserted that, after the first 25 minutes or so, "the movie stops being smart and savage and witty, and turns to some of the most brutal, unremitting, nonstop violence ever filmed."[32] He continued:

> "Fight Club" is the most frankly and cheerfully fascist big-star movie since "Death Wish," a celebration of violence in which the heroes write themselves a license to drink, smoke, screw and beat one another up.
>
> Sometimes, for variety, they beat up themselves. It's macho porn—the sex movie Hollywood has been moving toward for years, in which eroticism between the sexes is replaced by all-guy locker-room fights. Women, who have had a lifetime of practice at dealing with little-boy posturing, will instinctively see through it; men may get off on the testosterone rush. The fact that it is very well made and has a great first act certainly clouds the issue.[33]

With negative reviews such as this, and with the legacy of the Columbine massacre still fresh in many minds, the edgy, unique, and, ultimately anti-corporate and materialist tale suffered at the box office, grossing a mere $37 million in the United States.[34] Did it deserve such criticism? Did its message get bogged down in a barrage of sex and violence? Is *Fight Club* a penetrating, agitating film with a serious political edge, or is it, as Roger Ebert suggested, merely a violent, misogynistic "thrill ride masquerading as philosophy"?[35] You be the judge. But whatever your analysis of the sex, violence, and its merit (or lack thereof), the film's political connotations and cultural commentary on modern American consumerism, corporate manipulation, and capitalism run amok is unmistakable. And, perhaps, a tad unsettling.

An International Economy?
Globalization and Liberalism

The imperatives of an international economy in the modern era demand that countries open their markets. An emphasis on reducing barriers to goods coming into a country,

especially tariffs (or taxes), has meant that materials produced by smaller manufacturers are often at a disadvantage
to larger, more efficient manufacturers. This is because the
larger manufacturers have an economy of scale that makes
their production much cheaper than smaller manufacturers.
Often this means that multinational corporations can lower
their prices so much that small manufacturers cannot sell
their products at a profit.

By opening their markets, countries are no longer able to
protect some of their most vital industries. There have been
calls to protect the cultural industries of some countries. For
example, there have been calls in the past to have the French
government protect the French film industry by requiring a
certain percentage of movie screens to show French-
language films.[36] Some would argue that this leads to a situation where there is a temptation that economically disad-
vantaged cultures would be pushed out of the arena by
wealthier and seemingly more influential cultures.

On the other hand, increased global interaction and globalization allows for an exchange of ideas and cultures that
has never existed before. As this book demonstrates,
foreign films, once only seen in major metropolitan areas of
the United States, are now available around the country by
way of videocassettes, DVDs, and cable and satellite television. American film, television shows, music, and literature
are available in nearly every country in the world. Sometimes this interaction provides us with learning situations;
sometimes it provides us with entertaining situations.

At the beginning of the film The Gods Must Be Crazy
(1980), Xixo (played by N!xau) is walking in the Kalahari
desert when a strange animal flies over the sky. Xixo, a
member of a small bush tribe in Botswana, has never seen
a white man technology, nor does he know anything harder
than the scrub wood that is occasionally found in the Kalahari. As the strange animal flies overhead, it drops something from the sky that is at once beautiful and the hard-
est thing Xixo has ever seen. The animal flying overhead
is what we would call an airplane, and the wonderful,

beautiful, hard object that Xixo believes the gods have given him is a Coca-Cola bottle. After the bottle causes great trouble among the members of his clan, Xixo sets off on a journey to throw the bottle off the edge of the world. During his journey he encounters a world that he never knew existed and the resulting culture shock, both for him and those he encounters, provides one of the classic comedies of the art house circuit.

Another film with a similar theme is the first film ever made in the country of Bhutan, *Phörpa* ("The Cup"). Made in 1999, the film is based on a true story of two Tibetan Buddhist monks who are avid soccer fans and go to extraordinary lengths to pull off their plan to watch the 1998 World Cup final, which is being televised from Paris. While funny and sweet, the movie also says a lot about the world in which we live: Tibetan monks, in one of the most remote regions of the world, obsessed with a soccer game that is played halfway around the world. The interaction between cultures is significant.

The Big One: Debating the Human Costs of the Global Economy

On the other hand, it would be a mistake to think that all of the effects of globalization are sweet and funny. Several scholars and pundits, notable among them Thomas Friedman, Benjamin Barber, and Ignacio Ramonet, have debated the benefits and drawbacks to globalization. The one conclusion that they seem to come to is that there are both benefits and drawbacks.[37] Guerrilla filmmaker Michael Moore's documentary, *The Big One* (1998) follows the satirist, agitator, and social commentator on his nationwide book tour in support of his 1996 bestseller *Downsize This! Random Threats from an Unarmed American*.[38] Moore, the man behind 1990's lauded *Roger & Me,* which catalogued the disastrous effects of GM layoffs in Flint, Michigan in the 1980s, uses his book tour to examine downsizing and economic misery in the 1990s. As he trots from bookstore to theater to university campus to radio show—and hotel to airport to hotel—he runs into Americans who have been downsized (i.e., lost their job) in the midst of unprecedented national prosperity. From Centralia to Rockford, from Milwaukee to Minneapolis, and many places in between, Moore chastises corporations for laying off workers in times of rising profits, presents corporations with checks for their first hour of Mexican wages, criticizes a welfare-to-work program in Wisconsin, and asks Pillsbury—on a "Post-It Note"—why they need millions of dollars in federal subsidies to promote their "Doughboy" overseas. In Des Moines, Iowa he shows solidarity with Barnes & Noble employees who work to form a union, and at the Mall of America outside Minneapolis, he finds a murderer who worked for TWA while in prison. It turns out that, across the country, prisoners perform labor for severely reduced wages.

All of these experiences on the road in the U.S. reinforce Moore's central interpretation of what he sees as the darker, or more extreme, side of liberal economics: that many corporations do not care—but should care—about the health and well-being of their employees; and, moreover, that the social contract demands that people should not lose their jobs when the company is doing well. It is a theme accented in length in *Roger & Me,* and *The Big One,* while essentially a series of pit stops on a promotional book tour, echoes the same message.

While Moore provides the audience with some comic and entertainment relief, such as a visit with Cheap Trick's Rick Nielson where Moore does his best Bob Dylan impersonation, these are merely entertaining distractions from he heart of the film, which asks the fundamental question: What is the human cost of the global economy—both here in the United States and around the world? In the spirit of this question, Moore winds up at a Nike protest in Portland, Oregon, where the shoe giant's corporate headquarters are located. Activists came to protest working conditions at shoe factories in Vietnam and Indonesia. Unlike GM CEO Roger Smith, who never agreed to a legitimate sit-down with Moore in *Roger & Me,* Phillip Knight, the CEO of Nike, actually *invites*

Moore to his home to discuss his inclusion in the "corporate crook trading cards" section of Moore's *Downsize This!* When they meet, Moore presents Knight with two airplane tickets to Indonesia so that he and Knight can inspect the factories where Nike shoes are made. Knight politely declines the invitation. Throughout their discussion of Nike's factories and corporate citizenship, Knight is affable and accommodating to his muckraking guest, but clearly does not share Moore's view that 14-year-old girls should not be working in Indonesian factories making Nikes. He also rejects Moore's contention that Americans would, if paid a decent wage, manufacture shoes in the states.

In the end, their views of the global economy are not in sync, though Moore does get Knight to match his $10,000 gift to Flint, Michigan's public schools. One critic's review summarizes Moore and Knight's—and many other CEO's—opposing interpretations of corporate responsibility and the costs of globalization:

> Moore's overall conclusion: Large American corporations care more for their stockholders than for their workers, and no profit level is high enough to satisfy them. If he'd been able to get more top executives on camera, I have a feeling their response would have been: "Yes. And?"[39]

In the final analysis, these closing remarks get to the heart of *The Big One* and the issues it raises. What should the proper balance be between workers' rights, wages, health and safety standards, and environmental standards, on one hand, and efficiency and profit, on the other? Would it be better to pay workers in the Third World higher wages and pay more for shoes here at home so that the workers would take home more money? Are corporations doing underdeveloped states a favor by bringing jobs to countries starved for economic investment? Who benefits more from the economic relationship in globalization: the corporations, the American consumers, or the workers in factories—whether it's Indonesia, Vietnam, or China? What do you think? Clearly, *The Big One* is a vehicle for Moore's perspective. But whether one accepts his view of the social contract, corporate power, and worker's struggles in the global economy one thing is clear: Moore brings essential dynamics and penetrating questions to the political table for all to ponder.

Conclusion

The United States, as the most prosperous and powerful country in the world for the latter half of the twentieth century, frequently saw its values and worldview displayed on the screen. Even before the Second World War, the United States had a domestic audience sufficient enough to insure that its film industry could out-produce any of its rivals in Europe. Consequently, the American film industry became the standard by which other industries were measured. As this chapter has indicated, however, there have been warnings about the excesses or limitations of both democracy and capitalism coming even from the United States. Other parts of the world have been less sure about the assumptions that capitalism and democracy necessarily go hand in hand.

For example, Fritz Lang's 1926 science-fiction masterpiece *Metropolis* depicted a world of the year 2026, where growing disparities between haves and have-nots leads to a physical separation between the two. The "haves" lead an idyllic life in the Metropolis above ground. They are blessed with a lifestyle of wealth and leisure, largely unaware of the plight of those who live below the city. The "have-nots," those workers who live underground and run the city, work themselves to death in service to the Metropolis. While they are indeed employed, they are little more than automatons. The workers are forced to operate machinery in perpetual motion, in dangerous circumstances, and often die at their workstations. In one scene of the film, in the eyes of a person who lives above ground, the machinery is transformed into an altar for human sacrifice; where individuals are forced into the interior of the machine that resembles individuals being dumped into a volcanic pit.

Events during the course of the film force a showdown between those who live above ground and those who live below. A revolution ensues and the workers destroy the machine. However, in doing so, the workers also endanger their house and the lives of their children. The hidden message of the film seems to be that revolution hurts both groups, and therefore is not a proper course of action. Yet the explicit message of the film is contained in the phrase, *"There can be no understanding between the hands and the brain unless the heart acts as mediator."* In some prints of the film there was a quote from Thea von Harbou's novel on which the film was based:

> This film is not of today or of the future.
> It tells of no place. It serves no tendency, party or class.
> It has a moral that grows on the pillar of understanding:
> The mediator between brain and muscle must be the heart.

By the end of the film, both sides are reconciled by the love of a daughter of the underworld and the son of those who live on top. Interestingly enough, both fascists and communists claimed the film. In fact, it was also said to be Adolph Hitler's favorite film, although both the director of the film, Fritz Lang, and the author of the novel, Thea von Harbou, claimed that Hitler misunderstood the meaning of the film.

Some films, as this chapter has indicated, provide a clear message as to how society should be governed, and what ideology should be the driving force: liberalism, fascism, or communism. Other films, such as *Metropolis,* provide a seemingly ambiguous message. That being said, *Metropolis,* its director Fritz Lang, and its author Thea von Harbou, centered the story on the domestic relationship of capital and labor. While claiming no particular ideology, the film nevertheless focuses the attention of the audience on a particular relationship within society. It is important to remember that films, documentaries, and television programs each carry a message, stated or unstated. If they had no story to tell, no message to convey, then the piece or work would not have been made. Our job as students of politics and film is to mine the fertile earth of film to discover all of these messages, and discuss their application and relevance to the real world of politics, governmental institutions, and international relations. Whether you're watching film classics, PBS, primetime television (*The Simpsons* is an especially good place to start!), or sitting at the multiplex, this critical approach to studying film and our world will set us on the intellectual path of "seeing the bigger picture."

CHAPTER 3

Alternative Ideologies: Communism and Fascism

One of the seminal debates in any society is how that society is best governed. Many would argue that in European societies the politics have been moving from a time when one individual has been the sovereign, toward the incorporation of all people in the society into the decision-making processes. But debates still occur as to what decisions are in the public sphere and which are best left to the private individuals. In many societies, those that we tend to think of as "Western," societies are guided by liberal ideologies, meaning a reliance on a market system of economic governance as well as an understanding of fundamental freedoms and human rights as necessary and proper for the maintenance of good governance in society. In this chapter we will explore two of the more prominent theories on this subject that challenge liberal ideals.

In a seminal piece written as the Cold War was coming to an end in 1989, Francis Fukuyama wrote that we are entering a phase where great battles over ideologies were over. Liberal democracy was "the end of history" because, aside from technical modifications, it was a system of governance that could not fundamentally be improved upon.[1] If one is to consider the course of history, then one notices that there are an ever-increasing number of people participating in the decision-making process. Once the number of people participating reaches its maximum, all adults, then there is no way to fundamentally enlarge the number of people who participate in society. Fukuyama argues that over the course of the twentieth century liberal democracy experienced two great challenges: communism and fascism. This chapter will focus on those two primary philosophic challenges to liberalism, beginning with films that advocate Marxist/communist perspectives and then how films were used to criticize the tenets of communism. Next the chapter will examine films made by fascist regimes, films that advocate a fascist agenda, and those films that attempted to refute fascist ideology and ideals.

Alternative Views: Marxism

Writing in the mid-nineteenth century, Karl Marx observed the growing economic inequality between those that provided labor and those that own capital. Marxists argue that this system of economics was a structurally unfair system and one that privileged those who were lucky enough to own capital such as factories. Those that own the factory actually did no labor or work, but existed and profited from the hard work of those who were employed by the factory. In essence, many Marxists argued that the relationship between the two classes was parasitic, with the owners living off the labor of the working classes. Marx argued that the capitalist system was one that would gradually privilege fewer and fewer people while at the same time drive more and more workers to the brink of desperation.

Thus, Marx predicted that history was moving toward a time when workers would finally revolt against the upper classes and create a system of governance that would be fair to workers. Since everyone would then be a laborer, what would emerge would be a classless society. Marx had originally thought that the workers' revolution that was to come would occur in an industrialized society where the inequalities between labor and capital classes were most pronounced. However, the first successful Marxist, or communist, revolution occurred in imperial Russia, a largely agricultural state that lacked significant industrialization. As an adherent to Marx's ideas, Vladimir Lenin, the leader of the Bolsheviks (communists) in Russia, expounded on Marx. Lenin suggested that in order for capitalism to continue it would necessarily have to expand in order to gain access to increasing capital and markets. In order to do this it would use the state to create colonies and use force if necessary to insure the protection of the capitalist class's interests.

After the Russian Revolution of 1917, the Bolsheviks would use the relatively new medium of cinema to "educate" the population. While many of the films of this period can and are considered propaganda, there is general agreement that the films produced during the silent era of the Soviet Union (roughly 1917 to 1930) are some of the most imaginative and innovative films ever made. Early Soviet cinema also visualized the ideals of a workers' revolution most clearly. In many ways it is too bad that these films are not more widely known because they are excellent commentaries about how the Soviets saw the world in the first thirty years of the twentieth century.

Potemkin (1925)

Consistently ranked among the top ten films ever made, *Potemkin* (or *Battleship Potemkin*) tells the story of the failed 1905 Russian Revolution. The film, made in honor of the twentieth anniversary of the event, recounts the story of the battleship *Potemkin* on which, while in the Black Sea, a mutiny breaks out. Sailors are given maggot-infested food for their rations and when some sailors protest the captain orders the protestors to be shot. One sailor, Vakulinchuk, implores those who carry the rifles not to follow orders because they would only be shooting their brothers. The sailors lower their weapons and join in a general mutiny against the imperial czarist officers. During the struggle for the ship, Vakulinchuk is killed; however, the mutiny is successful.

The sailors take the body of Vakulinchuk to Odessa, where the citizenry of the city come to pay respects. While a crowd is gathered on the steps heading down to the sea a czarist militia appears and begins shooting. A massacre occurs, and in particularly moving imagery, even babies and old women are deliberate victims of the massacre. The *Potemkin* returns to the sea to face a group of battleships sent to subdue it. As the sailors ready the guns of

An advertisement from the *New York Times* for the film *The Fall of the Romanoffs* (1917). Films such as this were very popular in the United States following the Russian Revolution and sought to exploit the sensationalism of those events. They also laid the groundwork for anticommunist films by associating the revolution with the violence and brutality of these events.

the *Potemkin,* they signal the other ships not to fight but instead to join them. In the face of a destructive battle the other ships relent and add their support to *Potemkin.* The film ends with the jubilant crews of all the ships cruising off to face their adversaries.

Potemkin may be the best example of Marxist filmmaking achievement. Note that there is no real protagonist in the film other than the Russian people. The only other potential protagonist is Vakulinchuk who is killed off early in as a sacrifice for the good of the people. Also, coming just eight years after the revolution, the films serves as a document and a reminder to citizens (and others) of the brutality of the czarist regime. In the famous Odessa Steps sequence, one of the most famous and important scenes in film history, director Sergei Eisenstein focuses on the viciousness of the regime using a baby carriage to symbolize all the innocents. The officers in the navy are particularly brutal and dismissive of the needs of the sailors. Essentially Eisenstein is making a comment on how the aristocracy and the upper class in general (bourgeoisie) treat workers, the masses, and the nation, with contempt and disregard in favor of their own selfish interests.[2]

The Fall of the Romanov Dynasty (1927)

Part of the appeal of the early Soviet cinema was the use of innovative editing techniques. The use of these techniques is evident in the work of Eisenstein, especially in the creation of the Odessa Steps sequence. Esther Shub, one of the early female pioneers in world cinema, would use old newsreel footage and archival footage to create a commentary on the czarist regime before the revolution and the need for a Marxist revolution.[3] Shub searched the Soviet Union for several films to put together a montage of film to create a historical film document of the events from 1912 up to the 1917 revolution organized to create a communist commentary on the events. Shub's efforts are particularly noteworthy not only because of the statement she is making about the czarist regime and the need for the Bolshevik revolution, but also Shub's work probably saved a number of scenes that would not have otherwise been seen by people today.

Shub creates a number of running themes through *The Fall of Romanov Dynasty,* the most prevalent of which is the opulence of the czar and the aristocracy juxtaposed with the poverty of the average Russian citizen. The film opens with documentary footage, shot by the czar's own cameramen, of the celebration of the tricentennial of the Romanov Dynasty. The film employs title cards to raise questions as to why some Russians (the czar and his court) are allowed to enjoy such privilege and wealth, while in the meantime newsreel footage shows peasants suffering from various natural disasters, such as floods and drought, and barely eking out an existence. In a particularly biting commentary, Shub shows a party on a cruise liner on the Black Sea where members of the court are having a dance. Shub next shows footage of peasants suffering from a drought and are on the verge of starvation. Title cards explain the desperate situations in which the peasants find themselves, when the footage cuts back to the dance on the cruise liner, and a title card reads, ". . . and the aristocracy dances on."

Regardless of how one views Marxist ideology, it is hard to deny that both Eisenstein and Shub created films that make an impassioned plea for a change from the czarist regime. Both provide evidence of the brutality of the czarist regime and the need for a new order within the Russian society. However, where many will depart from their line of thinking is how society should be ordered after the fall of the czar. Many Russians though saw the aristocracy and merchant classes as complicit in the subjugation of the Russian people.

First Reactions to the Communist Revolution

By the 1930s revolutionary experiments in the Soviet films were over. The film industry in the Soviet Union turned primarily to a reconstruction of revolutionary events in terms of social realism such as in *Lenin in October* (1937) and *Lenin in 1918* (1939).[4] Of course, outside the Soviet Union there were immediate reactions to calls of worldwide revolution. Many are familiar with the more blatant anti-communist films of the 1950s; however, "red scare" films have their genesis in the late teens and 1920s in American film history. Later, in the 1950s, Hollywood would develop a more sophisticated response to a perceived communist threat. Europeans would offer an even subtler critique that would even come from communist societies themselves.

Hollywood would begin reacting to the Russian Revolution almost immediately. In the same year as the revolution,

1917, the American film industry produced a number of films about the subject. Two of the more prominent were *The Fall of the Romanoffs* (1917) and *The Rose of Blood* (1917); copies of neither of the films survive today. These films would concentrate on the events in Russia at the time and were not specifically critical of Marxism per se. Instead the Soviet Union was used as a backdrop of drama, terrorism, and political intrigue. Later, the films would focus more on the stereotypes of the regime rather than the revolution itself. In *The Tempest* (1927), a John Gilbert vehicle, the film took viewers "inside" the Soviet Union to show the brutality of the regime.

During the Second World War, because of the wartime alliance between the Soviet Union and the United States, American films sometimes reflected some of the points of views of the Soviet leadership. In *Mission to Moscow* (1943), former ambassador Joseph E. Davies, whose memoirs the film was based upon, offers an almost apologist view of the Soviet system. The film gives a Soviet view of the war and attempts to garner support for the Soviet Union as an ally. The controversial film even goes as far as offering a sympathetic view of the army purges of the 1930s. Other films, such as *Tender Comrade* (1943), directed by Edward Dmytryk (see "Who Were the Hollywood Ten" box on page 68), portrayed collectivism in action in everyday life. The film tells the story of five women, whose significant others are engaged in war duties, sharing a house together. The women use democracy to run the house, while Jo Flanagan (played by Ginger Rogers) sets about to organize the house and to provide moral chats and to keep everyone devoted to the war effort and the missing men.

Battling Communist Ideology: The Red Scare Films

Soon after the death of President Franklin Roosevelt and the end of World War II, relations between the Soviet Union and the United States, once staunch allies in the fight against Nazi Germany, fascist Italy, and the empire of Japan, frayed considerably. Competing values, economic systems and ideologies—namely liberalism and Soviet communism—vied for moral superiority and world prowess. Severe disagreements and misunderstandings over several pressing issues—especially the shape of post-war Europe and, specifically, control of Eastern Europe—fostered increasing hostility and contempt between the superpowers. In the midst of this ideological warfare, both states readied and expanded their conventional and nuclear arsenals,[5] and embarked upon nearly five decades of expensive, nerve-racking "Cold War."

In the meantime, Hollywood film studios also entered the ideological fray of the Cold War, using their arsenal of writers, producers, and directors to promote liberalism and Western-style capitalism and denigrate communism. Responding to the extensive and, at times, violent labor struggles between Hollywood studios and the writers' and actors' guilds in the late 1940s, the growing animosity and distrust between the U.S. and the U.S.S.R., the political ascendance of the House Committee on American Activities (HUAC), and, by 1950, the war in Korea and the loss of American lives, film studios produced a series of films condemning communism and warning of its insidious spread in the United States. Thus, studio heads were not driven entirely by altruism and ideology—be it absolute faith in individual liberty or the gospel of the free market—but by the shifting winds of domestic politics, business interests, and blatant opportunism. In this new era, out were the unabashedly pro-Soviet films—such as the propagandistic *Mission to Moscow* (1943), which had been produced with active support from the Roosevelt administration—and in were movies that featured American innocents duped by the lies of communism.[6] The message of these films is clear: the vigilant rooting out of subversives, socialists, and communists at home is vital to winning the worldwide war against communism.

In the midst of this ideological warfare, Americans were encouraged, via a variety of new movies, to stand guard against the poisoning of children's minds, to be wary of academic elites indoctrinating students with Karl Marx's theories, and, if need be, to turn in family members suspected of being traitors to liberalism and American values. From the late 1940s through the mid-1950s, Hollywood produced a plethora of anti-communist "red scare" films that reflected the paranoia and hysteria concerning real and imagined domestic communist subversion and the fear of worldwide communist domination. A slew of films—such as *The Iron Curtain* (1948), *The Red Menace* (1949), *I Married a Communist* (1949), *I Was a Communist for the FBI* (1951), *Big Jim McLain* (1952), *My Son John* (1952), and, to a lesser and more curious extent, *Invasion of the Body Snatchers* (1956)— represent this genre of political films.

Big Jim McLain (1952)

One significant film that highlights many of the plot devices inherent in this genre of movies is the quintessential "red scare" anti-communist film *Big Jim McLain* (1952). Directed by Edward Ludwig and produced by John Wayne and Robert Fellows (the "Wayne-Fellows" production company), *Big Jim McLain* is a blatant propaganda tool for the House Committee on Un-American Activities (HUAC). Made with the explicit help and blessing of HUAC, the film stars Wayne as Jim McLain, a HUAC investigator who, along with his partner (James Arness), is sent to Hawaii to break up the communist infiltration of a longshoreman's union. Not unlike other red scare films, the communists are portrayed as sleek, well dressed, occasionally effeminate sophisticates (some with decidedly Eastern European accents) who are willing to murder and drug innocents and even sacrifice their own "comrades" if it advances their worldwide crusade. The film is also unabashedly anti-intellectual. At the start of the film, determined, patriotic HUAC investigators at a congressional hearing grill suave economic professors about their communist beliefs, only to be thwarted by the university intellectuals exercising their Fifth Amendment right to protect themselves against self-incrimination.

McLain scoffs at these un-American tactics, chastising the professors for "hiding behind the Constitution" just so they can continue to manipulate and poison the minds of American students. Some film critics have argued that the movie gives the impression that the sacred liberties of the Bill of Rights are reserved only for certain Americans.

As in other classic red menace movies of the era, *McLain* features parents who cooperate with HUAC investigators and willingly turn in their children who have been brainwashed by the communists and have become Soviet agents. In this film, the parents are retired, God-fearing, working class people who have settled in Hawaii after years of toiling for modest wages in San Francisco. They feel it is their duty to inform HUAC of their son's descent into communism. What makes *Big Jim McLain* unique among this group of films, however, is the prominence and drawing power of its leading man. While the vast majority of the red scare films featured moderately famous and B-movie Hollywood players, *Big Jim McLain* featured a bona fide Hollywood superstar— "The Duke," John Wayne. This immediately gives the film stature and an audience other red scare films could only dream of. Moreover, while most of the aforementioned red scare films were mildly successful, *McLain* was a major box office success. With a budget of $800,000, the Wayne-Fellows produced *McLain* grossed over $2.4 million dollars, earning a very healthy profit.[7]

Invasion of the Body Snatchers (1956)

In the sci-fi Cold War classic *Invasion of the Body Snatchers* (1956), alien seedpods infiltrate Middle America, quietly turning the citizens of Santa Mira into heartless, loveless drones. Released in the midst of anti-communist panic, the political implications would seem to be clear: the pods represent the communist menace, calmly and deliberatively turning trusted neighbors into uncaring communists. This development is especially alarming, as the neighbors look the same, dress the same, and inhabit the same houses, but something is wrong—*terribly* wrong. Their individuality and vitality has been sapped and been replaced with passion-less adherence to the communist cause. One by one, once vivacious, individualistic Americans are now dressed in a suit of subversive, Soviet skin.

Upon another careful viewing, however, Don Siegel's film may speak to another dynamic in post-war America. Rather than solely espousing the fear of insidious, Godless, soulless communism taking over the bodies of everyday suburban Americans, the film may very well be an *indictment* of Eisenhower-era conformity, McCarthyism, and mindless anticommunism. In this interpretation of the film, the pods that take over innocent Americans do not represent the evil of *communism,* but, rather, the peril of *anticommunist conformity* run amok. Political scientist Philip Gianos advances this alternative—and increasingly accepted—theory of the overriding political message of *Body Snatchers:*

> But one can as easily see *Invasion of the Body Snatchers* as an al-legory on another cold-war era concern: the drive toward a de-humanizing conformity in behavior and orthodoxy of thought in the service of opposition to communism. It was this interpre-tation that director Don Siegel gave to his own film. . . . arguing that the film was designed as a warning about the price in free-dom to be paid by demanding political and social orthodoxy.[8]

Similarly, political scientist Ernest Giglio includes *Body Snatchers* in the category of fifties films that indirectly ques-tion the pervasive anticommunist hysteria of the day. While there were few films that dared to overtly criticize the red scare and McCarthyism, *Body Snatchers* is cited as a movie in a category of films that "challenged the communist para-noia and the effects of McCarthyism allegorically, express-ing . . . condemnation of HUAC and the blacklist in plots that dealt with subjects ranging from space aliens to west-erns."[9] The pods, therefore, represent "the three dominant forces of the fifties: conformity, paranoia, and alienation."[10] While saturated in American popular culture at mid-century, the fifties sci-fi classic with powerful political undertones has remained popular with subsequent genera-tions of moviegoers. Gianos asserts that the film's staying

Invasion of the Body Snatchers

©1956 Republic Pictures Corporation

Are they humans or alien seedpods?! Many believe the alien seedpod invasion in the 1956 sci-fi classic *Invasion of the Body Snatchers* is a metaphor for the spread of anti-communist hysteria and rampant conformity in 1950s America.

power—it was remade in 1978 and 1992—is due, in large part, to the story's enduring appeal and its applicability to the politics and concerns of Americans on both sides of the ideological spectrum:

> The continuing power of the story is its attractiveness both to those who see the film as anti-Communist allegory and those who see it as a cautionary tale about conformity—an "anti-anti" Communist fable. Indeed the film may be easily seen as reflecting both of these concerns simultaneously, as such concerns were felt

simultaneously by many Americans of the time. . . . The subtle
implication was that there might be deep similarities as well as
differences between the contending parties of the cold war.[11]

Indeed, other later films would dare to directly criticize
and even lampoon McCarthyism and anticommunist conformity, as well as the self-serving, cynical politicians who
propagated fear and paranoia to further their careers. John
Frankenheimer's chilling Cold War political assassination
classic, *The Manchurian Candidate* (1962), is a perfect example. In one infamous scene, the loudmouthed McCarthy-
esque Senator Iselin (a hilarious James Gregory) rants and
raves on the Senate floor about the growing number of
communists serving in the U.S. government. However,
when pressed by reporters outside of Senate chambers for
more specifics, Sen. Iselin responds by giving several different numbers of communists. He finally settles on one number to suit his domineering political operator and wife (Angela Lansbury): 57. Why 57 communists? Because he tops
his hamburger with Heinz's 57 Ketchup at dinner the night
before his next anticommunist diatribe![12] This snippet from
the movies mirrors the historical record—and is clearly an
indictment of Senator Joe McCarthy, who, during a famous
speech in Wheeling, West Virginia in 1950 made headlines
by claiming he had a list of communists serving in the
government. Said McCarthy in Wheeling: "I have a here in
my hand a list of 205 [card-carrying communists] . . . who
are still working and shaping policy in the State Department." Secretary of State George Catlett Marshall was also
the target of McCarthy's ire; the Republican senator from
Wisconsin asserted that Marshall avidly participated in a
"conspiracy so immense and an infamy so black as to dwarf
any previous such venture in the history of man."[13] Like the
fictional Senator Iselin, McCarthy also occasionally had
trouble remembering the *precise* number of communists
selling out the United States. But, much like films critical of
America's involvement in Vietnam—most of which appeared years *after* the war—it is important to note that it
took several years for Hollywood to overtly question and

criticize the almost sacrosanct anticommunist ethos of the late 1940s to mid-1950s. Indeed, identifying communists and furthering the fear of domestic subversion became increasingly popular and bipartisan, as evidenced by the passage of the McCarran Act in 1950. Passed over the veto of Democratic President Harry Truman, the McCarran Act

> required communists to register with the government, revoked the passports of those suspected of communist sympathy, and established provisions for setting up concentration camps for subversives in the event of a national emergency.[14]

The Legacy of the Red Scare: HUAC, the Blacklist, and the Hollywood Ten

In 1938, the House Committee on Un-American Activities—soon known to many simply as the "Dies Committee" (the select committee was chaired by Rep. Martin Dies)—was formed to probe a variety of dangerous "Un-American" right and left wing ideologies and movements, from fascist kidnappers to the Ku Klux Klan. Soon after Dies ascended to the chairmanship of the committee, however, the targets became largely left-wing individuals and groups, especially those associated with President Franklin Roosevelt's (1933–1945) New Deal programs.[15] What was the legislative basis for the congressional examination of subversive groups? Specifically, the new House committee was authorized to—"from time to time"—conduct investigations of

> (1) the extent, character, and objects of un-American propaganda activities in the United States, (2) the diffusion within the United States of subversive and un-American propaganda that is instigated from foreign countries or of a domestic origin and attacks the principle of the form of government as guaranteed by our Constitution, and (3) all other questions in relation thereto that would aid Congress in any necessary remedial legislation.[16]

Cradle Will Rock (1999)

In particular, Dies and his investigators targeted suspected communist and socialist playwrights, actors, and directors in

Franklin Roosevelt's Federal Theatre Project, part of the New Deal's ambitious Works Project Administration (WPA). *Cradle Will Rock* (1999), written and directed by Tim Robbins, is a semi-fictional retelling of the congressional investigation of FDR's controversial jobs program as well as the creation and staging of Marc Blitzstein's 1937 left-wing Depression-era musical drama *The Cradle Will Rock*. The play's

> story line describes a union-organizing drive in the mythical city of Steeltown, USA. Its characters included a handsome union organizer named Larry Foreman, a rich industrialist named Mister Mister, and a streetwalker aptly named The Moll. . . . The climax of the play is a dramatic confrontation between the forces of good and evil personified by Foreman and Mister Mister. The play ends with a stirring massed chorus of union supporters . . . singing the title song.[17]

Among other plots, Robbins' 1999 film follows the extensive difficulties faced by the director of the Federal Theatre Project, Hallie Flanagan (Cherry Jones), as well as the challenges faced by the likes of writer Blitzstein (Hank Azaria) and producers Orson Welles (Angus MacFadyen) and John Houseman (Cary Elwes), who were attempting to stage the pro-union musical in the midst of enormous political pressure and threatened (and later, real) censorship. Robbins' *Cradle Will Rock* is clearly sympathetic with the government activism of the WPA and the Federal Theatre Project, and, moreover, defends the rights of artists to practice their craft free from government censorship. As such, the film stands as a cautionary tale of how reactionary politics can stifle creativity, and forcefully defends the artistic vision and liberal politics of the playwrights, directors, actors, and producers who worked in the Federal Theatre Project.

By the late 1940s, however, HUAC's main targets were no longer New Deal programs (the Federal Theatre Project was eventually discontinued after a series of congressional investigations) but left-wing actors, writers, and directors—some of whom were active in organizing the various unions in the film industry. In October 1947, after several closed-door hearings and investigations over a six-month period, HUAC

Chairman J. Parnell Thomas began public hearings designed to root out communists in Hollywood. The first to appear before the committee were so-called "friendly witnesses" trotted out by the motion picture industry to denounce communism and to suggest names of suspected Communist Party members and sympathizers in Hollywood. Witnesses representing "The Motion Picture Association for the Preservation of American Ideals" included actors Gary Cooper and Adolphe Menjou, and studio heads Jack Warner, Louis B. Mayer, and Walt Disney. The studio heads were eager to stem the rising tide of unionism and strikes in their industry, and Thomas' hearings served their purpose well.

After the "friendly witnesses" testified, a list of writers and directors who were suspected communists were called before the committee. The first ten of these witnesses were outraged at being called before a hostile, politically charged committee and refused to cooperate with Thomas' inquiry on constitutional grounds. They were later sent to prison for contempt of Congress, and several of them lost years of work in the industry, effectively "blacklisted" by studios and producers. This group of writers and directors became known collectively as "The Hollywood Ten." In alphabetical order, The Hollywood Ten are: Alvah Bessie, Herbert J. Biberman, Lester Cole, Edward Dmytryk, Ring Lardner, Jr., John Howard Lawson, Albert Maltz, Samuel Ornitz, Adrian Scott, Dalton Trumbo (see box *Who Were the Hollywood Ten?*)

Hollywood eventually directly examined the legacy and fallout of HUAC's hearings and the blacklisting of artists in the poignant dark comedy *The Front* (1976). Directed by blacklisted director Martin Ritt, written by blacklisted screenwriter Walter Bernstein, and starring a host of blacklisted actors, including Zero Mostel (Hecky Brown/Herschel Brownstein) and Herschel Bernardi (Phil Sussman), *The Front* stands as a major achievement: it is the first studio film to directly criticize the blacklist and address its myriad effect on writers, actors, producers, and their families. For instance, in the film, we see how the lack of work, loss of income, mounting depression, and pressure to "name names"

WHO WERE THE HOLLYWOOD TEN?

In October 1947, HUAC Chairman J. Parnell Thomas' conducted hearings aimed at rooting out communism and subversion in Hollywood (as well as gaining political points and smearing labor unions and left-wing sympathizers). The first ten witnesses that appeared before the committee were uncooperative, refusing, on constitutional grounds, to answer the question *"Are you are now or have you ever been a member of the Communist party?"* The ten witnesses were found in contempt of Congress for refusing to answer chairman Thomas' questions. The "Hollywood Ten" were sentenced to prison for their refusal to cooperate with HUAC.

The Media Resources Center at UC Berkeley, Moffitt Library: http://www.lib.berkeley.edu/MRC/blacklist.html
Biographies and filmographies of the "Hollywood Ten"—as well as excellent HUAC and Blacklist-era links and suggested readings—provided by The Media Resources Center at UC Berkeley (Moffitt Library at UC Berkeley, phone number: 510–642–8197).

For further reading, see:
"Hollywood and the Movies in the 1950's: A Short Bibliography of Books and Articles in the UC Berkeley Libraries"—http://www.lib.berkeley.edu/MRC/50sbib.html

The Hollywood Ten
(in alphabetical order)

Alvah Bessie (novelist, journalist, screenwriter)
Herbert J. Biberman (director, screenwriter, producer)
Lester Cole (screenwriter, playwright)
Edward Dmytryk (director)
Ring Lardner, Jr. (screenwriter, reporter, publicist)

John Howard Lawson (screenwriter)
Albert Maltz (author, short-story writer, playwright, screenwriter)
Samuel Ornitz (screenwriter)
Adrian Scott (producer, screenwriter)
Dalton Trumbo (newspaper reporter, editor, screenwriter)

causes the talented comedian Hecky Brown, a blacklisted actor, to commit suicide.

The film stars Woody Allen as Howard Prince, a simple debt-ridden bookie who is a "front" for his friend Alfred Miller, a blacklisted writer. Prince routinely meets with Miller and other blacklisted writers at a local deli, where the out-of-work artists give Prince scripts for television shows. Prince gets a ten percent cut from each of the scripts, and winds up becoming a celebrity as he pads his modest gambling revenue. Even Prince's high school invites the bumbling bookie-turned-star writer back for a school assembly, where he is introduced as a bonafide American success story. The deli scenes have direct political resonance, as the three fictional writers depicted in the film—Herbert Delaney (Lloyd Gough), Bill Phelps (David Marguiles), and Alfred Miller (Michael Murphy)—are actually composites of real life blacklisted writers Walter Bernstein, Arnold Manoff and Abraham Polonsky, who collaborated on the 1953 Walter Cronkite television segments *You Are There*. It is perhaps poetic justice that in 1977 Bernstein's script for *The Front* was nominated for best screenplay by the Academy Awards and the Writers Guild of America.[18]

In later years Hollywood would revisit many of the same issues addressed in *The Front,* albeit less successfully. *Guilty by Suspicion* (1991), written and directed by Irwin Winkler and starring Robert De Niro as an unjustly accused communist, attacked the blacklist and its pernicious consequences on writers, directors, and their families. However, the film failed to garner the critical accolades and audience size earned by Ritt and Bernstein's film. A few documentaries do an excellent job of detailing the social, political, and cultural legacy of HUAC's investigations, the red scare films of the late 1940s to mid 1950s, and the blacklist. *Hollywood on Trial* (1976), an Oscar-nominated documentary directed by David Helpern and written by Arnie Reisman, is the most in-depth and impressive blacklist documentary, featuring extensive archival footage of HUAC investigations of 1947 and revealing interviews with members of the Hollywood Ten. *Blacklist: Hollywood on Trial* (television, 1996) narrated by Alec Baldwin, re-examines many of the themes covered in *Hollywood on Trial*. The documentary, produced for the American Movie Classics network, earned the President's Award at the 1996 Emmy's and the "Gold Apple" award from the National Educational Media Network, USA.

Challenging Communist Ideology: The Czech New Wave

While the films that confronted communism in the United States tended to rely on scare tactics and overblown characterizations, criticism from within the Communist block had to be more muted and subtle. Filmmakers in the Communist block had to make criticism of their regimes and societies surreptitiously. One of the great eras of filmmaking was the Czech New Wave, which flourished in the 1960s and took particular advantage of the loosening of government censorships that culminated in the Prague Spring of 1968. While not being able to attack the communist regime of Czechoslovakia directly, filmmakers like Miloš Forman and Jan Němec used simple stories to explore issues of deeper political meanings. On the surface, one might not see the political significance, but understanding the context of these films provide a richer appreciation of the work of Czech New Wave directors.

Loves of a Blonde (1965)

Initially, *Loves of a Blonde* (1965) appears to be a simple tale of a young girl and her adventures following a boy who she has spent the night with. However, the film is more of an indictment of the monotony of Czech society under the Communist regime. As the film opens, Andula is working at a shoe factory in her hometown of Zruc. The manager of the factory is sympathetic to the fact that there are not enough men around for the two thousand or so women who work in the shoe factory. He implores the local military commander to move the base closer to the factory so that the women can meet some men. Initially the military

MILOŠ FORMAN

Forman may be the most celebrated director to emerge from the Czech Republic. After he emigrated to the United States following the Soviet invasion of Czechoslovakia in 1968, Forman went on to direct a series of highly acclaimed films. Taken by themselves, the films are some of the most celebrated films of the last several decades. Taken together, and considering his biography, Forman's filmography may provide an interesting body of work to consider.

Forman's parents were killed in a Nazi concentration camp outside Prague during World War II. After attending film school in Prague, Forman made two of the most important films of the Czech New Wave: *Loves of a Blonde* (1965) and *The Firemen's Ball* (1967). Both films ran into trouble with government censors, and some volunteer fire fighters in Czechoslovakia reportedly were offended by the ineptitude of the firemen in *The Firemen's Ball*, although this may be propaganda from the communist Czechoslovak regime.

Consider some of Forman's U.S. films:

One Flew Over the Cuckoo's Nest (1975)—Nominated for nine Academy Awards, and winner of five, including best picture and best director. The film examines the abuses of authority inside a mental institution. Lead actor Jack Nicholson finds that the head nurse is more dangerous than the patients.

Hair (1979)—A musical that celebrates individuals' choices and the counter-culture. Being drafted into the Vietnam War interrupts the happiness and contentment of the protagonist.

Amadeus (1984)—The phenomenally successful film biography of Wolfgang Amadeus Mozart, examines the unique individuality of the great composer. The film was nominated for eleven Academy Awards, and was the winner of eight, including best picture and best director.

The People vs. Larry Flynt (1996)—A highly controversial film, which examined the right of the famous pornographer and his exercise and defense of free speech. The film used the tagline, *"You may not like what he does, but are you prepared to give up his right to do it?"* Forman was again nominated for an Academy Award for best director.

In the first two films listed here, the director examines the abuses of authority. In the latter two films, Forman examines the exercise of free expression, whether that be from an 18th century composer who was censored because of the subject manner of his operas, or a 20th century pornographer. Forman did receive a great deal of criticism for his defense of Larry Flynt. For further reading consider Forman's reasoning behind taking on the project:

Miloš Forman's Address to the National Press Club: http://www.mit.edu/activities/safe/writings/people-v-flynt

commander balks, arguing that soldiers are needed at the border rather than to entertain young women. The factory manager implores him, asking what good is peace if people cannot live fulfilling lives. The train arrives and off come men who are not very appealing; one of the women comments that the army sent them veterans rather than young soldiers.

At a dance held as a mixer for the women and the soldiers, three soldiers approach Andula and her friends. The women are not really interested in the men, but they are polite, and the encounter results in a comedic exercise. Meanwhile, Andula finds herself drawn toward the piano player, Mila, in the band. She meets him after the dance, and is later seduced by him. After her tryst with the young piano player, she becomes enamored with him and dumps her oft-absent boyfriend.

In a scene that is perhaps telling of the society that Forman is trying to represent, the film depicts how the trappings of democracy can be twisted. After an incident in which Andula's former boyfriend comes to the factory dormitory, the women get a lecture from the housemother about morals. She argues that by "giving into boys," women cheapen themselves and make the prospects of having a happy and fulfilling live with a happy family more remote. After the lecture, two of the women step forward and say that the housemother has made a lot of sense and they propose to take a vote to mend their ways. The women in the dormitory vote to mend their ways without opposition or abstentions.

Seeing her life in Zruc as monotonous, Andula travels to Prague to with her luggage to drop in on Mila. When she arrives at Mila's apartment, Mila's parents confront her about why she is there and who invited her to Prague. While the father is a little more sympathetic, Mila's mother interrogates her unmercifully. Meanwhile, Mila is out trying unsuccessfully for another sexual conquest. When Mila arrives home his parents confront him: Mila denies inviting Andula to Prague. His mother insists that he sleep in their bedroom, and goes on and on about him, saying that he will be the death of her. At the same time, Andula listens in the next room tearfully to the conversation.

When she returns home, Andula remains upbeat and hopeful of her love life and future. She tells how nice Mila's parents were, and what a great person in particular his father is and how happy Mila was to see her. She whispers to her roommate that she will be making several trips to Prague now, and the close of the film shows her back on the assembly line working on the shoes. While initially we might think that Andula is naïve, one could argue though that she is coping with her plight as optimistically as possible.

Forman has said that he got the idea of *Loves of a Blonde* when he was driving home one night and saw a young girl on the street corner in Prague with her bags. When he stopped to see why she was there she confessed that she had traveled to Prague to find a young man whom she had met in her village and had slept with. However, the address he had provided was false.[19] While the film focuses on the love life of the blonde, Andula, Forman is also commenting on the society in which she exists. Andula's isolation and her reliance on married men, one-night stands, and absent boyfriends for company is a function of her employment. She works in an all-women factory, remote from social functions. In the scene where the women are subjected to lectures on morals, we presume that the women who propose the vote to mend their ways are operatives of the state. The vote is an opportunity to publicly shame the women into changing their behavior. Clearly no one is going to vote against higher morals, and the vote is essentially meaningless. But, in the end, those in charge can argue that they have provided a democratic "choice" for the women in the dormitory.

The Firemen's Ball (1967)

Forman's next film went farther in its criticism of the ineptitude and banality of Stalinist regimes. *The Firemen's Ball* (1967) is again on the surface a simple tale of a party for a former fire chief. But the conformity of the society and the inability of the bureaucracy to rationally organize society are at the heart of the film. The main plotline of the film is a party to award the former police chief a golden axe in recognition of his years of service. The occasion is his 86th birthday; his 85th birthday would have been more appropriate, but as one reviewer observed, "procrastination is important to any functioning bureaucracy."[20] But before the awarding of the gifts and the raffling off of various prizes, the firemen are called away on a fire.

One of the funniest scenes of the film is when another old man in the town's house is burning down and the firemen arrive to extinguish the flames. The man is sitting in a chair in front of his house, in the snow, watching the house burn when his neighbors come out and decide that he should be turned away from the house so that he does not have to watch it burn. The neighbors then decide that since it is cold that they should move the man closer to the house so that he does not get cold. Forman is making a comment here about the society's inability to make decisions that are rational. Instead of the neighbors taking the old man inside, to offer him comfort, they search for an idea that is relevant to the man yet does not put any burden on themselves.

Once the firemen return to the party, they find that the guests have stolen all the gifts. The firemen attempt to have all the presents returned, only to find that they must protect one of their own. The proceedings descend into comedy while the aging chief is left to list from side to side patiently awaiting his award. In the midst of this ball to honor the former chief, several other activities are going on, including a beauty contest and the various raffles. The story calls into question not only how people should behave, but also the reasoning behind the ball in the first place.

Notice that neither of the two Forman films reviewed here are attacks directly on the regime in Czechoslovakia at the time. They are simple stories of everyday life, the life of common people in Czechoslovakia, that have overtones that go to the heart of Czech society. But behind the story is an exploration of the one of the most sensitive debates of the late 1960s in Czechoslovakia. When the end of Stalinism in the Soviet Union and the progress of de-Stalinization throughout Eastern Europe occurred, the question became what should be done with those who committed the brutality of the 1950s, particularly those who were still in power. *The Firemen's Ball* was released in December 1967, just a few weeks before the Novotný regime was to be replaced by the more liberal Dubček regime, which ushered in what became known as the Prague Spring. During most of 1968 Prague flourished under increasing political and economic liberalization. Journalists, writers, and academics were given enough freedom and were allowed to speak about the abuses of the past. Television shows, newspapers, and commentators outlined the excesses and abuses of the Stalin and the Novotný regimes. As the liberalization continued other East European regimes, and most importantly the Soviet Union, worried about the end result. Questions were raised as to whether Czechoslovakia would even remain a member of the Warsaw Pact (the defensive organization of European Communist countries). Finally in August 1968, Warsaw Pact troops, led by the Soviet Union, invaded Czechoslovakia to replace the Dubček regime and restore a more hard-line government whose policies would be more in line with that of the Soviet Union.[21]

A *Report on the Party and the Guest* (1966)

Perhaps the most bizarre film discussed in this book is *A Report on the Party and the Guest [O slavnosti a hostech]* (1966). While the narrative and plot seems rather odd, understand that director Jan Nemec was making a very pointed criticism of the Czechoslovak regime while at the same time not directly mentioning politics at all. While the *New York Times* named it one of the top ten films of the 1960s, Czech President Novotný declared the film "banned forever." As the film opens, a group of people is having a picnic. Each agrees that it is a beautiful day and the food is delicious. The group reminisces about their previous

outings and what their host has done in the past. One remarks, "Remember the time he had the wine?" Almost im-
perceptibly to the picnickers and the viewer, a man comes
out of the woods with a bottle of wine.

Later the group is making their way through the forest
when a strange man (Rudolf) approaches them and asks if
they are enjoying their outing. Rudolf is very insistent on
gaining the groups' attention, but he makes the group feel
very uneasy. Soon a number of severe-looking men come
out of the woods and prevent the group from reaching their
destination. Eventually, they lead the group to a clearing in
the forest where Rudolf reappears and forces the group to
conform to his wishes. The men bring a desk and chair to
the clearing, where Rudolf sits and directs the group to organize, à la communist apparatchik. Members of the group
attempt to address him, but Rudolf only responds when
they are organized as he desires them to be organized. Finally, the intellectual of the group organizes the group, di-
viding men from women by an imaginary line, and addresses Rudolf with the deference he is seeking. While the
group makes progress with Rudolf, some are still resistant.
When one of the men refuses to be bound by imaginary
walls and incoherent rules he attempts to run away, only to
be stopped by Rudolf's men and roughed up.

The group is finally "rescued" by the "host," who explains
that Rudolf enjoys acting and that the whole thing has been
staged for entertainment purposes. The host says he is
deeply distressed that his guests were unhappy or scared;
his only desire is to make his guests very happy. The host
leads the group to where his birthday party is to occur, but
one of the group (Karel) decides not to attend the party; he
does not like that he was made to endure "the joke" of
being held captive in the woods. His wife continues on to
the party, but word soon spreads that one has left the party
to return home. Eventually the group arrives at the lakeside,
where several beautiful and elaborate tables are set for the
birthday celebration. Everyone begins the feast, but the
host soon turns inconsolable, saying that this was not how

he imagined his birthday. How can one enjoy their birthday party with a guest running out on him? The members of party agree that the host has provided them with an exquisite banquet and that everyone should enjoy it. They resolve to go after Karel to bring him back so that he can enjoy the party, and the guest can enjoy his birthday. In preparing to go after the missing guest, the group gets bloodhounds and guns to retrieve Karel. In the end, the host has organized the party to stifle free will with the rights of the individuals subservient to the group.

The point of director Jan Nemec is very clear. While the story on the surface is seemingly very bizarre, what Ne˘mec is portraying is a very clear indictment of the way repression was used in Czech society during the Novotný regime. The *New York Times* film critic Vincent Canby noted that the picnickers collapsed in the face of a smiling tyrant, "with only the vaguest suggestion of menace—and meeting only the slightest resistance—the host assimilates the picnic."[22] The story is even more poignant when one realizes that director Evald Schorm, whose film *Return of the Prodigal Son* was banned by the government at that time, played the role of the guest who was not happy. The film is a study in conformity in the face of oppression and brutality. Ultimately the film is an explanation of how and why the Stalinist regimes managed to stay in power without significant opposition.

After the Soviet invasion of Prague in 1968, many film directors that made up the Czech New Wave left out of fear. Both Forman and Nemec left for the United States shortly after the invasion. Forman continued to make films in the United States, capturing Oscars for films like *One Flew Over the Cuckoo's Nest* (1975) and *Amadeus* (1984), and receiving accolades for the politically charged *The People vs. Larry Flynt* (1996), a spirited biographical sketch of the life, times, and free speech court cases of the peculiar pornographer and First Amendment crusader Larry Flynt (see Miloš Forman box on page 71). Nemec lived in relative obscurity for a time in the United States, but returned to the

Czech Republic after the collapse of the Communist government in 1989. Since his return he has made a handful of films in his home country.

Alternative Views: Fascism

Fascism finds its roots in the 1922 parliamentary crisis in Italy. When the institutions of the Italian State were seemingly paralyzed, an attempt to streamline and make the state more efficient was introduced. Many people saw it as an economic alternative to both liberalism and Marxism. Fascists argued that the community has the right to determine what national interests are. To that end, the conflicting interests of workers, owners, technicians, and the state should be brought together under a single unit, operating under the control of the public, called the corporation. The use of strikes or lockouts is to be forbidden. Ultimately, the primacy of the expert and the technician should outweigh the desires and needs of politicians. Consequently, the divisiveness of politics should be replaced by the unity of expertise. However, fascists seemed to be more interested in building power than in building theoretical coherence.[23]

While the examination of fascist forms of governance begins with Italy, it is ultimately applied to several totalitarian regimes that sacrifice individual liberties in exchange for efficiency and national prosperity. The most famous examples of fascist regimes tend to be Germany under the Nazis and Italy under Mussolini. Yet other regimes fall under this category as well such as Spain under Franco and Argentina under the military dictatorships. There are main four tools of powers that fascists attempted to develop and refine: charismatic leadership, single-party rule, terror, and economic control.

During the Nazi regime, the German film industry was under the control of information minister Joseph Goebbels. Yet unlike the Soviet Union, the German film industry was not nationalized until 1942, almost a decade after the Nazis had come to power and three years into the war. The German government was more interested in the populace being entertained,[24] provided that entertainment was in the form of escapism, than being educated about the benefits of National Socialism.[25] Thus, films concerning fascism are relatively rare even from the most recognizable fascist regime.

Films that carried the message of National Socialism to the masses generally fell into one of a number of categories: newsreels, historical dramas of great national leaders or events, films that glorified the Nazi regime or racial propaganda. The most recognizable films to advocate a fascist ideology come from the films of Nazi Germany. Of particular note is *Triumph of the Will* (1934), which was filmed by the famous and controversial female director Leni Reifenstahl. Essentially, the film is a pure propaganda piece in which Hitler delivers a speech to the Nuremberg Party Convention. However, the entire event was staged for the camera. Complete plans for marches, parades, and architecture were drawn up in advance.[26] The opening of the film depicts Hitler arriving on an airplane in Nuremberg, almost as if he were descending from the clouds to address the convention. While the speeches made at the convention were designed to appeal to emotion rather than intellect, officials of the day thought the film effective enough to have the film banned in Britain, Canada and the United States.[27]

What may be surprising to many people is how fascism has crept into other films over the years. In the depths of the Depression some Americans were actively seeking alternative forms of government to help relieve the dire economic crisis of the 1930s. As seen in the film *The Nazis Strike* (1943), a number of Americans were in attendance at a huge rally for the German-American Bund in Madison Square Garden. In fact, there were several rallies during the late 1930s that supported Germany, Hitler, Nazism and fascism across North America.

Many Americans in the 1930s were looking for ways to escape the economic deprivations that were brought on by the Depression and some were willing to sacrifice individual liberties for economic well-being. One such suggestion is found in the 1933 film *Gabriel Over the White House*. In the film (also discussed at length in chapter two, Liberal Ideologies) a playboy president, Judson C. Hammond (played by Walter Huston), leads a reckless lifestyle while the country suffers through the Great Depression. After suffering a near-fatal automobile accident, Hammond has a remarkable recovery and sets about to solve the problems of the country. The President assumes almost dictatorial powers, dismissing both his cabinet and ignoring Congress, creating jobs for the unemployed and threatening countries that owe the United States money into reducing their arms and paying off their debt. In one scene that is almost unbelievable in its brashness, Federal agents raid the headquarters of gangsters in New York, take the criminals outside, line them along the wall and use machine guns to carry out instant death sentences. As the Federal agents begin firing their machine guns, the camera pans up to the Statute of Liberty, which is overlooking the scene. In the end, the film suggests that either the Angel Gabriel or God had inhabited the body of the president to solve the problems of the United States.

Even in recent years, there has been an examination of fascist-type governance that does not necessarily reflect the negative attitudes often displayed in films associated with the Nazi regime. The Paul Verhoeven film, *Starship Troopers* (1997), depicts Earth in the near-future in a world that fights alien bugs from half-way across the galaxy. As the film opens, a news report/commercial over the Federal network, a worldwide news service, gives an overview of the war with the "bugs" of the Klendathu system. The news update tries to get volunteers to sign up for the infantry in order to fight the bugs saying, "service guarantees citizenship."

The film then tells in flashback, beginning a year earlier, how the war with the bugs came about. The story opens in a high school classroom where a history teacher summarizes the lessons of the year. He reminds students that the failure of democracy was the overreliance on social scientists that led the world to the brink of chaos. "Veterans," whose identity is left open, seized power and imposed a stability that lasted for generations. The earth society is based on the idea that only citizens are allowed to vote and participate in the body politic, because citizens are willing to fight and die in defense of it while civilians were not. Violence and naked power are seen as the ultimate, supreme authority from which all other authority is derived. The teacher asserts that naked power has solved more issues throughout history than any other method.

The film chronicles the development of the students in the classroom in their pursuit of military careers. Throughout the film, the students espouse different reasons for joining the military. Some of the students want to start families, some want to enter politics, other want to escape poverty, all of them see the military as the only way to achieve any status in the society. The military, particularly brutal, serves its interest and there are some hints that it has fostered the war with the bugs. While most of the film falls in an action-adventure, or sci-fi genre, the opening sequences that detail earth society provide a back story that touts some of the detriments of a fascist society, but also point to some of the perceived benefits as well.

Starship Troopers received some criticism from the press because of its perceived pro-fascist sentiment.[28] To be fair, there is some effort to lay out how a fascist form of government can lead to a violent and militant society; however, that message is muted in the film in order to concentrate on special effects and building a feeling of animosity toward the bugs. In the end, the question of the film's stance on fascism is muted. The film provides a fairly sympathetic portrayal of fascist ideology and reasoning with the debate in the classroom, with little or no real debate to the contrary. As such, *Starship Troopers* is one of the few films to provide a message concerning fascism and its possible benefits in the post–Second World War era.

On the other hand there have been plenty of films that have decried fascism as a bad, or even evil, form of government. A number of wartime propaganda films during the

1940s took their shots at Germany and Italy. The ever-popular cartoon short features are an excellent source of antifascist rhetoric. Unfortunately a number of these films dwell on personalities or racial stereotypes rather than on an exploration of why fascism is perceived to be "bad." Cartoons such as *You're a Sap Mr. Jap* (1942) starring Popeye, *Herr Meets Hare* (1944) starring Bugs Bunny, and *The Spirit of '43* (1943), starring Donald Duck, are all example of this type of cartoon. However, as forms of propaganda, this type of cartoon was highly effective, if not particularly accurate.

Other films have tackled the same subject in much more subtle ways. For instance, the British film *It Happened Here* (1966) explores the hypothetical result of Germany winning the Second World War. The film explores what life would be like in 1960s Britain under a Nazi regime.[29] Directors Kevin Brownlow and Andrew Mollo's film explores the hypothetical effects of a fascist government on everyday life in Britain, using the tagline, "The story of Hitler's England." American films such as *I Was a Captive of Nazi Germany* (1939), *Confessions of a Nazi Spy* (1939), *The Man I Married* (1940), and *Hitler's Children* (1942) all used similar techniques as the red scare films to make their not-too-subtle points. Some of the best antifascist statements came from the American government produced propaganda films such as *Why We Fight: The Nazis Strike* (1943). However, perhaps the most damning of all the anti-Nazi films is *Judgment at Nuremberg* (1961). In this three-plus-hour film the war crimes trial at Nuremberg in 1948 is recreated with incredible effectiveness.

Conclusion

This chapter has focused on two ideologies that challenged the tenets of liberal democracies and market-based economies. The discussion above has focused on a limited number of films, and the authors encourage you to think about other films. What has not been discussed is how often ideologies are embedded in films without ever being discussed. Take for example several American films and note how there is an automatic return to liberal democratic principles. When a narrative film presents a situation for a group, the scene often includes some kind of voting procedure or attempt to achieve consensus. The film *Lifeboat* (1944), directed by Alfred Hitchcock and discussed in the chapter on war, follows this pattern more decidedly than others, because it is about ideology as well. However, notice how many times, when a decision is to be made by the group, the members of the lifeboat take a poll over what to do. Often Americans take this for granted, but still it is an expression of ideas about how we govern ourselves. Similarly, films in other parts of the world do not necessary follow American practices. Often films from the Soviet Union embedded ideas about collectivism and socialist norms. When watching films from other parts of the world, especially non-Western films, we encourage you to think about the underlying ideologies that might be present and not readily apparent.

CHAPTER 4

The American Presidency

Introduction

Film, Popular Culture, and American Political Institutions[1]

Historians, long interested in tracing change through examples from popular culture, have frequently used literature, art, and music as sources for studying change in American society. In the past two decades historians have given increasing attention to another valuable source—Hollywood movies. They have examined the ways in which themes developed in the movies sometimes reveal or verify shifts in the public's interests, hopes, fears, and prejudices.[2]

There are so many political institutions worldwide that it hardly seems fair to focus on one. Yet despite the importance of Congress and the Supreme Court to the American political system, and various Parliaments, executives, and tribunals to political systems around the world, one institution alone has been the focus of numerous movies and television programs: the American presidency. It is probably a safe assumption that the presidency has been the institution that has been depicted the most on screens around the world. In this section we will focus on the American presidency, charting how the institution has been portrayed in the past and in more recent films. We will also consider how films have depicted real presidents versus the way they have portrayed fictitious presidents. Moreover, we will address the explosion of presidency films in the 1990s, most of which portrayed the institution in a negative light. The chapter then examines the possible variables responsible for this significant shift in tone. Finally, we shift gears to review the present phenomenon the "television presidency"; namely, NBC's hit drama, *The West Wing*. *The West Wing*, with its sweeping musical score, patriotic images, and attention to passionate, enlightened, and well-intentioned public servants, stands as a grand exception to the seismic shift toward a more cynical and negative depiction of the presidency. Martin Sheen's dignified President Bartlet is neither a shyster, sycophant, nor sexual deviant. Throughout this chapter be conscious of how the institution of the presidency has been presented, what this says about Hollywood, ourselves, and the political and social fabric of the country, and what consequences these portrayals may have for the body politic and its perceptions of a traditionally venerated institution.

Films in the 1920s, 1930s, and 1940s regularly featured some depiction of the presidency. However, in later years, passion for producing such films seems to have faded somewhat. And while Hollywood never outright abandoned presidency-themed films (there were a slew of presidents in the Cold War movies of the 1960s), decades later

there was clearly something of a renaissance of presidency films in the 1990s. The proliferation of recent movies featuring presidents is a trend that, since the release
of Ivan Reitman's Capraesque box-office hit *Dave* in 1993,
shows little sign of reversing itself. In fact, joked one columnist, the period between 1993–1998 brought the
movie-going public "more Presidents onscreen than, say,
strippers and volcanologists combined."[3] Yet such a statement, however tongue-in-cheek, is actually quite accurate
when considering the barrage of 1990s films that feature,
in major or significant supporting roles, the President of
the United States. *In the Line of Fire* (1993), *Dave* (1993),
Clear and Present Danger (1994), *The Pelican Brief* (1994),
Canadian Bacon (1994), *My Fellow Americans* (1996), *Mars
Attacks!* (1996), *Wag the Dog* (1997), *Murder at 1600* (1997),
Absolute Power (1997), *Amistad* (1997), *Shadow Conspiracy*
(1997), *Deep Impact* (1998), *Armageddon* (1998), *Enemy of
the State* (1998) among many others, illustrate this trend.
Running the genre gamut from thrillers to comedies to box
office hits to B-movie, straight-to-video wonders, these
films are evidence of Hollywood's renewed fascination
with the politics and personalities consuming and inhabiting the White House.

The Hollywood Presidency:
The Pre-1990s Model

President as Redeemer and Hero

In order to consider how the presidency is perceived today,
we must first revisit the Hollywood presidency prior to the
1990s. By and large, American films prior to the 1990s presented a very positive portrayal of both the individual and
the institution. Presidents were commonly depicted as
steadfast and heroic in times of crisis and common men
who rose to uncommon greatness. Even when presidents
were initially depicted as flawed or less than extraordinary,
they often, when faced with certain serious situations,
could rise to the occasion and redeem themselves and the

country. Moreover, the presidency was generally a revered institution, one that—even if occasionally threatened by conniving, self-serving special interests or disingenuous presidential hopefuls—would ultimately regain or retain its prestige and honor. In short, on screens throughout the country, the president was more often than not a redeemer and hero, and the office he inhabited was sacred and renowned. Many prominent films illustrate variants of these themes, including: *Gabriel Over the White House* (1933), *Young Mr. Lincoln* (1939), *Abe Lincoln in Illinois* (1940), *Yankee Doodle Dandy* (1942), *Wilson* (1944), *State of the Union* (1948), *Sunrise at Campobello* (1960), *PT-109* (1963), *Fail Safe* (1964), *The Best Man* (1964), and *Seven Days in May* (1964).

Prototypical Hollywood Presidents

Henry Fonda, Fredric March, and Spencer Tracy

The positive image of the presidency was reinforced by Hollywood via the deliberate and skillful casting of certain actors. In particular, three legends of the silver screen—Henry Fonda, Fredric March, and Spencer Tracy—stand out as the prototypical heroic Hollywood president (and presidential candidate) through their memorable onscreen performances in the 1930s, 1940s and, especially, in the 1960s.

Henry Fonda, having already portrayed the revered Abraham Lincoln in John Ford's *Young Mr. Lincoln* (1939), was perhaps the perfect choice to play America's chief executive; or, as was the case in Gore Vidal's play-turned-movie *The Best Man,* a leading presidential candidate. Fonda, as William Russell, the principled, progressive presidential candidate in *The Best Man* (1964), ultimately takes his name out of the running at the Democratic national convention, even as he is the front-runner, when he realizes that a mud-slinging battle and crafty innuendo campaign engineered by his chief rival—demagogue Joe Cantwell (Cliff Robertson), whose tactics and ruthlessness recall

PAST PRESIDENTS PORTRAYED ON FILM

George Washington (1789–1797)

Films, Shorts, and Television

The Life of George Washington (film short, 1909)

Washington Under the American Flag (film short, 1909)

Washington Under the British Flag (film short, 1909)

The Spy (1914)

The Battle Cry of Peace (1915)

Betsy Ross (1917)

The Spirit of '76 (1917)

The Beautiful Mrs. Reynolds (1918)

Alexander Hamilton (film short, 1924)

America (1924)

Gateway to the West (1924)

Yorktown (1924)

Flag: A Story Inspired by the Tradition of Bets y Ross (film short, 1927)

The Road Is Open Again (film short, 1933)

Give Me Liberty (film short, 1936)

Sons of Liberty (film short, 1939)

The Howards of Virginia (1940)

The Remarkable Andrew (1942)

Don't You Believe It (film short, 1943)

Where Do We Go from Here? (1945)

Monsieur Beaucaire (1946)

Unconquered (1947)

Williamsburg: The Story of a Patriot (film short, 1956)

Lafayette (1961)

Sing Out, Sweet Land (television, 1970)

Valley Forge (television, 1974)

Independence (film short, 1976)

The Rebels (television mini-series, 1979)

George Washington (television mini-series, 1984)

A More Perfect Union: America Becomes a Nation (1989)

George Washington: The Man Who Wouldn't Be King (documentary, television, 1992)

Liberty! The American Revolution (documentary, television, 1997)

"Histeria!" (television series, 1998)

The Crossing (television, 2000)

Founding Fathers (television, mini-series, 2000)

The Patriot (2000)

Founding Brothers (documentary, television, 2002)

Benedict Arnold: A Question of Honor (television, 2003)

PAST PRESIDENTS PORTRAYED ON FILM

Thomas Jefferson (1801–1809)

Films, Shorts, and Television

The Slacker's Heart (1917)
The Beautiful Mrs. Reynolds (1918)
My Own United States (1918)
America (1924)
Janice Meredith (1924)
The Declaration of Independence (film short, 1938)
The Howards of Virginia (1940)
The Remarkable Andrew (1942)
Williamsburg: The Story of a Patriot (film short, 1956)
Sing Out, Sweet Land (television, 1970)
1776 (1972)
The Rebels (televisions mini-series, 1979)

"Pursuit of Happiness" (television series, 1987–1988)
A More Perfect Union: America Becomes a Nation (1989)
Reflections on Liberty (film short, 1997)
"Liberty's Kids" (television series, 2002)
Jefferson in Paris (1995)
Thomas Jefferson (television mini-series, 1997)
"Histeria!" (television series, 1998)
Founding Fathers (television, mini-series, 2000)
Founding Brothers (documentary, television, 2002)

Andrew Jackson, 1829–1837

Films, Shorts, and Television

My Own United States (1918)
The Gorgeous Hussy (1936)
The Buccaneer (1938)
Man of Conquest (1939)
Old Hickory (film short, 1940)
The Remarkable Andrew (1942)
Lone Star (1952)
The President's Lady (1953)

Davy Crockett, King of the Wild Frontier (1954)
The Buccaneer (1958)
Houston: The Legend of Texas (television, 1986)
War of 1812 (documentary, Canada, 1999)

PAST PRESIDENTS PORTRAYED ON FILM

Abraham Lincoln (1861–1865)

Films, Shorts, and Television

The Battle of Gettysburg (1913)

The Battle Cry of Peace (1915)

The Birth of a Nation (1915)

The Heart of Lincoln (1915)

Her Country's Call (1917)

My Father (1917)

My Mother (1917)

Myself (1917) 4-part film

Madam Who (1918)

The Copperhead (1920)

The Dramatic Life of Abraham Lincoln (1924)

The Iron Horse (1924)

Hands Up! (1926)

The Heart of Maryland (1927)

Abraham Lincoln (1930)

The Road Is Open Again (film short, 1933)

Are We Civilized? (1934)

The Littlest Rebel (1935)

The Perfect Tribute (film short, 1935)

Calvary (1936)

Hearts in Bondage (1936)

The Plainsman (1936)

The Prisoner of Shark Island (1936)

Trailin' West (1936)

Wells Fargo (1937)

Of Human Hearts (1938)

Lincoln in the White House (film short, 1939)

Young Mr. Lincoln (1939)

Abe Lincoln in Illinois (1940)

Hi-Yo Silver (1940)

The Mad Empress (1940)

Abe Lincoln in Illinois (television, 1945)

Abe Lincoln in Illinois (television, 1964)

The Faking of the President (1976)

The Lincoln Conspiracy (1977)

The Blue and the Gray (television, mini-series 1982)

"Police Squad!" (television series, 1982)

North and South (television mini-series, 1985)

Dream West (television mini-series, 1986)

Lincoln (also known as Gore Vidal's Lincoln, television, 1988)

Bill & Ted's Excellent Adventure (1989)

The Civil War (documentary/mini-series, 1990)

The Perfect Tribute (television, 1991)

Lincoln (documentary, 1992)

Late Night with Conan O'Brien (television series, 1993–1999)

Tad (television, 1995)

Abraham and Mary Lincoln: A House Divided (documentary/mini-series, 2001)

Zoolander (2001)

Clone High (television series, 2002)

the red-scare monger Joseph McCarthy—would demean the country. Rather than take America down the road of personal scandal and vitriolic campaigning, he opts for the high road. Thus, in this campaign for the highest office in the land, Russell's principled departure from the race proves that he is definitely "the best man." The political process, the presidential campaign and the presidency remain dignified thanks to the actions of William Russell.

With regard to *The Best Man,* it should also be noted that ex-President Art Hockstader (portrayed by Lee Tracey, who garnered a Best Supporting Actor nomination), ultimately chose to endorse and fight for Russell's (i.e., Fonda's) nomination at the convention, even as the president's policies and decision-making style more closely mirrored those of conservative Cantwell. Yet, President Hockstader couldn't stomach the utter deviousness of Cantwell's below-the-belt tactics, and he did everything he could—before dying during the convention—to see that "the best man" would secure his party's nomination.[4] President Hockstader may have been a cagey, street-smart old codger willing to use hardball tactics, but, in the final analysis, his aim was pure and his intentions virtuous.

Further cementing Fonda's image as "the best man" was his portrayal of President of the United States in Sidney Lumet's stirring Cold War drama *Fail Safe* (1964). As a nuclear first-strike is accidentally triggered by the United States against the Soviet Union, it is up to the president to prevent the attack and convince the Russians that the launch was entirely a mistake. Sweating it out in intense negotiations in a closed room, accompanied only by his special assistant Buck (Larry Hagman), Fonda's president is steadfast under the most intense anxiety humanly possible, negotiating one-on-one with the Soviets in order to prevent a pending nuclear holocaust. Ultimately, the President ignores advice from the Pentagon and from the hard-nosed realist Groeteschele (Walter Matthau)[5] to use the opportunity as a fortuitous sneak attack to roll back the Iron Curtain and insure American military and ideological supremacy for generations. Fonda's president in *Fail Safe* displays humility and sincerity, and condemns the arms race that has triggered the imminent nuclear Armageddon that haunts the entire film.[6]

Fredric March, as the honorable and earnest President Jordan Lyman, advanced the positive image of the presidency in John Frankenheimer's *Seven Days in May* (1964). Faced with a near certain right-wing coup d'etat masterfully engineered by the sinister General James Mattoon Scott (Burt Lancaster), President Lyman courageously stays and fights the plot until the bitter end, using close aides and friends, such as Senator Raymond Clark (Edmond O'Brien) and the ever-faithful Colonel "Jiggs" Casey (Kirk Douglas) to thwart the coup. Again, the American movie audience is reassured by the onscreen presence of a strong, steadfast leader—and virtuous, if slightly imperfect close presidential aides—in the midst of national chaos and constitutional crisis.

In Frank Capra's *State of the Union* (1948), also discussed in chapter two, Spencer Tracy portrays Grant Matthews, an aviation tycoon and idealistic Republican candidate for president who pledges to use blunt talk ("plain ordinary garden-variety honesty," in his words) to solve the problems of the day. However, Matthews is quickly swayed by crooked and ambitious politicos, namely his political adviser (Adolph Menjou), and a power-mad newspaper tycoon with whom he has had an affair (Angela Lansbury), to abandon his pledge of probity and not antagonize any of the entrenched interests (i.e., big business, labor, farmers) that he will need to secure the nomination. However, as "one could comfortably predict from a Capra-Tracy-Hepburn film, Matthews eventually sees the light and withdraws from the race," swayed by the devotion and encouragement of his wife.[7] Moreover, Matthews assures a live nationwide radio audience that—while he is no longer a presidential candidate in *this* election—he will be going to *both* party conventions to make sure the candidates are accountable to the people's interests. Thus, by withdrawing from the race and maintaining his integrity and principles, Matthews upholds the sanctity and integrity of his candidacy and the presidency, and strengthens an electoral process in serious need of purification.[8]

Certainly, however, there are some exceptions (and comedic interludes) to the generally positive portrayal of the presidency. Not all presidents or candidates-who-would-be president were Fondas, Marches, or Tracys. *Tennessee Johnson* (1942), *Dr. Strangelove* (1964), and *The President's Analyst* (1967), for example, stand out in this regard. We see the beleaguered and impeached 17th president, Andrew Johnson, as a court-marshaled slovenly drunkard *(Tennessee Johnson)*, and the leaders of nuclear doomsday-America as peculiar, mentally unstable zealots *(Dr. Strangelove)*. At the same time, the portrayal of President Andrew Jackson in *The Gorgeous Hussy* (1936) is one of an eccentric individual who has the best interest of the common man at heart. In the film, Jackson is portrayed as a man whose quick tongue gets him into trouble with more seasoned politicians. Because of this, Jackson is portrayed as a flawed person, but with a heart of gold.

But even in the darker films that point out imperfections and personal failings, the presidency does not completely sink into the depths of utter depravity. For example, *Dr. Strangelove*'s president, Merkin Muffley (Peter Sellers), may be rather intellectual and egg-headish (note his uncanny resemblance to Adlai Stevenson, the Democratic Party's presidential nominee in 1952 and 1956) in the midst of a nuclear crisis, but a devious criminal he is not. In *Strangelove,* Stanley Kubrick's dark, absurd, and humorous treatment of the nuclear age and presidential leadership stands in stark contrast to the other Cold War era films that deal with the same subject. As stated before, the presidents in *Fail Safe* (Fonda) and *Seven Days in May* (March) are reasonable and seasoned public servants who fare pretty well in the midst of national emergency. Moreover, satirical send-ups of the Cold War and the nuclear age, such Kubrick's black comedy, largely reflect "a certain levity of outlook" evident in several other films

In John Frankenheimer's *Seven Days in May* (1964), President Jordan Lyman (Fredric March) thwarts a *coup d'etat* engineered by General James Mattoon Scott (Burt Lancaster). Unlike most films of the 1990s, this Cold War era political thriller represents a heroic portrayal of the presidency.

during this period which questioned the merits and morals of the Cold War.[9]

For most of the history of popular film in the United States—from the 1930s to the 1990s—the prevailing image of the office and the individual presented to the American public (and, in many cases, the world) was a most positive one. The likes of Abraham Lincoln, Franklin Roosevelt, and Woodrow Wilson—as well many of Hollywood's fictional presidents—were treated with the utmost respect on screen. Aside from a few notable exceptions, the president and the presidency received reverential treatment from Hollywood. In those films that showcased the flaws of human nature specifically and the U.S. political system generally, the dignity and goodness of the office ultimately prevailed, even if wayward people did occasionally roam its corridors of power. Such was the case, for example, in

1933's *Gabriel Over the White House*.[10] Thus, for decades, Hollywood succeeded in establishing a few prototypical heroic presidents and presidential candidates—Henry Fonda in *Young Mr. Lincoln, The Best Man,* and *Fail Safe;* the stoic, diligent and dignified Fredric March in *Seven Days in May;* and Spencer Tracy in *State of the Union*—that largely depicted the institution and individual in a very positive fashion. We will now examine the portrayal of presidents and the presidency in the 1990s, and in the process determine if there is a continuation of this established Hollywood presidency.

The Hollywood Presidency in the 1990s

Action-Hero Presidents and Positive Depictions

In the massive summer blockbuster *Independence Day* (1996), Bill Pullman portrays Gulf War veteran and alien-blasting President Thomas J. Whitmore, a chief executive who helps save the United States and the world from certain annihilation at the hands (or antennae?) of sinister, invading aliens by personally manning an F-18 and fighting the alien menace. In another summer action-infused blockbuster, *Air Force One* (1997), perennial top-draw Harrison Ford is President James Marshall—"a blend of Han Solo, Woodrow Wilson and Jackie Chan"—who saves his plane, family, and several members of the press corps and cabinet from death at the hands of a terrorist (Gary Oldman) and his fellow sadistic henchman who hijack Air Force One as it prepares to leave Kazakhstan.[11] Certainly President Bill Clinton could not have imagined a more flattering portrayal of an American Chief Executive. Thus, it is perhaps not surprising that a year before the film's release, Clinton himself gave Harrison Ford a tour of Air Force One in August 1996 while vacationing in Jackson Hole, Wyoming. However cartoonish and over-the-top, both Pullman and

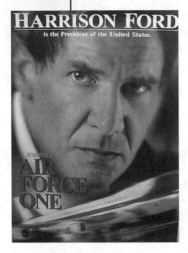

The President as Action Hero!
Unlike the majority of films of the 1990s, the summer 1997 blockbuster *Air Force One,* starring Harrison Ford, depicted a heroic presidency in which America's chief executive personally battled terrorists.

Ford's action-hero presidents stand as examples of principled, heroic figures that harken back to a less cynical age.

Another unambiguously positive depiction of the presidency in the 1990s is Rob Reiner's *The American President* (1995). Here, Michael Douglas is President Andrew Shepherd, a Midwesterner, father, widower and liberal who faces demagogues (Richard Dreyfuss as pesky, conservative Senate Majority Leader Bob Rumson) ranting about family values and patriotism when he decides to commence a relationship with the attractive environmental lobbyist Sydney Ellen Wade (Annette Bening). Reiner's film is significant in that both the president—as well as most of his closest White House aides (Michael J. Fox, Martin Sheen, and Anna Deveare Smith—the latter two going on to portray characters on the NBC hit series *The West Wing)*—are portrayed in a most glowing manner. They are dedicated to their jobs and care passionately about public policy issues. As president, Shepherd does not relish or exploit for political gain an attack on a Libyan terrorist base, and furthermore, he refuses bow to the pressure from conservative politicians and end his relationship with Wade. At the film's dramatic conclusion, the president announces at a live, unrehearsed press conference that he will fight for gun control and environmental legislation—two pieces of legislation that he previously abandoned due to political pressure and compromise.

In *Deep Impact* (1998), Morgan Freeman portrays a president (President Beck) seeking to prevent the destruction of the United States due to an impending meteor. While not the over-the-top hero president of *Independence Day* or *Aiar Force One,* Freeman's sober, somber, and steady chief executive reflects a fairly positive view of the presidency.

Portraying Past Presidencies:
Mixed Messages

While the aforementioned films present fictitious contemporary presidencies, other films in recent years have addressed past presidents, their administrations, and the central scandals and major issues that defined their tenure. Oliver Stone's *JFK* (1991) and *Nixon* (1995), and Steven Spielberg's *Amistad* (1997) are examples of such films. The depictions of the presidents in these films are both positive and negative, and thus the overall presentation of the presidency is quite mixed indeed. *JFK,* while unabashedly romantic in its fondness for Kennedy, his policies, and leadership, for instance, is entirely about the 35th president's assassination in Dallas on November 22, 1963, the Warren Report and investigation, and the various conspiracy theories—such as those advanced by New Orleans D.A. Jim Garrison—that shed serious doubt on the veracity of the Warren Report. The only real depictions of the office are negative innuendoes concerning Lyndon Johnson's willingness to engage in a full-scale war in Vietnam in the aftermath of Kennedy's death. In fact, pressure from the military-industrial complex—the marriage of defense contractors, big business, the defense department, and politicians tied to these interests—is tied to LBJ's decision to appease the Pentagon (and shadowy defense contractors) by enlarging the conflict in Southeast Asia. This message is conveyed by LBJ's conversation in a smoke-filled military-planning room, assuring generals "you'll get your damn war" in Vietnam.

In Oliver Stone's presidential psycho-history *Nixon* (1995), Anthony Hopkins portrays a haunted, embittered version of the 37th president, and Stone goes to great detail to present nearly all of the presidential aides, rogue players and other key Watergate and Washington players who dominate Nixon's presidency and political life. Perhaps surprisingly, given Stone's past movies and outspoken politics, *Nixon* is largely a character study . . . that aims for, and often achieves, the dimensions of classical tragedy. . . . Stone's Nixon is appalling and strangely moving, a man whose private and public demons bring him down with an almost Shakespearean thud.[12]

In fact, while, Stone does not gloss over the sins and cynical political maneuvering of the oft-vilified president—the "Checkers" speech, divisive campaign tactics, and paranoid rants about the Kennedys, East-coast elites, "niggers," leaks, Jews, homosexuals, and his political enemies are included—there is also ample sympathy for the hardships endured by the Whittier graduate and Quaker from Yorba Linda, California. For example, considerable screen time is devoted to Nixon's humble upbringing, his devout mother, the loss of his brother, and the condescension and prejudice endured at the hands of the Yale and Harvard elite when he sought a position in a prestigious law firm. Stone himself has commented that Nixon, like "every one of the protagonists" in his films, "goes through a crisis of conscience and ultimately achieves some form of enlightenment through the travails of this life."[13] Ultimately, the image of the presidency in this film is quite mixed; there is extensive evidence of lawlessness, selfishness, and self-induced wounds—yet there is also room for sympathy and redemption.

Amistad (1997), belongs in the mixed message category of films because of its contrasting depictions of two eighteenth-century presidents—Martin Van Buren and John Quincy Adams—and their respective roles in aiding or opposing slaves in their attempt to gain freedom after their slave ship, *La Amistad,* is captured off the U.S. coast (the film is based on actual events). Van Buren (Nigel Hawthorne) is presented in a negative light, as he and his close advisers—especially Secretary of State Forsyth (David Paymer)—attempt to aid Queen Isabella of Spain in her quest to regain the slaves. In large part, Van Buren and his advisers take this approach due to crass political considerations, as southern states threaten to deny Van Buren the Democratic nomination for a second term if he does not intervene to uphold the principle of slaves as property.

When it appears as though the slaves may win their freedom, the president intervenes and has the case taken to the
Supreme Court. John Quincy Adams, conversely, is portrayed favorably as an old anti-slavery crusader and states-
man who, when called upon by abolitionists, lawyers and
supporters of the slaves, gives an impassioned plea for the
slaves' freedom before the Supreme Court. Some critics
have charged that Hollywood's version of real life events in
Amistad takes too many liberties with the historical record,
and perhaps applies the norms of twentieth-century politics
to a far different age. What do you think? Does *Amistad* represent filmmakers' attempts to deliver later twentieth-
century justice to a nineteenth-century problem? Are such
charges unfair or accurate? After viewing the movie and reviewing the historical record, you be the judge.

Finally, one portrayal of a past presidency that is *not*
mixed is the unabashedly upbeat and highly-acclaimed biographical film *Truman*. *Truman,* premiering on HBO in 1995,
starred the award-winning theater veteran Gary Sinise as
the plain-spoken, bespectacled 33rd president and Diana
Scarwid as Bess Truman. The tagline for the film—*"A Simple Man . . . A Legendary President"*—sums up the film's
positive treatment of the feisty Missourian. Whether winning World War II, rising from obscurity through the Pen-
dergast political machine, firing the immensely popular
Douglas MacArthur, or chewing out a reporter for criticizing
his daughter's artistic talents—Harry S. Truman is primarily
depicted as an heroic, honest, tell-it-like-it-is leader. He may
be occasionally uncouth or ill-tempered, but is nearly always unflinching in the face of grave challenges.

Shysters, Sycophants and Sexual Deviants: The Hollywood Presidency in the 1990s

Portraying the Presidents

In the soundtrack to the 1967 classic, *The Graduate,* Paul Simon and Art Garfunkel lamented the disappearance of baseball great Joe DiMaggio from the national scene:

> Where have you gone Joe DiMaggio? / A nation turns its lonely eyes to you

Reflecting upon the depiction of the presidency in the films of the 1990s, it may well be prudent to lament: "Where have you gone Henry Fonda, Fredric March, Spencer Tracy, and Ralph Bellamy?/a nation turns its lonely eyes to you."

In the taut political thriller *In the Line of Fire* (1993), the comments, inferences and innuendoes of veteran Secret Service agent Frank Horrigan (Clint Eastwood) clearly indicate that he finds the current president to be all pomp and circumstance and no substance. Horrigan, who had protected JFK in 1963, remains haunted by the events in Dealey Plaza in Dallas as he is harassed by a maniacal would-be assassin (John Malkovich) who threatens the new president (Jim Curley). Yet, it is clear that the weathered agent has little to no regard for the current chief executive. When asked to remember that he willingly lied on several occasions in order to protect Kennedy's sexual liaisons some 30 years previously, Horrigan responds: "That's different. I was different. *He* was different. *The whole damn country* was different." Moreover, the jaded agent no longer bothers to get to know the presidents he protects, as he may find out "they're not worth taking a bullet for." Moreover, in the current era, it seems not even the president's security detail is above crude political and image manipulation: Horrigan complains that female Secret Service agents are now assigned to the president merely to energize "feminist" supporters.

The big screen version of John Grisham's *The Pelican Brief* (1994) is illustrative of the trend towards negative depictions of the White House and its most notorious inhabitant. Here, the president (Robert Culp) is engaged in sordid and criminal activity—actively subverting the FBI and CIA's investigations of anti-environment, big-business campaign donors directly tied to the assassination of two Supreme Court justices. In his attempts to cover-up the scandal and bury a legal brief implicating his rich benefactors, the president and his Chief of Staff Fletcher Coal (Tony Goldwyn) enlist the support of a secret supra-governmental association of thugs and killers. Car bombs, top-notch surveillance, and shootings are routinely provided by the covert cabal. Likewise, in the film adaptation of Tom Clancy's *Clear and Present Danger* (1994), the president (Donald Moffat) is hardly a candidate for memorialization on Mount Rushmore. This president is dishonest and shows contempt for the nation's veterans, planning and executing covert military operations in South America not for the nation's security but rather to settle a personal vendetta with drug lords. In the meantime, brave military veterans and protagonist Clancy Jack Ryan (Harrison Ford) are left for dead in an operation that the administration denies ever transpired. When Jack Ryan finally confronts the wayward president about the crimes he has committed in the name of national security, the president yells: "How dare you come in here an bark at me like I'm some junkyard dog—*I'm the President of the United States!*" Ryan, indignant and utterly disgusted with the lowlife president before him, bellows "How dare *you,* sir!"

In the 1990s, even light-hearted, seemingly innocuous comedies are not above portraying presidents as scheming, murderous jerks or just plain bizarre characters. In the comedy *My Fellow Americans* (1996) two flawed ex-presidents (James Garner and Jack Lemmon) redeem themselves by thwarting power-grabbing and money-laundering schemes engineered by the slick, crooked President Haney (Dan Akyroyd) and his seemingly befuddled (but also crooked) vice-president Ted Matthews (John Heard). In this film, like several

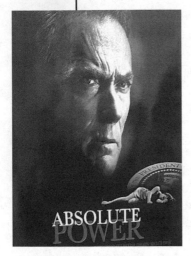

ABSOLUTE
POWER

Typical of the films of the 1990s, Clint
Eastwood's *Absolute Power*, released
in early 1997, paints a very negative
portrait of the presidency.

others, the thugs enlisted by the president are not above murder or planting evidence. In Tim Burton's deliberately campy *Mars Attacks!* (1996), however, Jack Nicholson is a wacky commander-in-chief who is *not* engaged in murder, extortion, or private gain—but *is* an all-around bizarre alien-battling and gambling chief executive who *definitely* inhaled.

In 1997, a slew of sexually deviant presidents and close associates hit the screen with reckless abandon. In *Murder at 1600* President Jack Neil (Ronny Cox) is a weak but fairly honest chief executive, but his rich, spoiled playboy son likes to sow his wild oats by engaging in rough sex on the floor of the oval office—on the presidential seal, no less. While neither the president nor his son are ultimately guilty of the murder that soon takes place at the White House, they are surrounded by treacherous, back-stabbing aides—especially the National Security Adviser (Alan Alda) and the Director of White House Security (Daniel Benzali), who vie for advancement at the expense of others. *Absolute Power,* released in the early months of 1997, features the reigning king of sexually deviant presidents, President Alan Richmond (Gene Hackman). Richmond's dirty-talk-laced sexual tryst with the wife of a loyal supporter (E.G. Marshall) ultimately leads to her death when the encounter turns ugly and rough; the Secret Service, sworn to protect the president's safety at all times, shoots the president's paramour as she tries to stab the overly aggressive Richmond with a letter opener. In addition, the B-movie *Shadow Conspiracy,* also from 1997, is rife with an evil shadow government threatening to rise to power, including a duplicitous Chief of Staff (Donald Sutherland) and Vice-President (Ben Gazzara). Not surprisingly, bombs, murders, and car chases follow those who try to expose the crimes committed by those in and around the White House.

Perhaps not surprisingly, the year 1997 ended the way it began with *Absolute Power* et al.—with the big screen filled with a scandal-ridden, sex-addicted chief executive—in this case, in the ultra-cynical farce *Wag the Dog*. After the president's sexual liaison with a girl scout in the oval office is exposed, a cunning White House aide (Anne Heche), cagey spin doctor (Robert De Niro) and Hollywood producer (Dustin Hoffman) are called in to create and orchestrate a fake war (the chosen opponent is Albania) to divert attention from the scandal. In addition to producing their own propaganda—such as bogus video clips of Albanian refugees (they were actors shot on a sound stage!)—the PR gurus then hire Willie Nelson and Pops Staples to write catchy songs to sway the American public in favor of the war. The images, songs, sound bites, and chicanery work like a charm: the press and the public buy and digest the war story hook, line, and sinker and the President hangs on to power.

"Warm. Direct. Straightforward. Sincere. Comforting"[14] Such was John Travolta's description of President Bill Clinton—whom he had personally met twice (once at an Italian American awards banquet and another at a volunteerism summit) before portraying him (or rather, a fictionalized facsimile of him) on the big screen in *Primary Colors*. Though Travolta has commented that he hoped the movie-going public would view the Bill Clinton he created on screen as a "very caring and genuine character, flawed but real and wonderful,"[15] and while White House Press Secretary-turned television pundit Dee Dee Myers commented after seeing the film that "It's really not half-bad for the president"—and generally good reviews for the movie notwithstanding—the depiction of presidential candidate Jack Stanton is hardly flattering.[16] In many ways the film is, as director Mike Nichols asserted, essentially about "honor."[17] And in nearly all of the tests, the lead character—smooth-talking presidential candidate Jack Stanton (John Travolta)—fails all of the tests. From impregnating a young African American girl, to a string of other marital in-

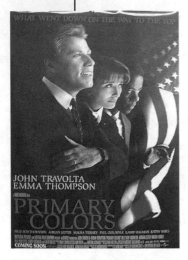

"What went down on the way to the top": Mike Nichols' *Primary Colors* (1997), based on the novel by Anonymous (AKA journalist Joe Klein), follows the deals, compromises, sordid peccadilloes, and serious ethical lapses surrounding a Clintonesque Southern governor and his headstrong wife as they do what it takes to win the presidency.

fidelities, to his (and his wife's) decision to use damaging information to blackmail and destroy a rising competitor (Larry Hagman), Stanton displays a penchant for half-truths, cover-up and dirty tricks. His attributes—such as his empathy, love of public service, and understanding of the key issues—ultimately cannot make up for the dearth of character.

One may characterize these films as simply escapism entertainment. And as the success of big-budget summer blockbusters and the health of box-office receipts generally indicate, Americans value their escapism. However, in a culture constantly saturated in electronic media, with images and sounds in every direction, it seems pertinent to ask: Are there problems with portraying the presidency in a negative light? Does exposure to negative portrayals of the presidency lead us to take a jaded and jaundiced view of the office and those that inhabit it? Will this affect our voting levels, willingness to participate in presidential politics, or understanding of a complex institution? Are we, or can we, be unduly swayed by film's portrayals of the presidency—or do we have an automatic switch that allows us to keep the facts from the fun and fiction? The jury may be out. However, one thing is certain: there is no denying that how presidents were portrayed towards the end of the twentieth century was markedly different from those earlier in the century.

Portraying the Presidency: The White House Staff and Cabinet

There is another strategic element concerning the recent Hollywood renderings of the presidency that warrants mention.

It is increasingly evident that, in addition to the shysters, sycophants and sexual deviants occupying the Oval Office, deviancy, criminal behavior, and general ineptitude are every bit as common in the men and women who advise and counsel the president. The following films—running the gamut from comedies, dramas, to thrillers—illustrate this trend.

In the *Naked Gun 2 1/2: The Smell of Fear* (1991), real life Chief of Staff John Sununu (Peter Van Norden) in addition to George Bush (John Roarke), is portrayed as seemingly inept and, moreover, prone to kowtow to business interests that threaten the environment. Ivan Reitman's Capraesque box-office smash *Dave* (1993) finds the Chief of Staff (Frank Langella) and Press Secretary (Kevin Dunn) overseeing a massive conspiracy, placing a Midwestern everyman, Dave Kovic (Kevin Kline), in the Oval Office when the real president, Bill Mitchell (Kevin Kline) suffers a massive stroke during a sexual encounter with a White House aide (Laura Linney). While Dave and the White House press secretary eventually find an honorable way out of the conspiracy and cover-up, the power-hungry, conniving Chief of Staff continues the cover-up, and even attempts to blackmail Dave en route to running for president himself.

The Pelican Brief (1993) depicts a scheming Chief of Staff (Tony Goldwyn) at the vortex of executive corruption, engineering an elaborate illegal cover-up for the president nearly entirely by himself. Likewise, in *Clear and Present Danger* (1994), it is not only the President, but also his Chief of Staff, who masterminds cover-ups and illegal activity. *In the Line of Fire* (1993), not only suggests that the current president is of questionable character, but his domineering Chief of Staff (Fred Dalton Thompson, from 1995–2003 a Republican Senator from Tennessee!)[18] is recalcitrant and shortsighted, and blatantly puts crass political consideration above the security of the president. When asked by Secret Service agent Horrigan (Eastwood) to consider limiting the president's public appearances due to the serious threat posed by a menacing assassin, he scoffs as the thought of frisking "people going into

In Michael Moore's satire *Canadian Bacon* (1995), starring John Candy, a U.S. President in the 1990s wages a phony war with Canada in order to gain high approval ratings and distract Americans from a sagging economy.

$10,000-a-plate dinners," suggesting that fewer presidential appearances "would be political suicide." After all, comments the Chief of Staff, he had already helped to narrow the president's deficit in the polls to a measly five points. Thus, election-year politics wins out over the safety of the president.

Canadian Bacon, a satire written and directed by Michael Moore, finds a "touchy-feely" president (Alan Alda), a bumbling, gung-ho general (Rip Torn), and an ultra-cynical Chief of Staff (Kevin Pollack) seeking to divert attention from a stagnant economy, poverty and pollution by reviving the arms race and going to war with Canada. Far more serious and sinister, however, is President Richmond's Chief of Staff, Gloria Russell (Judy Davis) in *Absolute Power* (1997)—a sycophant who uses two Secret Service agents and members of the FBI to do whatever it takes (including attempted murder) to cover-up the murder of the president's lover. Further evidence of deceptive, villainous and/or traitorous Chiefs of Staff include *Shadow Conspiracy* (1997) and *Wag the Dog* (1997). In *Murder at 1600* (1997), most of the evil and illegalities are perpetrated by the National Security Adviser and Director of White House Security, and in *Primary Colors* (1998), campaign staff, aides and friends of candidate Jack Stanton assist in the bribing and dirt-digging designed to protect their boss.[19]

In addition to being portrayed as sycophants, cover-up experts, and overly ambitious jerks, several films portray top White House officials as less-than-qualified. In many of the aforementioned films—especially *In the Line of Fire, Clear and Present Danger, Absolute Power, and Murder at 1600*—ineptitude ruins even the best attempts at cover-up or arrogance. Even in the McDonald's-endorsed big-budget summer

blockbuster *Armageddon* (1998), starring action movie sta-
ple Bruce Willis, the president (Stanley Anderson) and his
top Defense Department adviser, General Kimsey (Keith
David), make the hasty—and wrong decision—to fire nuclear weapons at an incoming meteor, and in the process
nearly destroy all of life as we know it. It takes a NASA official (Billy Bob Thornton) *outside* of the President's inner-
circle to make the correct decisions. Moreover, in the end, a
gang of Joe six-pack oil-drillers and petty criminals turn out
to be more dedicated and shrewd in their efforts to stop the
deadly Texas-sized meteor than the White House and all of
its key advisers. (One of whom—the top science expert to
the president received "a C- in astro-physics," according to
one of the NASA officials.)

Explanations for the 1990s Hollywood Presidency

After the release of 1997 box-office hit *Air Force One, Newsweek* reporter Howard Fineman pondered:

> . . . it may say something about the state of America—or Holly-
> wood—that it took a Japanese studio (Sony) and a German-born
> director (Petersen) to bring to the screen a creature that we
> Americans can barely imagine: a president as hero.[20]

Considering the avalanche of 1990s films portraying presidents and the presidency in a negative light, it may not be
much of a stretch to concur with Fineman's sentiments, as
well as those of former Clinton aide George Stephanopoulos, who asserts that the "new presidential thrillers have a
common premise: crime and corruption are routine at the
highest levels."[21] It is clear from this survey of American
film that a variety of comedies and dramas alike have chosen to depict the presidency as running amok with ambitious, duplicitous, self-serving, and, at times, sexually
deviant criminals. These figures are also generally portrayed as more inept and less honest than those outside
the Washington, D.C. corridors of power and influence.

What does this trend mean, if anything, for citizenship and public perceptions of our most fundamental governmental institutions? Why has such a shift occurred and why should it merit our attention? Scholars and public servants offer several suggestions on how to go about answering these questions:

> *George Stephanopolous:* In an era when journalism employs the techniques of fiction ("The Agenda," "Blood Sport") and novels employ the techniques of journalism ("Primary Colors"), it's not surprising that movies are doing the same thing. . . . But what looks true on the screen is rarely what's happening behind the screens.[22]

> *Michael Seagow:* . . . it's true that American movies are largely about escape. But that's what American public life has been all about, too—form and symbol over substance, and the orchestration of video-images rather than truth-telling. . . . [23]

> *Christopher Sharrett:* Cinema as amusement, rather than springboard for audience debate, always will separate our films, and our art over all, from that of Europe and the rest of the world.[24]

It is hard to deny that there has been a seismic shift in the way that the president and the institution of the presidency have been portrayed by Hollywood. In the first three quarters of the century, the typical portrayal was of a president who was rational, trustworthy, and prone to do the "right thing." The outliers were those films that showed the presidency as "cartoonish" or deviant. Such films as *Dr. Strangelove* were among the few that portrayed the whole institution in a negative light.

At the end of the twentieth century the exact opposite seems to be true: it is rare to find a movie that shows the institution of the presidency in a positive and heroic light. The norm is to depict a president or his advisors as deviants, perverts, or, at the very least, self-absorbed Machiavellian calculators. Therefore, the key questions that need to be addressed are: Why has this shift occurred, and what effect does it have on the public's attitudes toward the presidency?

THE MEDIA'S FOCUS ON "CHARACTER" AND PRESIDENTS

After Watergate, the media became obsessed both with the "character" of our elected officials and cynical regarding politics. As Thomas Patterson argues, the press focuses on character as a keystone to leadership, even though the public tends not to view it as one of the more important attributes when coupled with a candidate's stand on the issues or experience and qualification.[25] Character was the issue that drove front-runner Gary Hart from the Democratic Primaries in 1988, and character has been an issue that has dogged Bill Clinton from the primaries of 1992 to the end of his presidency. Indeed, the drama of "Monicagate" in 1998–1999 brought the question of presidential character to the fore.[26] During the course of the Clinton presidency, polls seemed to register the media's concentration on the character issue. When asked about Bill Clinton's performance as a president, the American public tended to give him relatively high marks. However, when asked about Bill Clinton as a person, his poll numbers were dismal.[27]

Add to this seemingly paradoxical mix of public opinion the stream of numerous sensational allegations involving devious cover-ups in the death of Clinton White House counsel Vincent Foster, and one finds additional media obsession with the issue of character. Clinton critics and certain media outlets—especially Rev. Jerry Falwell (who sold anti-Clinton video tapes during his *Old Time Gospel Hour*) and the *Pittsburgh Tribune-Review* (owned by staunch Clinton-critic Richard Mellon Scaife) and its star journalist Christopher Ruddy[28] (who featured several lead stories on the subject)—have asserted that Foster's death was not a suicide, and that the White House engineered an intricate plot to kill the White House counsel and then cover it up. Such allegations have turned conspiracy theories concerning Vincent Foster's death and the former First Family's personal and public peccadilloes—both real and imagined—into somewhat of a cottage industry.[29] Could the persistent rumors and coverage of these allegations surrounding the Clintons give Hollywood the means and context to direct their attention to an executive branch that has given way to the "dark side of the force"?

Discussion Questions: "Character" and the Presidency

Character
How would you define "character"?
How has the media defined "character"?
Is "character" a useful framework for reporting presidential politics and behavior?
Is there a universal definition of character? Explain.

Presidential Character
Read James David Barber's classic *Presidential Character*. What are his four classifications of "presidential character"? How is Barber's notion of presidential character different from, or similar to, media definitions? Based on Barber's classifications of presidential character, how would you classify George W. Bush? Bill Clinton? Past presidents?

Richard Lacayo, writing for *Time,* notes that "[I]t's odd that so much has been made of Bill Clinton's friendship with the Hollywood crowd. It doesn't seem to have done him much good as far as movies are concerned."[30] In a description of the change in presentation of the presidency, Mr. Lacayo picks up on the same themes that we have addressed in the paper. However, Lacayo points to Watergate and the release of *All the President's Men* (1976) as the turning point in which the president is portrayed as a villain. Yet the film largely reaffirmed what the public had already been led to believe—that checks and balances ultimately will rein in a political actor who usurps his constitutional authority. It should also be noted that political scientists were themselves reevaluating the notion of executive power after the revelations of Watergate (i.e., Arthur Schlesinger's *Imperial Presidency* in 1973). *All the President's Men* was a depiction of an actual event, and as such, fails in its comparison to the movies released in the 1990s. So to consider it the first of the movies that have led to a negative portrayal of the presidency is, in our opinion, erroneous. It is better classified as an outlier in the pre-1990s model of the presidency.

The End of the Cold War

So why did Hollywood alter its depiction of the presidency in such a drastic way in the 1990s? One possible hypothesis is that with the end of the Cold War, there was no longer the need to show a president as a cool, calm, rational actor with the nerve and wisdom of Solomon. This hypothesis holds that since the U.S. was now lacking an enemy, Hollywood could now make films that closely examine the executive branch. It is easy to see a close connection in proximity to the end of the Cold War and the onslaught of negative movies about the presidency. But the Cold War on its own does not seem to be a sufficient reason to explain this shift. A better explanation has to do with the very nature of the media itself, both as a result of the consolidation of corporate ownership in the 1980s and as a shift in professional norms of what is considered "newsworthy."

"Priming" and the Hollywood Presidency

Flawed characters make great subjects for books and for movies, and Hollywood has used this as a springboard to produce a number of reasonably profitable movies that have dominated the post-1990s model. But does the presentation of these movies have any effect on how the public perceives a traditionally venerated institution? We argue that, just as a perceptively negative bias toward politics in the media has done much to shape the public's attitude towards politics (see Patterson 1993), the manner in which the presidency has been portrayed in the last decade also shapes the public's attitude towards the executive branch. Thomas Patterson refers to this process as "priming," which he defines as "the capacity of the press to isolate particular issues, events, or themes in the news, as criteria for evaluating politicians."[31] He suggests that when primed, the public will view politicians and candidates in the manner in which they have been portrayed by the media. For example, Patterson points out that "A Times Mirror poll in May (1992) showed that half of the public believed Clinton was not trustworthy. There was only one way they could have come to this conclusion; the media, in effect, had said so. Clinton had been unknown to the general public a few months earlier."[32]

Can this priming effect be extended to Hollywood? It is our contention that it can. Former Clinton aide George Stephanopoulos notes that in the absence of a Soviet threat, "we can fantasize about the enemy within. After all, conspiracy theories—from Vince Foster to crack in the inner city—are now part of the popular imagination."[33] Such stories help feed the public's imagination that something sinister is going on inside the White House. If the media have already primed the public to be largely negative and cynical towards politics,[34] then Hollywood has reinforced such views via several films from the 1990s, further priming an audience willing to believe that corruption and deviousness is rampant inside the Oval Office. Further, the drive in the media towards "infotainment," the rise of "punditocracy," and the popularity of [conservative] talk radio has pushed legitimate news stories aside for cryptic and sordid tales about our elected officials, including the institution of the presidency, regardless of whether they are true or not.[35]

Finally, to borrow from Richard Harwood's censure of the media and apply it to Hollywood: "Their failure to put things in perspective is perhaps their greatest sin."[36] So great is this sin that Joe Eszterhas, the screenwriter behind *Showgirls* and *Basic Instinct,* peddled a screenplay (entitled *Sacred Cows*) that portrayed the president having a "transspecies tryst in a barn."[37] When asked if the script is too vulgar to ever be made, Eszterhas agrees, but adds: "I hope it has something to say."[38]

The Presidency on Television

Television has had a much different history in its portrayal of the American presidency. Starting in the 1950s, the

American president and the office of the presidency has been regularly featured on television, but usually in terms of news rather than storytelling. Presidents have used the medium of television as a vehicle to impart important messages to the American public, and in some cases, the world. Some events surrounding U.S. political history are etched in the American mind because of television. President Kennedy's announcement of the Cuban Missile Crisis, President Nixon's resignation from office in the wake of the Watergate scandal, President Johnson's dramatic announcement that he would not seek reelection at the end of a speech on Vietnam, and President Reagan's comments memorializing the Space Shuttle Challenger astronauts are all examples of how presidents have used the medium in an effective manner. Similarly, the presidential debates between Kennedy and Nixon in 1960, the annual broadcasts of the State of the Union, and news footage of the assassination attempt on President Reagan are all examples of events in which television pictures have helped shape the American public's image of the presidency and the individuals who have occupied the office.

While presidents appear almost daily on news programs across the television dial, it is relatively rare that presidents have been seen on regular entertainment programs. Yet there have been a few instances when the presidency figures prominently on television screens. One memorable example was when President Nixon appeared for a few brief seconds on the 1970s hit *Laugh In,* saying simply, "Sock it to me?" The presidency has also figured prominently in programs that have had quite a short history. A 1977–78 television program called *Carter Country* fictionalized the hometown of President Jimmy Carter during his first year in office. Similarly, prior to the September 11, 2001 terrorist attacks, Comedy Central's *That's My Bush* fictionalized and satirized the presidency of George W. Bush. And shortly after leaving office, former president George H.W. Bush appeared on an episode of *Saturday Night Live* hosted by his perennial comedic nemesis, Dana Carvey.

Presidential *candidates,* however, at least in recent years, are not as reticent to use strictly entertainment to their advantage. As the last few election cycles illustrate, candidates have increasingly turned to late night comedy to get their message, or at least image, out to the masses. From Bill Clinton playing the saxophone on *Arsenio Hall,* to George W. Bush nagging David Letterman about his heart surgery, to Al Gore bringing his own top ten list to read on Letterman's *Late Show,* presidential candidates have been seeking the additional visibility and press offered by such appearances. And, in the fall of 2000, Democrat Al Gore and Republican George W. Bush both appeared on NBC in primetime to introduce *Saturday Night Live*'s "Presidential Bash," a collection of 25 years of presidential parodies and political sketches. Yet despite these examples of presidential *candidate* appearances, regular appearances by current presidents on purely entertainment programs has been extremely rare.

The West Wing—The Grand Exception

Television's Positive (and Often Realistic) Portrayal of the American Presidency[39]

While many of Hollywood's contemporary forays into presidency films have been anything but flattering or inspiring, television has provided one grand exception to this trend. Winning an army of Emmys in its first several seasons, earning the prestigious George Peabody award in its inaugural and second season, and named "TV show of the year" by *Entertainment Weekly* in its inaugural year, NBC's political drama *The West Wing* has been a ratings bonanza and cultural phenomenon. It has been praised in many media circles for its prime-time family-friendliness, lauded by one cultural critic as "a magnificent episodic series that depicts the tension and backroom drama of presidential politics with an unusual mixture of maturity and humanity," and has been discussed at length by politicians, academics, prominent radio personalities, columnists, and the intelligentsia.[40] Its portrayal of the inner-workings of the presidency and treatment of controversial issues—from the death penalty to school vouchers to gays in the military—has sparked debates among teachers, scholars, students, pundits, and politicians alike. Increasingly analyzed in depth by academics, used by educators in high school and university classrooms, and featured on countless fan web sites, *The West Wing* is especially relevant to presidency scholars and students of politics—and political scientists generally—given its attention to politics, public policy, and the myriad institutional dynamics of the modern presidency.

To make sure that the show presents an authentic rendering of White House politics, institutional dynamics, bureaucratic snafus, and routine presidential dilemmas, *The West Wing* has received consultation from prominent White House insiders—including Democrats such as former Clinton White House Press Secretary Dee Dee Myers, Carter pollster Pat Caddell, and Clinton economic policy adviser Gene Sperling, as well as Republican White House stalwarts Peggy Noonan (Reagan and Bush speechwriter) and Marlin Fitzwater (press secretary for Presidents Reagan and Bush). Nonetheless, this has not insulated the show from allegations of ideological heavy-handedness and bias. Indeed, Aaron Sorkin's award-winning presidential drama has been a lightning rod of controversy, as some have accused the show of a pervasive liberal bias. Indeed, in a May 4, 2000 speech before the National Press Club, no less than Majority Leader Tom DeLay (R-TX) derided NBC's celebrated series as more "left wing" than "west wing," arguing that the program was yet another exercise in cultural imperialism from liberal Hollywood elites hostile to core American values.

Praise for *The West Wing*

Media Critics, Academics, and Politicians Weigh In

The TV/politics nexus is far from new. John F. Kennedy added sparkle to his presidential hopes by visiting Jack Paar's "Tonight Show" before the 1960 campaign. Richard Nixon gained a measure of hipness by uttering "sock it to me" on "Laugh-In" in 1968. And Clinton's June 1992 appearance on "The Arsenio Hall Show," playing "Heartbreak Hotel" on his saxophone, was arguably a key moment in his summertime sprint from third to first place in the polls. And yet it's hard to summon a non-news show from TV's past that has the political edge of NBC's "The West Wing." Focused on the doings of the top aides to President Josiah Bartlet, "West Wing" does an amazingly effective job of dramatizing the moral and ethical questions surrounding politics and government.[41]

Former Clinton press secretary Mike McCurry asserts that *The West Wing* is "the only television show" that he watches, and commends the popular program for treating "those who work in politics . . . as human beings."[42] Media scholars have applauded the weekly drama's ability to "complement journalism by offering an entertaining reality of the White House that sharpens the image of the presidency and national politics."[43] Syndicated columnist and former Clinton White House aide Matthew Miller praises the show for providing a truer rendition of White House service and politics than most journalists,[44] while Jay Rosen, chairman of New York University's journalism department, suggests that *The West Wing* "conveys a truth about the White House that we don't get from other sources," especially because the "humanity of the participants" in the White House gets lost in the vast majority of the media's coverage.[45] In addition, the show's detailed attention to domestic and international issues—and the complexity of developing and implementing policy—has been lauded by many inside and outside of the power corridors of Washington, D.C. No less than Clinton Secretary of State Madeleine Albright offered a ringing endorsement of *The West Wing* after an episode from season one dealt substantively with the intricacies of India-Pakistan relations and the ongoing conflict in Kashmir.[46]

West Wing aficionados include Republican public servants as well. Reagan and Bush press secretary Marlin Fitzwater is an enormous *West Wing* enthusiast. A friend of Clinton press secretary Dee Dee Myers, Fitzwater was brought on as a consultant for the show's second season (2000–2001)—along with Reagan and Bush speechwriter Peggy Noonan. Fitzwater gladly climbed aboard the NBC vehicle to offer insight into White House–press relations and presidential governance in general. Fitzwater has high praise for the show and the program's creator, Aaron Sorkin, telling PBS' Terence Smith:

> I like it because I think it accurately portrays so many of the aspects of the White House that people never get to see and can't know about. . . . I think Aaron Sorkin is brilliant. The way he captures attitudes and nuances of issues and people's attitudes toward each other in the White House is truly remarkable.[47]

Amidst the positive feedback from politicians, academics, television critics, and the American public, a deluge of awards, statuettes, and critical acclaim keep rolling in. Yet beyond winning the prestigious Peabody award in each of its two seasons and receiving an avalanche of Emmy and Golden Globe nominations, perhaps most important is the size and enthusiasm of weekly audiences glued to their television sets: an average of thirteen million Americans tune in each week to follow the political, policy, and personal twists and turns that envelop President Jed Bartlet (Martin Sheen), Chief of Staff Leo McGarry (John Spencer), Communications Director Toby Ziegler (Richard Schiff), Deputy Communications Director Sam Seaborn (Rob Lowe),[48] Deputy Chief of Staff Josh Lyman (Bradley Whitford), Lyman's assistant Donna Moss (Janel Moloney), Press Secretary C.J. Craig (Allison Janney), and Presidential Assistant Charlie Young (Dule Hill).[49]

Criticism for The West Wing

> On a show called "The West Wing," a wise and humane president of the United States heads a White House staff devoted to making nice and serving the best interests of the public, special interests be damned. Experts agree. This impossibly sentimental confection is the most preposterous premise on TV, hands down.[50]

Not all West Wing feedback and critiques from the Atlantic to the Pacific have been positive, however. Several prominent Republican politicians and strategists—as well as media critics and academics—have charged the award-winning show with painting a grossly unfair and one-sided picture of the White House, national politics, and social issues that aggressively highlights and praises liberal policy positions, demonizes conservatives, and even challenges America's core values. Television critics more concerned with quality entertainment than ideological biases have chastised *The West Wing* for being sappy, sentimental tripe that is heavy on stirring musical scores, hokey idealism, and moral uprightness.[51]

During his "Challenge of Cultural Renewal" address at the National Press Club in Washington, D.C. on May 4, 2000, House Majority Whip Tom DeLay (R-TX), the third-highest ranking Republican in Congress, declared his disdain for public policies, cultural trends, media elites, and entertainment that mocked Christianity, faith, religious conservatives, and American values. Asserting that "the American people are trying to resist a cultural *coup d'etat*—a revolution launched by a privileged few who are determined to discredit and, ultimately, replace core American traditions"[52]—DeLay offered this assessment of the media in general and *The West Wing* in particular:

> In short, in the name of liberation, the fashionable elite created their own perverse ideology; in the name of "tolerance," they are profoundly intolerant. . . . The media show this disdain for faith by the way they depict religious conservatives: as either hypocritical totalitarians on shows like NBC's "The West Wing"—or as "poor, uneducated and easy to command," as *The Washington Post* once put it.[53]

Republican campaign strategist (and McCain 2000 guru) Mike Murphy has blasted the show for demonizing conservatives while canonizing liberals, and columnist and Bush and Reagan White House veteran James Pinkerton has complained of a brazen liberal bias on *The West Wing*, scoffing, "there's always an ideological hit there someplace."[54] Moreover, charges Pinkerton, creator Aaron Sorkin is "a liberal who believes in liberals" whose scripts religiously follow a smug "Republicans bad, Democrats good" plot line.[55]

Yet it is not only partisan elected officials and other stalwart Republicans that have been critical of the critically acclaimed Wednesday night drama. Other complaints have not centered on any liberal hijacking of American values but of basic believability. Caryn James, the chief television critic for the *New York Times* finds the show "wildly uneven" as it all-too-frequently shifts from complex sequences to "scenes of Martin Sheen making the right moral decision with the music swelling in the background."[56] Even some prominent Democrats (themselves avid *West Wing* devotees), have found certain small institutional aspects of the fictional Sorkin White House—such as the *GQ*-like appearance of nearly every low- or high-level White House staffer, and the size and comfort of the offices—to be rather unrealistic. And then there is the matter of the show's presentation of issues and agendas. Peter Rollins, president of the Film & History League, editor of the interdisciplinary journal *Film & History,* and co-editor of a volume of scholarly *West Wing* essays, stated that *The West Wing* "lays out a Hollywood political agenda sometimes so powerfully and passionately that it's offensive."[57] To illustrate this point, Rollins cited what he viewed as an unfair caricature of the religious right in the pilot episode—a treatment that he believed went "overboard" in its criticisms of religious conservatives.

Conclusion

For over a century the medium of film has been used to critique, glorify, vilify, lampoon, and analyze presidents and the presidency. For the first half of the twentieth century and more, the majority of these offerings, whether biographical or other feature films, were quite lavish in their praise of presidents. The office and its inhabitants were presented in a most positive light, and often featured classic leading men tackling the role of president or presidential candidate. Later, with the advent of the Cold War, and the post-Vietnam era, Hollywood became far less generous to

American chief executives. Many of the most extreme examples of this trend arrived in theaters throughout 1990s, when a majority of movies released in that decade depicted a White House run amok by shysters, sycophants, and sexual deviants. It is necessary that we take stock of this trend, examine the different perceptions of the presidency, and evaluate the root causes of this dynamic and the potential consequences for the body politic.

At the same time, we also see a tale of two presidencies, as television has not fully embraced wanton cynicism. NBC's *The West Wing* has humanized the White House and offered a sympathetic portrayal of public servants. At the same, the success of the show and the myriad salient public policy issues and political dynamics it has addressed has led to charges of ideological bias. Who is right and who is wrong? The best way to make an informed decision is to carefully watch the show, week after week—perhaps even reviewing some of the episodes discussed in detail in chapter two! In the meantime, whatever your ideological leanings—and *The West Wing* staff has prominent Democrats and Republicans who have served several presidents—one thing is for certain: *The West Wing,* with its romantic and fictional White House, has provided the viewing audience with a number of prescient insights into the everyday workings of the presidency, from the press room, to the war room, and all the pollsters, pundits, policies, filibusters, and bureaucratic inertia in between.

CHAPTER 5

Civil Rights and Social Justice

One of the enduring problems of any society is to make sure that all of its citizens enjoy, or at least have access to, the fundamental decency of civil rights and social justice. In narrative form, stories that depict the quest for political, social, and economic justice are often very compelling. Portraying the search for equality and dignity on the big screen, especially when it is done in a visually appealing manner, allows an audience to sympathize and perhaps even identify with protagonists, whether real or fictional. There are literally hundreds, perhaps thousands, of films and documentaries that chronicle the plight of people seeking civil rights and social justice in the United States alone. And while the search for equality is hardly limited to American society and the U.S. political system, for the sake of brevity, we have chosen to focus on film and television that examine the ongoing quest for civil rights and social justice in the United States. And within the context of American society and politics, we will highlight a few specific issues, groups, and dynamics. Therefore, in this chapter we explore the plight of African Americans, Jewish Americans, and homosexuals in American society. Finally, we turn to an exploration of labor strife and economic justice as portrayed on film and television.

Racism and the Civil Rights Movement

The issues of racism and the search for civil rights and social justice in the U.S. political system—and society as a whole—have been addressed on the big screen in a variety of ways. Whether it has involved a glowing tribute to the Ku Klux Klan in the Reconstruction-era South *(The Birth of a Nation)*, the trial of a black man falsely accused of raping a white woman in the Depression-era South *(To Kill a Mockingbird)*, a ritualistic lynching in Depression-era Mississippi *(O Brother, Where Art Thou?)*, the 1964 Freedom Summer murders of three civil rights workers in Philadelphia, Mississippi *(Mississippi Burning)*, the racially motivated bombing of the 16th Street Baptist Church in Birmingham, Alabama, in September 1963 *(4 Little Girls)*, the inability of African Americans to hail cabs in contemporary New York City in the 1990s (Michael Moore's series *TV Nation* and *The Awful Truth*), or the ramifications of racial profiling in today's America *(Murder on a Sunday Morning)*, commercial films and documentaries alike have provided citizens and students of politics with useful insights and different perspectives into the seminal political events and realities that have shaped attitudes, actions and public policy. In short, through their fictional and factual presentations, film and television can help us better understand the how and why—and occasionally the *"how not and why not"*—of America's ongoing struggle for civil rights.

As the long, gradual march toward equality continued

throughout the twentieth century, the Fourteenth Amendment's guarantees of equal protection and due process eventually became more fact than fiction, and the country's politics and values slowly evolved. And as millions of Americans' attitudes on race progressed and key elements of legal, state-sanctioned discrimination were eventually dismantled in the 1960s—via the Civil Rights Act of 1964, the Voting Rights Act of 1965, and the elimination of the poll tax through the Twenty-Fourth Amendment—Hollywood's portrayal of African Americans and the depiction of the issues at the heart of the struggle for civil rights evolved as well.

The Birth of a Nation: Depictions of African Americans and the Legacy of the Ku Klux Klan

The earliest and perhaps ugliest depiction of African Americans on film came in the form of D. W. Griffith's politically-charged silent epic The Birth of a Nation (1915). Griffith (1875–1948), an Oldham County, Kentucky, native and son of a lieutenant colonel in the Confederate army, often reminisced that he sat at his father's feet listening to stories about the glory that was the Confederacy. Later in life, remembering these stories, he clearly sympathized with the Confederacy and embraced many of the most insidious, and common, racial stereotypes of his day. Based on Thomas Dixon's (1864–1936) novel and play The Clansman, Griffith's controversial film portrays African Americans in Reconstruction-era South as sexually aggressive, deviant, barbaric slobs who possess neither the intellect nor civility to legitimately exercise their new-found freedoms. Throughout the film freed slaves terrorize the South, preying on innocent white women and bullying and beating Southerners and their "faithful servants" at will.[1] Dixon, an evangelical Baptist minister from North Carolina, was long obsessed with racial relations, especially the issues of integration, miscegenation and the perceived oppression of white Southerners in the Reconstruction era. He believed that political equality and the "black menace" threatened the very future of white womanhood, white civilization, and America itself.

It should not be surprising, therefore, that Dixon's story reinforces, and perhaps creates, many of the era's dominant—and most ominous—stereotypes of African Americans. In particular, the film makes the case that the right to vote and hold elected office had been abused by incompetent freed blacks. As discussed in chapter two, in one infamous scene, belligerent African American state legislators remove their boots, drink whiskey, and chomp wildly on chicken legs in the chambers of the South Carolina legislature. The film has the black majority pass a law allowing for whites and blacks to marry, as well as a statute mandating that whites salute black officials on the street. And while Dixon and Griffith depict slaves and servants (the vast majority of whom are portrayed by white actors in blackface) as obedient, moral, loyal, and intelligent, the freed slaves and the ambitious Northern political leader Silas Lynch (who is multiracial) are portrayed in the most negative manner possible. Lynch has an aggressive penchant for white women, as does a freed slave named Gus. Gus' primitive and violent pursuit of a white virgin ends in the woman falling to her death from a mountain cliff. She would rather preserve her virginity and purity than give in to the demands of the sexually aggressive black male. At the end of the film, the Ku Klux Klan arrive on horseback to save the South from raping and pillaging at the hands of the freed slaves, Silas Lynch, and pesky Northerners, and in doing so preserve white and Southern heritage and bring justice, hope, and redemption to a "new nation."[2]

The broad political implications of the film are unmistakable. In addition to the glowing portrayal of the Ku Klux Klan as redeemer and protector of the nation, and the film's reinforcement of some of the darkest and most destructive stereotypes of African Americans, Griffith's movie received a glowing endorsement from none other than the President of the United States, Woodrow Wilson (1913–1921). Wilson, a Staunton, Virginia native, who embraced racial segregation, stated that *The Birth of a Nation* "was like writing history in lightning. . . . My only regret is that it is all so terribly true"—and held a private viewing of the film at the White House.[3] It was the first time in the history of the presidency that a full-length motion picture was screened at the White House. Years later, after the film had clearly inflamed racial tensions across the country—at the time of the film's release, for example, the NAACP led boycotts of the film in several major cities[4]—President Wilson tried to distance himself from his previous effusive praise for the film, calling *The Birth of a Nation* "an unfortunate production."

As a Southerner who reflected the dominant views of his day, Wilson's acquiescence to segregation and racism is certainly understandable, however unfortunate. What is perhaps paradoxical—and should be cause for discussion, study and examination by students and scholars—is the fact that Wilson, as architect of the League of Nations and the Treaty of Versailles, was a champion of self-determination, human rights, and international law across the globe. Wilson the idealist, with an almost messianic zeal for self-determination and international peace—vs. Wilson the Southern segregationist who endorsed *The Birth of a Nation*—is one of the more interesting paradoxes and case studies in American politics.[5]

Griffith's epic was the highest-grossing motion picture of its time, and it signaled the advent of the motion picture as an art form, political statement, and major cultural event. The director's grandiose vision, groundbreaking cinematic techniques, budget, and innovative special effects—as well as the decades of raw emotions, picket lines, petitions, and protests that the film has spawned—have cemented *The Birth of a Nation* as one of the most influential and controversial movies in the history of film. As historian Leon Litwak has commented, "With the release of *The Birth of a Nation* in 1915, the motion picture as art, propaganda, and entertainment came of age."[6] The film would continue to be shown commercially into the mid-1920s, and from the time of its release on February 15, 1915 until 1946, it is estimated that roughly two hundred million people viewed *The*

Birth of a Nation in the United States and overseas.[7] The criticism that Griffith received prompted him to make an even more grandiose film the following year as an attempt to answer his critics. In *Intolerance* (1916), Griffith tells four simultaneous stories of man's inhumanity to man: the fall of Babylon, the passion of Christ, the 1572 St. Bartholomew's Day Massacre in France, and a modern story of a man falsely accused of murder. Perhaps it says something that this film, which was touted to be even bigger than *The Birth of a Nation,* failed miserably at the box office. All the money that Griffith made on *The Birth of a Nation* was lost in the making of *Intolerance;* in fact, *Intolerance* lost so much money that it took Griffith years to pay off his debts.

O Brother, Where Art Thou?

By identifying the worldview and key antagonists of the Ku Klux Klan, a riveting scene in the Coen brothers' otherwise farcical, frivolous *O Brother, Where Art Thou?* (2000), simultaneously lampoons the Klan's virulent racism and begs us to remember the horrific, violent legacy of lynching in the United States. In their box office hit, independent film giants Joel and Ethan Coen replicate Homer's *Odyssey* in Depression-era Mississippi against a backdrop of bumbling convicts, buried treasure, vintage Appalachian music, and a hotly contested governor's race between the incumbent Menelaus "Pappy" O'Daniel (Charles Durning) and Homer Stokes (Wayne Duvall). During a massive KKK rally designed to hang a black man named Tommy Johnson (Chris Thomas King)[8]—in which Klan members engage in a militaristic, nazi-esque march and an awfully strange, almost comical dance—the grand wizard of the KKK removes his red hood, revealing himself to be none other than Homer Stokes, the leading candidate for governor. After singing the unsettling, eerie strains of the traditional Appalachian ballad "O Death," the racist charlatan Stokes addresses his minions, condemning the enemies of the Ku Klux Klan and preparing his followers for a lynching:

Brothers! We are foregathered here to preserve our hallowed culture'n heritage! From intrusions, inclusions, and dilutions! Of colluh! Of creed! Of our ol-time religion! We aim to pull color up by the root! Before it chokes out the flower of our culture'n heritage! And our women! Let's not forget those ladies y'all, lookin' to us for p'tection! From darkies! From Jews! From Papists! And from all those smart-ass folk say we come descended from the monkeys! That's not my culture'n heritage. . . . and so . . . we gonna hang us a neegra![9]

Through the heroism of the kindhearted but simple protagonists Everett (George Clooney), Delmar (Tim Blake Nelson), and Pete (John Turturro), Tommy is rescued just before he is about to meet his untimely fate. This chilling, ghostly sequence—placed in the midst of otherwise light-hearted cinematic fare—is a vivid reminder of the prominence of the Klan and its impact on Southern politics and culture in the first half of the twentieth century. And while KKK membership dwindled in later years and it became less acceptable to publicly embrace the Klan's views in the 1950s onward, "White Citizens Councils" began to crop up throughout the South, quickly becoming a major political force in state politics. By the 1990s an obscure, political action committee (PAC) offshoot of the White Citizens Councils—the "Council of Conservative Citizens" (CCC)—existed in some areas of the South. Former Senate Majority Leader, Trent Lott (R-MS), and former Rep. Bob Barr (R-GA), among others, were criticized by Democrats and others in the mid-late 1990s for being associated with the CCC, which was viewed by some as the not-so-distant political progeny of the White Citizens Councils and the Klan.[10] In December 2002, Sen. Lott was roundly criticized in Democratic and Republican circles for praising the 1948 presidential campaign of South Carolina segregationist Strom Thurmond, who ran on the States Rights or "Dixiecrat" ticket.[11] Though merely a "moderate" hit by Hollywood blockbuster standards, it is worth noting that the Coen brothers' O Brother is the team's highest grossing film to date, far surpassing the Academy Award-winning Fargo (1996), among others.[12]

The Broken Code:
Battling the Cycle of Racism

To Kill a Mockingbird (1962)

Harper Lee's classic novel *To Kill a Mockingbird,* adapted for the screen by playwright Horton Foote in 1962, offers an insightful glimpse into the world of black-white relations and institutionalized racism in the Depression-era South. While *The Birth of a Nation* glorified the KKK as the saviors of white, Christian America, in *Mockingbird* principled lawyer Atticus Finch (Gregory Peck) tackles racism, cultural taboos (white women socializing with black men), stereotypes (African American males as sexual predators with a predilection for white women), and the Southern legal establishment head-on by defending an innocent black man charged with raping a white woman. While Finch's vision of justice and equality under the law ultimately loses to the irrationality of racism—as his client, Tom Robinson, is convicted by a white jury—audiences are presented with a strong, passionate voice against racial injustice and intolerance in an era dominated by such dynamics. Finch is not only a caring, doting, and widowed father raising two children, but he is willing to be shunned by white elites and spat upon by backward thugs in order to stand up for justice in his small Southern town. In his closing statement, Finch articulates the view that what was really on trial in the trumped-up rape case was the breaking of the time-honored racist code—the notion that white women and black men could not have relationships, emotional or sexual. And, in this case, a white woman and black man dared to, ever so slightly, break that code. *To Kill a Mockingbird* stands as a vivid example of popular literature—and then Hollywood— attacking the legitimacy of the racist code.

And, as the years passed by, and the civil rights movement picked up strength through the activism and sacrifice of thousands, film and television began to break down the barriers of racism and prejudice at an increased pace.

One of the most celebrated and popular sitcoms of the 1970s, Norman Lear's politically charged All in the Family *routinely examined race and social justice in America.* (The Bunkers and "Meathead": Maureen Stapleton, Carroll O'Connor, Sally Struthers, Rob Reiner)

Whether it was Stanley Kramer's *The Defiant Ones* (1958), starring Tony Curtis and Sidney Poitier; Norman Jewison's Academy Award–winning *In the Heat of the Night* (1967), starring Sidney Poitier and Rod Steiger; or the work of outspoken liberal writer and producer Norman Lear in the 1970s—who pushed the envelope by dealing with myriad aspects of race relations in hit series such as *All in the Family,*

The Jeffersons, and *Good Times*—Americans were finding that their popular entertainment on living room and theater screens was more willing to challenge the often unspoken codes of intolerance, fear, stereotypes, and prejudice. Fearful of challenging people's prejudice too directly, sometimes breaking racial barriers was done in an unthreatening manner. For instance, the first interracial kiss portrayed on American television was on the classic science-fiction show, *Star Trek.* The kiss was set in the twenty-third century, and against the will of the protagonists; presumably this was thought to be more tolerable to the American audience of the 1960s. Nevertheless, these codes, reinforced so blatantly in Griffith's *The Birth of a Nation* and in exclusionary (and legally sanctioned) Jim Crow tactics throughout the South, were increasingly facing stiff and subtle challenges from the world of film and television.

Monster's Ball (2001): "A lifetime of change can happen in a single moment"[13]

Breaking the cycle of deep-rooted generational prejudice is at the heart of Marc Foster's dark, compelling film, *Monster's Ball* (2001), which presents a harrowing tale of violence and racism surrounding a Georgia family. However, through risk taking, changes of heart, loss, and a series of tragic and unforeseen events, the cycle of racial hatred is ultimately broken. *Monster's Ball*—"whose title refers to the party wardens throw for prisoners on the eve of execution"[14]—concerns the life, times, and tortured family and social relationships of Hank Grotowski (Billy Bob Thornton), a racist, taciturn, violent prison guard who works on death row in a Georgia penitentiary. He has a volatile, hostile relationship with his son, Sonny Grotowski (Heath Ledger), who also works at the prison, and he has been taught to hate African Americans by his grotesque, frail father, Buck Grotowski (Peter Boyle). All three Grotowskis live in the same house, and the mix of racism, self-hatred, and dysfunction simmering within its walls ultimately leads to violence and tragedy. After a troubling turn of events, Hank begins an intense emotional and sexual relationship with Leticia Musgrove (Halle Berry), an African American woman who, unbeknownst to Hank, is the wife of the death row inmate that was just executed under Hank's watch.

While Hank loses his son in an ugly and vicious family fight—a fight which spirals into suicide—and faces the pressures imposed by his bigoted, belligerent, and ailing father, he is capable of breaking the code handed down by his father and so many around him. As both Leticia and Hank reach out for companionship and humanity in the wake of their pain, loss, and crises, they find each other. In the end, through their leap of faith and intense attraction, we see the code of racism, handed down from generation to generation, broken once again. Hank places his domineering father in a nursing home, and at the close of the film, Hank and Leticia sit beside each other on the steps of their humble home, quietly eating chocolate ice cream and gazing at the stars. We don't know for certain what will transpire in the future, but for now at least, they are one in spirit, and stand ready to stare down the future together. In *To Kill a Mockingbird* 40 years earlier, it was attorney Atticus Finch who exposed the evils of the code of racism when a white woman, Mayella, and an African American man, Tom, dared to be attracted to each other. In *Monster's Ball,* the roles are reversed as a white man Hank, and a black woman, Leticia, send the racist code to the scrap heap of history.

This gritty, bleak, but ultimately life-affirming journey through life's darkest corners of fear, brutality, prejudice, and dehumanization found itself on many critics "best of" lists in 2002. And, at the 2002 Academy Awards, it was an historic night, as, for the first time in the history of the movies, two African Americans took home the honors for Best Actor and Best Actress: Denzel Washington *(Training Day)* and Halle Berry *(Monster's Ball).* In this sense, *Monster's Ball's* tagline—*"A lifetime of change can happen in a single moment"*—may very well also apply to the Academy Awards.

Revisiting the Civil Rights Movement

Mississippi Burning (1988), directed by Alan Parker, and nominated for several Academy Awards, including Best Picture and Best Actor (Gene Hackman),[15] stands as Hollywood's definitive—though quite oversimplified and, at times, inaccurate—version of the 1964 Freedom Summer slayings of civil rights workers Mickey Schwerner, James Chaney, and Andrew Goodman. The three men were SNCC (Student Nonviolent Coordinating Committee) volunteers registering African Americans to vote in Mississippi, part of SNCC's concerted effort in the summer of 1964 to send idealistic college students trained in nonviolent civil disobedience to the South to help break down Jim Crow barriers at the ballot box.

Among the most common criticisms of the film are that it glorifies—or at least overstates—the FBI's commitment to solving the murders, and, moreover, that it unfairly and inaccurately portrays African Americans in Mississippi as passive and entirely void of brave, outspoken, and effective civil rights leaders.[16] For instance, it is now widely known that FBI director J. Edgar Hoover investigated and kept files on all of the Freedom Summer volunteers trained at the Western College for Women in Oxford, Ohio in 1964. Moreover, Hoover's penchant for wiretapping and harassing prominent civil rights leaders, especially Martin Luther King, Jr. (whom he despised and viewed as a communist and incessant womanizer), has been well documented. In addition, one of the great voices of the civil rights movement was Fannie Lou Hamer, an African American woman from Mississippi who founded the Mississippi Freedom Democratic Party, a movement designed to integrate the all-white delegation at the 1964 Democratic Party Convention in Atlantic City. There is also no mention of another great black civil rights leader from Mississippi, Medgar Evers, who was killed by an assassin's bullet in 1963. (See Rob Reiner's 1996 film *Ghosts of Mississippi,* starring Whoopi Goldberg and James Woods, for a chronicling of the state of

---

CIVIL RIGHTS, THE BROKEN CODE, AND *MISSISSIPPI BURNING*

Some questions to ponder when viewing several of the aforementioned films and videos:

What is the "Broken Code" discussed by Atticus Finch in **To Kill a Mockingbird**?
   Cite specific examples of this code being supported—and broken—in other films reviewed in this chapter (i.e., *Monster's Ball, The Birth of a Nation*) and in other movies or television series you have watched on your own.

What are the primary criticisms of 1988's *Mississippi Burning*?
   On what real life event(s) is the film based, when did the event(s) transpire, and what happened to the perpetrators of the crime?

According to the 1994 *Turning Point* special "Murder in Mississippi: The Cost of Freedom" what role did the KKK and the Mississippi State Sovereignty Commission play in this crime?
   Who was instrumental in helping the FBI ultimately infiltrate the Klan?

What major legislative victories followed this turning point in the civil rights movement, and what did they accomplish?

Mississippi's 30-year investigation and prosecution of Evers' alleged assassin, Byron de la Beckwith.) Despite these serious drawbacks, the film's taut direction, powerful depiction of pervasive institutionalized racism in Mississippi, and riveting performances by Hackman, William Dafoe and Frances McDormand (nominated for Best Supporting Actress), *Mississippi Burning* is a passionate, engrossing affair, and topped many "best of" film lists from 1988.

For a more specific, full, and accurate detailing of the events surrounding Freedom Summer and the FBI investigation of the slayings of Schwerner, Goodman, and Chaney, one can consult a 1994 installment of the ABC television news program *Turning Point*. The episode "Murder in Mississippi: The Cost of Freedom," hosted by Forrest Sawyer, follows on the heels of the 30th anniversary of the Freedom Summer, joining SNCC volunteers and their families as they make the journey back to Western College at Miami University in Oxford, Ohio, and Mississippi, to revisit this tumultuous turning point in the struggle for voting rights and equality. The events leading up to and following the murders, as well as all of the key players in the investigation—including all of the real life suspects, informants, and political leaders in Neshoba County, Mississippi—are reviewed in startling detail. Along with the historic voting rights March on Selma, Alabama, in March 1965, the Freedom Summer murders of Schwerner, Goodman, and Chaney—two Jews and an African American—stunned a nation and galvanized the civil rights movement and ultimately led to President Lyndon Johnson's signing of the historic Voting Rights Act of 1965. Among other things, the landmark legislation outlawed discrimination in voting, sponsored voter education and registration drives, and provided federal oversight of elections in areas where less than half of the minority voters were registered to vote. Within five years of the Voting Rights Act, the number of African Americans registered in the South doubled.

4 Little Girls (1997)

Documentaries, by their very nature, often delve into terrain where commercial films—so constrained by formulaic plots and the need to reach large audiences and optimize profits—dare not tread. Thus, for examining seminal political events and their effect on the body politic, documentaries can prove to be especially beneficial. Spike Lee's Oscar-nominated documentary *4 Little Girls* (1997), is an excellent case in point. Lee's moving film tells the riveting true story of the bombing of the 16th Street Baptist Church in Birmingham, Alabama on September 15, 1963. Four girls attending Sunday school at the church—Denise McNair, Carole Robertson, Cynthia Wesley and Addie Mae Collins—were killed in the racially motivated bombing, and the eyes of a nation were once again focused on the South. Featuring archival footage, interviews with surviving family members, and contextual commentary from national figures such as Walter Cronkite, Jesse Jackson, Andrew Young, Coretta Scott King—and a series of intriguing and odd ruminations from former Alabama governor, presidential candidate, and staunch segregationist, George Wallace *(see "The Many Faces of George Wallace" box)*—*4 Little Girls* carefully weaves reflections and realities, articulating the longstanding pain and the impact of the bombing on the slain girls' families and the American family. Clearly, students of American politics cannot understand the evolution and dynamics of the civil rights struggle without grasping the significance of this tragedy and its vital influence on the politics, events, and legislation that followed. Used in the proper context, Lee's documentary can be an invaluable educational tool in understanding the political and cultural dynamics surrounding the search for civil rights and social justice in the early- to mid-1960s. It is one very compelling chapter in the civil rights movement.

Racial Profiling and American Justice: *Murder on a Sunday Morning*

By the time the 2000 presidential election began in earnest, several presidential candidates addressed the issue of racial profiling in the primaries, openly discussing their opposition to the practice in speeches, debate appearances, and, in the case of Democratic candidate Bill Bradley, in their official policy platforms and web sites. Previously a topic of concern for a slew of civil rights activists, community leaders, mayors, and members of Congress, the issue now gained national prominence. Bradley, the three-term New Jersey senator and former New York Knicks star stated that the next president should immediately sign an Executive Order banning the practice. Other hopefuls—from Democratic Vice President Al Gore to Republicans such as Arizona Senator John McCain and Texas Governor George W. Bush—also expressed their distaste for racial

THE MANY FACES OF
GEORGE WALLACE, PART I

4 Little Girls on DVD: An Aging George Wallace "Unplugged"...

In the DVD edition of *4 Little Girls*, the "Making of 4 Little Girls" featurette contains illuminating commentary from Spike Lee concerning the making of the documentary, with special attention to the details and circumstances surrounding the lengthy and revealing, and at times, bizarre and barely audible, interview with former Alabama Governor and presidential candidate, George Wallace. George Wallace, whose health was in serious decline at the time of the documentary's filming, frequently speaks through a thick fog of Alabama accent burdened by age and illness.

In Spike Lee's documentary, the frail, aging Wallace attempts to make the case that he was never racist and that, as governor of Alabama, he passed legislation that paid for textbooks for African American students. He also demands to be filmed with his personal assistant, an African American man, at his side.

Evaluating the Legacy of George Wallace (1919–1998):
Unrepentant Segregationist, Southern Icon...

Wallace, like most Southerners of his era, started his political career as a states-rights Democrat. However, federal intervention in securing civil rights—as well as law and order issues—caused him to bolt the party in the late 1960s. After losing his first race for governor in 1958 to the race-baiting Governor John Patterson, who was openly backed by the KKK, Wallace confided to advisers that he would never be "out-niggered" again. When Wallace ran for Alabama governor in 1962 on a staunchly segregationist platform, he won, and become immensely popular throughout the South and a legend in his home state. In his infamous inaugural address on January 14, 1963, Wallace declared "segregation now, segregation forever." The speech was penned by Asa Carter, the founder of a KKK terrorist organization. Wallace later ran for president in 1968 as a member of the American Independent Party, capturing nearly 14 percent of the popular vote nationwide. He served as Alabama's governor from 1963–1967, 1971–1979, and 1983–1987.

Among other things, Wallace is famous for his stand-off with the Kennedy administration in June 1963 over the integration of the University of Alabama. (For more on the Kennedy-Wallace and federal-state showdown, see the 1963 documentary *Crisis: Behind a Presidential Commitment.)*

On June 11, 1963, after the federal-state dispute with Wallace over integrating the University of Alabama, President Kennedy addressed the nation from the Oval Office, calling civil rights a "moral issue" as "old as the scriptures" and as "clear as the Constitution." During the June 1963 crisis Wallace stood in the schoolhouse door and famously declared "segregation now, segregation tomorrow, and segregation forever!"

profiling, even as they did not endorse Bradley's specific Executive Order policy.

Murder on a Sunday Morning (2001), directed by French filmmaker Jean-Xavier de Lestrade, and winner of the Academy Award for Best Documentary in March 2002, weaves a compelling and disturbing tale of the real life consequences of racial profiling in Jacksonville, Florida in 2000. After the murder of a white female tourist outside of a Ramada Inn, a fifteen-year old African American male, Brenton Butler, is picked up and eventually charged with first-degree murder. On what grounds was he picked up? Did he confess to the murder? Were his constitutional rights violated? What was the outcome of the trial? *Murder on a Sunday Morning* answers all of these questions and poses many more as it meticulously follows the events in the immediate aftermath of the murder, examines the evidence at the crime scene, and gives the audience a firsthand view of the strategies of Butler's defense attorneys. We also see the effect of the trial on Brenton Butler and his family. The documentary allows the audience to see the trial, and in so doing, raises several penetrating questions about the veracity of the Jacksonville sheriff's office, the prosecution, and the practice of racial profiling. Roughly one week after capturing the Best Documentary Oscar, *Murder on a Sunday Morning* finally premiered in the United States, appearing as part of HBO's provocative "America Undercover" documentary series.

Michael Moore: Using Satire to Provide Alternative Perspectives on Television

For a much lighter and humorous (though perhaps no less disturbing or provocative) approach to examining the state of civil rights and race relations in contemporary America—in this case *de facto,* or non-state-sponsored discrimination—two segments from writer-director-producer Michael Moore work exceptionally well and should solicit animated reaction and spirited discussion among viewers. The segments come from Moore's two television series:

THE MANY FACES OF GEORGE WALLACE, PART II

Evaluating the Legacy of George Wallace (1919–1998):
Wallace: The Repentent Governor . . .

Later in life, Wallace disavowed much of his segregationist past and asked for forgiveness from prominent African American leaders. In 1979, for example, Wallace called civil rights pioneer, SNCC (Student Nonviolent Coordinating Committee) leader, and future U.S. congressman from Georgia, John Lewis, to ask his forgiveness for his past actions. Lewis accepted Wallace's apology.

By 1982, when Wallace ran for governor yet again, he actively sought the votes of African Americans throughout Alabama:

• *After a four-year political hiatus, Wallace returns to the Governor's Mansion, defeating his opponent easily, largely with the help of the majority black vote. During what would be Wallace's final term as governor, he appoints a record number of black Alabamians to government positions and establishes the so-called "Wallace Coalition," which included the Alabama Education Association, organized labor, black political organizations, and trial lawyers.*

•*Wallace addresses the Southern Christian Leadership Conference and pronounces his past stand on segregation in the schools "wrong."*[18]

To learn more about the life, times, politics, and paradoxes of George Wallace, see:

PBS's "American Experience" documentary *George Wallace: Settin' the Woods on Fire* (2000)
Website, *George Wallace: Settin the Woods on Fire:* http://www.pbs.org/wgbh/amex/wallace/
The TV film *George Wallace* (1997) starring Gary Sinise and directed by John Frankenheimer
Dan T. Carter's book, *The Politics of Rage: George Wallace, the Origins of the New Conservatism, and the Transformation of American Politics* (Simon & Schuster, 1995)

After viewing the 4 Little Girls DVD and the above films, consider these questions:

How did Wallace influence national politics and political party strategy in the 1960s–1980s?
What strategic roles did Wallace play in blocking integration and equality in Alabama in the 1960s?
What is "The Southern Strategy," what party employed it, and what did Wallace have to do with it?
In the 1970s–1980s, how and why did George Wallace ask forgiveness for his segregationist past?
Was Wallace sincere in his repentance?
What other actions did Gov. Wallace take in the 1980s to seek forgiveness and mend political fences?
What is his legacy?

You be the judge.

TV Nation (NBC and Fox, 1993–95) and *The Awful Truth* (Bravo Network, 1999–2000).

The Awful Truth's sketch "Whitey Can't Ride" (2000) follows Moore throughout Manhattan as he poses as a cab driver and refuses to pick up white people, stopping only to pick up African Americans. Need to get to East 86th Street and Lexington? Moore finds such upper class white neighborhoods "too dangerous" and leaves all Caucasians on his taxi route stranded without the ride they need. This sketch, which runs periodically throughout an entire episode, is an aggressive response and follow-up to his provocative *TV Nation* piece called "Taxi" (1994), in which Emmy–award winning African American actor Yaphet Kotto (*Midnight Run,* television's *Homicide*) tries to hail a New York City cab, but is routinely passed over for a convicted white felon named Louie Bruno! There are any number of discussions and debates that can follow Moore's use of satire to make a penetrating political statement.[17] Two volumes of Moore's Emmy-award winning *TV Nation* are available on VHS, and both seasons of *The Awful Truth* are available, in their entirety, on DVD, so that those interested can have the opportunity to discuss and debate the vital issues and questions posed by Moore.

The Struggle for Civil Rights and Social Justice Continues: Hollywood Addresses Anti-Semitism and Homosexuality

Anti-Semitism

Another chapter in the search for civil rights and social justice in the United States involves examining undercurrents of anti-Semitism in America. It may surprise some younger people to learn that two landmark films in this genre come not from the era of the civil rights movement in the 1960s, 1970s, or 1980s, but from 1947: Edward Dmytryk's *Crossfire* and Elia Kazan's *Gentleman's Agreement*. Both of these highly regarded black and white films address anti-Semitism, and its pernicious effects, head-on. *Crossfire* follows the murder of a Jewish man by a military man, and the twists and turns of the murder investigation. Boasting a stellar cast—including Robert Mitchum, Robert Young, and Robert Ryan, the gritty *film noir* pulls no punches. It exposes prejudice aimed at Jews and the lengths some will go to both exercise it and cover it up. It should be noted that original plotline of *Crossfire* involved the bashing and murder of a gay man, not a Jewish individual, but the topic was deemed too taboo or risqué in 1940s America. Thus, the plot was changed to anti-Semitism rather than homophobia in order to adhere to Hollywood's implicit and explicit film codes that kept explicit discussion of homosexuality, and prejudice and violence aimed at gays and lesbians, off the table for decades.

Elia Kazan's groundbreaking political drama *Gentleman's Agreement* (1947), winner of the Academy Award for Best Picture, follows a newspaperman (Gregory Peck) who poses as a Jew in order to catalog the obstacles presented by his faith. In so doing, he finds that neither his love interest nor workers at his very newspaper are immune to the stereotypical comments and sordid whispering campaigns that lie at the heart of anti-Semitism. Along the way he sees how a Jewish army veteran and close friend (John Garfield) is challenged to a fight at a restaurant just for being Jewish. He also discovers how hotels, clubs, and resorts find creative ways of keeping out Jews in favor of WASPS (white, Anglo-Saxon protestants). And, as he continues his journey as an "undercover" Jew in America, his son (a young Dean Stockwell) is taunted and harassed at school, coming home in tears after being called a "dirty Jew" and a "stinking kyke." In the end, the newspaper series at the heart of *Gentleman's Agreement* speaks for itself, exposing the myriad ways anti-Semitism is executed in the United States, whether in the home, businesses, the workplace, or school. It is an always present but not often discussed reality.

Homosexuality and Hate Crimes

Over the course of Hollywood's history, gays and lesbians have been depicted in various ways. It is difficult to briefly summarize the entire genre, however one documentary film covers the subject matter very well. *The Celluloid Closet* (1995), based on the groundbreaking book of the same title by Vito Russo, uses film clips from 100 years of film—from the silent era through 1993's *Philadelphia*—to examine stereotypes, recurring images, and the overall evolution of Hollywood's depiction of homosexuality on the big screen. Whether it is as a sissy, a violent predator, hopelessly depressed loner, or regular, everyday person, the documentary presents these images and stereotypes of gays and lesbians in a vivid, entertaining, and informative fashion. Narrator Lily Tomlin presides over this fascinating, illuminating review of film history that features insight and reflections from gay screenwriters and actors, including Gore Vidal, Amisted Maupin, and Harvey Fierstein, among others. In addition, Tom Hanks, Tony Curtis and several other prominent actors comment on their experiences performing in films that deal—implicitly or explicitly—with homosexuality. Insightful, disturbing, and at times hilarious, *The Celuloid Closet* is the ideal starting point for further critical analysis of Hollywood's myriad films that depict gays and lesbians.

HBO Films' *The Laramie Project* (2002), written and directed by Moises Kaufman, deals with the 1998 murder of gay University of Wyoming student Matthew Shepard. With a cast that includes the likes of Laura Linney, Steve Buscemi, Amy Madigan, Dylan Baker, and Christina Ricci, *The Laramie Project* is based on the play created by Moises Kaufman and the Tectonic Theatre Project based in New York City. After the murder of Shepard, Kaufman and his theatre project went to Laramie to discuss the murder and its ramifications with hundreds of townspeople. Did they know Matthew Shepard? Did they know the alleged murderers? How is homosexuality treated in the American West? How did the community respond to this brutal crime? What are the perspectives of clergy in the Laramie

HOLLYWOOD, HOMOSEXUALITY, AND HATE CRIMES

The Celluloid Closet (1995)

According to The Celluloid Closet, how has Hollywood depicted homosexuality over the years?

What are some of the major images—and stereotypes—of gays and lesbians on film?

How much has Hollywood's treatment of homosexuality evolved over the years?

What are the depictions of gays and lesbians in films from 1995–present?

The Laramie Project (2002)

What are your immediate reactions to the film and the main characters (townspeople, ministers, the police, Shepard's friends, those that committed the crime)?

What did you know about the Matthew Shepard case prior to the film?

Have you seen the play The Laramie Project?

Do you know anyone who has been on the receiving end of a hate crime or other forms of discrimination based on sexual orientation?

What did you do, if anything, to combat it?

How should we as a society (collectively via government policy)—and individually—work to understand those who are different?

How we can we collectively—and individually—work to stamp out discrimination based on sexual orientation?

How would you define "hate crime"? Is there such a thing as a "hate crime"?

For Further Study and Research

What are the pieces of federal legislation that have been introduced and debated in the last 10 years that deal with discrimination based on sexual orientation?

Does your state have laws that forbid discrimination based on sexual orientation?

Should they? Why or why not?

area? All of these penetrating questions, and many more, are explored in this play-turned-film. On any given day, *The Laramie Project* is performed on stages around the country, from college campuses to major public and private theaters. The HBO film provides a way for folks who may not be regular theatergoers to be exposed the important social, political, and cultural issues that surround homosexuality, hate crimes, and the specific case of Matthew Shepard.

"Whose Side Are You On?" Labor Struggles in the United States

Harlan County, USA

Another aspect of social and economic justice is the continuing struggle for dignity, worker's rights, and better wages. In examining the plight of the American worker and highlighting decisive, divisive battles between labor and business in the United States, seminal films—from independent film and documentary giants Barbara Kopple, John Sayles, and Michael Moore—stand out. Kopple's *Harlan County, USA* (1976), winner of the Academy Award for Best Documentary Feature, follows an acrimonious, protracted coal miners' strike against the Brookside Mine of the Eastover Mining Company in Harlan County, Kentucky—and its parent company, Duke Power—in the spring and summer of 1973. Throughout the two-hour documentary, Kopple provides the audience with ample political and historical context for the bitter standoff between the workers' union, the UMWA (United Workers of America), and the coal company, highlighting union struggles and violence that date back to the 1930s. This context arms the audience with important information about the nature of work in the mines (extremely dangerous), mine safety (often hazardous), black lung disease, and the disputes and violence between the union and coal company—and within the national union—that complicate and stymie the efforts of Kentucky miners to earn better wages, increased safety, a more democratic and responsive union, and dignity.

Not unlike Herbert Biberman's landmark blacklisted feature film *Salt of the Earth* (1953), which chronicled workers' struggle for economic justice during a zinc miners' strike in New Mexico, Kopple's documentary also focuses on the integral role—and plight—of miners' wives during strikes. *Harlan County, U.S.A.* also exposes corruption within the union, as the scandal-ridden UMWA president Tony Boyle has the democratic voice of the union, reformer candidate Joseph Yablonsky, killed. Yablonsky's murder is a blow to the miners who had been fighting for years for real political power within the union. Kopple also skillfully integrates archival footage of the mines and labor struggles with contemporary images of the miners' homes, poverty, and the general dismal socio-economic reality. Taken together, these images present viewers with a stark, realistic view of coal miners' lives, where lack of running water, electricity, and adequate health care are commonplace.

As the bitter 13-month long strike continues, the Duke Power Company, which controlled much of the mine operations, employed replacement ("scab") workers and hired gun-toting hooligans to threaten workers and break the will of the strikers. Violence begets more violence, and the already destitute town becomes polarized and shaken even further. The introduction of the hired guns presents local law enforcement and the strikers with further setbacks and dilemmas. In the end, while the struggles of the union and its strikers ultimately pay off—the new contract provided miners with a raise and more power within the mine and union—the film suggests that the struggle for better wages and basic dignity will be long and recurrent: just before the credits roll, miners strike yet again to protest the coal company's abuse of newly won grievance procedures. And the struggle for economic justice continues.

Matewan

Writer-director-producer John Sayles' *Matewan* (1987) is a semi-fictional retelling of real-life worker exploitation at the hands of a ruthless coal company in 1920s West Virginia.

UNIONS AND WORKERS' RIGHTS ARE FOR STRIPPERS, TOO: LOOK FOR THE UNION LABEL IN *LIVE NUDE GIRLS UNITE!* (2000)

Live Nude Girls UNITE!

Directed by:	Julia Query and Vicky Funari
Written by:	Julia Query and Vicky Funari
Distributed by:	First Run Features (USA)

Awards

San Francisco International Film Festival: Audience Award (2000)

Seattle Lesbian & Gay Film Festival: Best Lesbian Feature (2000)

Dubbed "A naughty *Norma Rae*" by *Entertainment Weekly* and called "wickedly funny, subversive, provocative" by the *Village Voice*, Query and Funari's documentary follows the efforts to unionize exotic dancers at San Francisco's Lusty Lady Peep Show during 1996–97.

The ladies at the Lusty Lady seek justice on a number of workplace issues and concerns, from sick leave, pay, and demotions to privacy, safety, and racial discrimination. While the picket line cries of *"2–4–6–8, don't go in to masturbate!"* may appeal to the audience's sense of humor, the film's inside look at the world of exotic dancing, labor issues in the sex industry, and the enormous struggle that goes into the collective bargaining and union building process, reveal a very serious side.

In addition to the exotic dancers' efforts to organize a union through the SEIU (Service Employees International Union), *Live Nude Girls UNITE!* also follows the relationship between the film's voice—Julia Query, stand-up comic and dancer at the Lusty Lady—and her mother, Dr. Joyce Wallace, a leading advocate of AIDS education for prostitutes.

For more information about labor and human rights in the sex industry, see: The Exotic Dancers Alliance (EDA): *http://www.edasf.org/*

Our mission is to address the lack of civil, human and labor rights on behalf of exotic dancers and other sex industry workers. Our primary objective is to support all sex industry workers by providing information, referrals and non-judgmental, empowerment-based services while collectively advocating for sufficient working conditions for everyone.... (Source: *http://www.eda-sf.org/EDAhome.htm.*)

Sayles acts in the film as well, portraying the local evangelical preacher who is more sympathetic with the coal company than the abused miners and their struggling union. As
historian Eric Foner writes, the labor struggles and corporate harassment in the southern West Virginia coal mines
depicted in the film "culminates in the Matewan Massacre, a
violent (and historically accurate) confrontation in which
the town's mayor, seven armed guards hired by the coal op-
erators, and two miners lose their lives."[19] The film, based
on this very real massacre and the general labor struggles in
the coal mines of West Virginia in the 1920s, depicts what
life was like in "company towns" and "company stores"
owned by powerful coal companies. During this time, mine
owners would pay workers in company script (money),
which could only be used at company stores—a situation
that invited corruption, maintaining a seemingly endless
cycle of poverty for the workers and profit for the company.
Matewan also examines some of the tactics routinely used
by coal companies to keep the miners and their fledgling
unions divided and ineffective. Race and ethnicity play a
major role here, as the coal company, aided by hired spies
and informants within union ranks, tries to paint the newly
arrived black coal miners as intent on stealing white
miners' jobs. This is not difficult to do in the midst of a poor
and worried population of white miners who are destitute
and, in many cases, have been inculcated with racial prejudice handed down through generations. In addition, the
coal barons also play on ethnic and religious differences to
create dissension within the union ranks by pitting Italian
immigrants against the native white West Virginians and
the African American miners.

Featuring riveting performances by James Earl Jones and
Sayles' stalwarts David Strathairn and Chris Cooper, *Matewan,* while a semi-fictionalized account of coal miners'
struggles—Sayles adds two fictional characters, Danny Rad-
nor, a union-supporting miner and boy preacher, and Joe
Kenehan, a union organizer and pacifist, to the cinematic

mix—covers much of the real world terrain of labor struggles in 1920s West Virginia. As *The Washington Post's* film
review surmised in the fall of 1987:

> "Matewan," based on events preceding the 1920 West Virginia
> Mine War, paints the struggle among the Stone Mountain Coal
> Company, its miners and a union organizer as a kind of "The
> Good, the Bad and the Wobbly." Joe Kenehan (Chris Cooper) is
> a former Industrial Worker of the World (they were known as
> "wobblies") who pulls into Matewan town, a place where the
> company owns everything. "You ain't with the Company,"
> Kennehan's new landlady Elma tells him, "there ain't no work."
> Stone Mountain has also infuriated the locals by recruiting
> southern blacks and immigrant Italians to keep labor cheap.
>   Kenehan has his work cut out for him. He must unite dispar-
> ate groups into strikers and, when the company forces them
> into a tent camp in the mountains, keep some very desperate
> people calm. And this company has not only firepower but eyes
> and ears in unexpected places.[20]

Sayles' attention to historical accuracy, gorgeous cinema-
tography, and riveting storytelling that provides context for
West Virginia politics and concentrated economic power in
the 1920s, combine to create one of the most memorable
film experiences documenting labor struggles in the United
States. It exposes injustice and poses questions about entrenched political and economic power that most films refuse to touch. It allows contemporary people to be trans-
ported to a time and a place that seems far removed from
our own socio-political reality, yet also reminds us that
some similar struggles remain. As Eric Foner asserts in his
praise of Sayles' masterpiece, to make *Matewan* during the
1980s, a time in which anti-labor sentiment was prevalent,
was an accomplishment, but

> In the hands of director John Sayles, *Matewan* offers a medita-
> tion on broad philosophical questions rarely confronted directly
> in American films: the possibility of interracial cooperation, the
> merits of violence and nonviolence combating injustice, and
> the threat posed by concentrated economic power to American
> notions of political democracy and social justice.[21]

American Dream

American Dream (1990), directed by Barbara Kopple, and winner of the 1991 Academy Award for Best Documentary, chronicles labor struggles and an eventual bitter strike in Austin, Minnesota during 1984–1986. The site of struggle here is the Hormel slaughterhouse and meat-packing plant in Austin. Hormel, the makers of Spam and a wide variety of meat products, while posting a healthy profit of $29 million in 1984, offered the workers at its Austin plant a contract that cut wages from $10.69 to $8.25 an hour. The contract also cut benefits by 30 percent. Kopple's film documents the ensuing battle of wills between Hormel and the local union, P-9, of the UFCW (United Food & Commercial Workers), who strike in order to win back the wages and benefits. It also chronicles the dissension among local P-9 members as the strike wears on, and, most of all, the rancor and severe disagreements between the P-9 and the international UFCW leadership. It is, as the VHS box cover of *American Dream* asserts, a "strike which pitted worker against management, worker against worker and even brother against brother."[22]

Refusing to take the salary and benefits cut, local P-9, led by president Jim Guyette and activist public relations guru Ray Rogers—who was hired by P-9 to orchestrate a "corporate campaign" aimed at gaining national solidarity and sympathy for the strike—work to organize labor, galvanize their union, and oppose Hormel's cuts. National attention comes to Austin, as Jesse Jackson and other political and labor leaders—including the future U.S. Senator from Minnesota, Paul Wellstone (1991–2002), then a political science professor at Carleton College—come to Austin to rally behind P-9's cause. However, as the strike continues with no end in sight, P-9 suffers a number of mortal blows. Hundreds of Hormel workers in other plants, who, in a show of solidarity with P-9 refuse to cross the picket lines at their plant, are fired. In addition, rancor and disagreements over strike and negotiation tactics between P-9 and the international union, led by Lewie Anderson, tear apart any hope of one united union front. In the end, Hormel hires back less than 20 percent of the Austin

plant workers who went on strike and honored the picket line. But that is not the end of the saga. Ultimately Hormel contracts out their plant to an independent company, and promptly slashes wages to $6 an hour. It is a painful, sorrowful chain of events for the workers and their families, and the film captures the struggles—within the union, among the families in Austin, and between labor and business—in dramatic fashion.

At the same time, many intimately involved with local P-9 efforts take issue with *American Dream*'s depiction of events. Peter Rachleff's 1993 account of the bitter Hormel strike, *Hard-Pressed in the Heartland,* strongly disagrees with Kopple's version of the strike and its presentation of key players. Rachleff, a history professor at Macalester College in St. Paul who was actively engaged in strike efforts on behalf of local P-9, finds the final film version of the labor dispute to cast an unfairly negative light on the local P-9, its members and its leadership, while praising International UCFW leaders who were, in his mind, destructive to the workers' cause:

> *American Dream* presents the International Union's hatchet man, Lewie Anderson, as a tough-talking, hard-nosed union bargainer in contrast to P-9's leadership and advisers who are presented as confused, inexperienced, and out of touch with reality. Worse than these character distortions, *American Dream* also gives Anderson one opportunity after another to predict that this strike will fail, without ever exploring the critical role he and the UFCW played in undermining it—in discouraging other unions from sending assistance, in denying P-9 the right to block production at Hormel's seven other unionized plants, in rejecting P-9's call for a boycott of Hormel products, and in organizing a minority of dissident P-9 members to disrupt union meetings and even to cross sanctioned picket lines. *American Dream* actually implies that the UFCW had the "right" position—not to take on Hormel at all, or to return to work on the company's terms when they began to hire "permanent replacements"—at the same time it whitewashes the union's role in destroying a strike it publicly claimed to support.[23]

eff viewed P-9's intense labor organizing at the local be "just what the doctor ordered as an antidote for a

moribund labor movement," and was amazed by the "large number of people participating, the involvement of families, the spirit and imagination . . . and the determination not to back down before what appeared to be unreasonable demands being made by a profitable company."[24]

Roger & Me: The Debate Over Corporate Responsibility and the Social Contract

Perhaps no labor-oriented film has garnered more universal acclaim or provoked as much controversy as Michael Moore's *Roger & Me* (1989). Made for a paltry $260,000, *Roger & Me* quickly became one of the highest grossing narrative documentaries in the history of film. A native of Flint, Michigan, Moore returned to his hometown after an unsuccessful stint at the liberal journal *Mother Jones* in San Francisco. His mission? To document the layoffs of thousands of GM workers and its effects on the local economy, crime, mental health, and the overall quality of life. The "Roger" is Roger Smith, the CEO of General Motors; the "Me" is Michael Moore.

Using his settlement from *Mother Jones* and scores of bingos and fundraisers, Moore scraped together funds needed to make his film. He had no film experience whatsoever. The son and grandson of GM auto workers, both union men from the UAW (United Auto Workers), Moore is especially interested in the plight of GM workers, and his repeated visits t plant closings to chat with workers bear this out. Along quixotic journey to plant closing after plant closing, he r to the increase in crime, the building of new jails, th exodus of workers, the evictions of citizens from th the rise of the rat population, the jobs people re ends meet (Taco Bell, Amway, blood and plas rabbit-butchering), and—most of all—he tri General Motors CEO Roger Smith and ask *Why, in a time of profits, is GM laying off*

While he is stymied at every attem one meeting with Smith, Moore i Kay, a spokesman for GM. During

agrees wholeheartedly with Moore's belief that GM has a special responsibility to the community in which it operates. This kind of "cradle to grave" care is, according to Kay, not the job of corporations.[25] The corporations are businesses, and, as such, are concerned with one thing: being as efficient and profitable as possible, and if it means laying off 20,000 or 80,000 people in order to achieve such goals, then that's what corporations must do. In the meantime, Kay suggests, there is as much economic opportunity in 1980s Flint as ever before, and cites the success of a lint roller company. Not surprisingly, Moore finds this contention to be laughable.

While *Roger & Me* was a huge critical and commercial success (at least by documentary standards, not all shared Moore's progressive view of corporate responsibility). Still others charged Moore with playing too loose—or deliberately and deceptively loose—with the facts when he cites Flint job losses at 30,000. Critics have countered that Flint only lost 3,000 jobs in the time period examined in the film. Film scholar and political scientist Ernest Giglio discusses this controversy:

> Moore considered his film a documentary, but eventually it was revealed that he had taken liberties even beyond editing and the rearranging of scenes. For example, Moore charged that the plant closings resulted in 30,000 workers being laid off but the actual figure for the Flint plant was a more modest 5,000. The 30,000 figure actually referred to jobs lost in plant closings in four states over a twelve year period.[26]

Moore has responded that the film gives no specific dates and that his film was meant to convey a larger picture about the devastating effects of layoffs on a region over the entire decade of the 1980s.[27] Whatever your view of these criticisms and Moore's response, and whatever your politics or interpretation of Moore's work (there tends to be a love-hate reaction to Moore's style and politics!), the serious issues he raises via his art should spark hours and days of serious debate and deliberation over corporate and government responsibility in the quest for economic and social justice in America.

Michael Moore: Still a Man with a Camera and a Point of View

In the years following *Roger & Me*, Moore has gone on to write, direct and produce films that examine social and economic justice, as well as other issues, such as gun violence and institutionalized violence: *Canadian Bacon* (1995), *The Big One* (1998), and *Bowling for Columbine* (2002). *The Big One* (1998) is discussed at length in chapter two (liberal ideologies). Moore examines many of the same issues addressed in *Roger & Me* via his satirical television shows *TV Nation* (1993–1995) and *The Awful Truth* (1999–2000). He has also written three books, *Downsize This! Random Threats from an Unarmed American, Adventures in a TV Nation* (co-authored with Kathleen Glynn), and *Stupid White Men*. But Moore's greatest commercial and, arguably, critical success arrived in October 2002 with the release of *Bowling for Columbine*. The controversial documentary, which examines the roots and consequences of American violence and obsession with guns, cost roughly $10 million to make and by early 2003 had grossed over $30 million, surpassing *Roger & Me* and *Hoop Dreams* to become the highest grossing documentary of all time. In December 2002, The International Documentary Association (IDA) named *Bowling for Columbine* the best documentary of all time, and in February 2003, Moore's unsettling film garnered an Academy Award nomination for Best Documentary Feature. As the accolades continued to roll in, on February 16, 2003, CBS's *60 Minutes* profiled Moore, *Bowling for Columbine*, and his entire body of film, television, and literary work.[28] Then, on March 23, 2003, Moore's film won the Academy Award for Best Documentary Feature.

In the meantime, other filmmakers, in addition to Moore, Kopple, and Sayles, continue to address labor struggles and economic justice in the United States. *American Standoff* (2002), for example, which debuted on HBO's premiere documentary series "America Undercover" in 2002, follows the state of the Teamsters Union by examining the notori-

DOCUMENTARIES, FEATURE FILMS, AND LABOR STRUGGLES: COMPARING *ROGER & ME* AND *AMERICAN DREAM*

What happened to Flint, Michigan, and Austin, Minnesota, in the 1980s?

How are the concepts of political economy and economic policy relevant to the issues raised in *Roger & Me* and *American Dream?*

What responsibility, if any, do corporations have to their workers and the community?

What is GM spokesman Tom Kay's view of corporate responsibility to communities?

Should *Roger & Me* be classified as a "documentary," "narrative documentary," or "feature" (i.e., "commercial") film? Why? Why not? Are such definitions arbitrary? Justify your position.

Compare and contrast *Roger & Me* and *American Dream:* In what ways are they alike and different in *style and substance?* Augment your response with specific examples from the films.

What do you believe the rabbits in *Roger & Me* symbolize?

Why did Moore include the "rabbits" sequence? Was it necessary? Unnecessary? Why?

Do you side with Hormel and GM or the unions? In *American Dream*, do you side with the local P-9 or the International UFCW leaders? Why?

ous union's internal politics under the new Hoffa regime, and by reviewing their extensive efforts in 1999–2002 to unionize the Overnite trucking company. The documentary was directed by Kristi Jacobson.

Conclusion

As this chapter illustrates, whether it is the legacy of racism, the history of the civil rights movement, anti-Semitism, the homosexual experience in America, or the struggle for economic justice, American film and television have increasingly provided a wealth of images and perspectives that provoke, challenge, offend, advocate, and, above all, tell the extraordinary stories of ordinary people searching for civil rights and social justice. Social and political action aimed at aiding this quest and realizing the dream of equality has indeed taken a long time and has been fueled by the sacrifices of many. However, the legitimizing and reinforcing of racial stereotypes in early American films such as *The Birth of a Nation* have given way to a wide array of artistic expressions that have openly—or in many more subtle ways— challenged the prevailing codes of racism, anti-Semitism, and homophobia. We are then free to evaluate these films and their points of view, reviewing them to learn more about ourselves and our political past and present. This examination of film also reveals that several directors and documentarians continue to ask unsettling questions about our past, present, and future, providing students and citizens alike the means by which to debate and discuss our republic's ongoing search for civil rights and social justice.

CHAPTER 6

Campaigns and Elections

While explicitly political films make up a small percentage of Hollywood's overall output—the best estimates are five to ten percent, at best—the industry, along with emerging independent filmmakers, has devoted a fair share of these films to campaigns and elections.[1] Several of these films—whether commercial ventures depicting fictional campaigns, or behind-the-scenes documentaries—examine a number of key dynamics and realities that underlie American elections in the media age. In exploring campaigns and elections, this chapter samples movies and television segments which present revealing, and, at times, controversial, portraits of candidates and the campaign process. They explicitly and implicitly offer provocative commentary on vital issues connected to campaigns and elections, including:

strategizing, politicking and machines, media power and behavior, ideology, Americans' political participation, and the role of—and obstacles faced by—third parties.

Reel Candidates: Mayors, Governors, Senators, and Presidential Candidates

The Last Hurrah:
Big City Mayors and Old-Style Politicking

John Ford's 1958 black and white classic *The Last Hurrah,* based on the novel by Edwin O'Connor, looks back with fondness on big city machine politics. The protagonist in this colorful tale of campaigning and patronage is the mayor of a large New England city (assumed to be Boston), Frank Skeffington (Spencer Tracy). Skeffington, who grew up in one of the working-class sections of the city and rose to greatness through hard work and party loyalty, is a back-slapping, big-hearted man of the people who sets aside entire days to meet and greet constituents in his office. The film follows Skeffington's last campaign, a battle against the new television-driven politics and the vacuous, superficial blow-dried opposition candidate Kevin McCluskey (Charles B. Fitzsimons). The smiling, attractive puppet-like McCluskey uses television ads with his wife and children to promote an image of an upstanding, honest, family man. However, the ad in question—which parodies Richard Nixon's famous "Checkers" speech, among other popular political ads—goes horribly awry when McCluskey's dog barks incessantly and his wife has trouble reading the cue cards. The message is clear: this new breed of image-making political stunt is as staged and fake as the day is long. It is an elaborate, well-lit, slickly produced manipulation of the American voter.

Throughout the film, the ebullient Skeffington shows Adam Caulfield (Jeffrey Hunter), a journalist and the mayor's nephew, the ropes of glad-handing campaigning and constituent politics. In one famous scene, Skeffington takes Caulfield to the wake of local man, "Nocko" Minnihan, and the gathering quickly becomes a political event, as the mayor's attendance brings out various constituencies—such as firemen and police—to impress Skeffington. At face value, this may seem like shameless, heartless politicking. However, Skeffington's presence brings a huge crowd to pay respects to Nocko, which soothes his grieving widow, Mrs. Minnihan. In addition, Skeffington gives Mrs. Minnihan money to help her along, and uses his stature to strong-arm the funeral director into providing funeral services and burial for a minimal fee. In the process, the mayor transforms his nephew from skeptical critic to adoring fan—of both his uncle and his style of big city politicking. When the larger than life mayor ultimately loses the election to the clueless but media-savvy McCluskey, it signals the end of a type of politics and campaigning once so prominent across the country. With the advent of television and the accelerated use of staged events, calculated confessionals, and carefully planned testimonials, this is a sign of things to come. *The Last Hurrah* clearly presents the positive potential of machine politics. While the context is quite different (mayoral politics aimed at helping constituents and winning elections), this celebration of patronage is a far cry from the intensely negative portrayal of the Taylor political machine in Frank Capra's *Mr. Smith Goes to Washington*.

An excellent real-world companion piece to *The Last Hurrah's* send-up of political ads would be Richard Nixon's notorious 1952 "Checkers" speech. Appearing immediately after the popular *Milton Berle* show, the beleaguered vice presidential candidate Nixon used his well-placed television slot to defend his usage of a political slush-fund provided by supporters, and to hurl allegations of impropriety at his Democratic rival. Nixon's television event was a huge success, rallying Republicans and forcing Dwight Eisenhower, the 1952 Republican presidential nominee, to keep the young U.S. Senator from California on the ticket. In the decades since Nixon's primetime confessional, such direct appeals have become quite commonplace. In the midst of allegations of infidelity in the heat of the 1992 New Hampshire primary, for example, Bill and Hillary Clinton appeared on CBS' long-running news magazine *60 Minutes* in January 1992, after the Super Bowl, to address questions of extramarital affairs. During the interview, Bill Clinton admitted to causing "pain" in his marriage. This real-life scene is repeated in fictional form in Mike Nichols' 1998 film *Primary Colors,* which follows the presidential campaign of a Clintonesque southern governor.[2]

The Candidate: U.S. Senate Campaigns in the Media Age

In 1972's *The Candidate,* directed by Michael Ritchie, starring Robert Redford, and featuring a stellar performance from Peter Boyle, there is an explicit connection to the real world of modern American politics: the screenplay was penned by Jeremy Larner, an aide to 1968 Democratic presidential candidate, Sen. Eugene McCarthy. "The Candidate" in the film is Bill McKay (Redford), the liberal son of a former backslapping, deal-cutting California governor (Melvyn Douglas). McKay is an activist, antipoverty lawyer who is talked into running against popular incumbent U.S. Senator Crocker Jarmon. McKay enters the race an idealistic individual who speaks his mind and offers substantive policy initiatives. However, as the long-shot McKay begins to rise in the polls and provide a stiff challenge to Jarmon, his team of advisers and image men take over, molding the once-outspoken, authentic insurgent candidate into a conventional, managed contender who drops his bold proposals and specifics and switches to the safe but cynical terrain of empty slogans and sound bites. He even placates his advisers by trimming his sideburns and hair. As Ernest Giglio observes, *The Candidate* "warns the audience of the pitfalls of contemporary electioneering where . . . personal appeal is celebrated over intelligence and ethical principles, and thirty-second sound bites are favored over detailed analysis of complex issues."[3]

In a telling scene at the close of the film, when the young McKay wins the election, his father approaches him and says, "Congratulations, son. You're a politician now." It is crystal clear from his tone and facial expressions that he doesn't mean politics in the noble, idealistic sense of unselfish public service. Larner's script is razor sharp, and, in many ways accurately echoes the stale, manipulative direction of modern campaigns in a media-saturated age. Nonetheless, this significant moment in *The Candidate* presents a potential problem for students and citizens alike. In a country with steadily declining voter turnout, where healthy skepticism too often gives way to wanton cynicism and alienation, such scenes reinforce the most negative perceptions of politics and our governing institutions: namely that politicians are self-serving snake-oil salesman and that politics is a sleazy cesspool unworthy of vigilant civic involvement. This cynical view, often propagated by popular media, can be disastrous for promoting citizenship and political involvement. Referring to this scene at the end of *The Candidate,* Ernest Giglio reminds us:

> The scene's cynicism offends two vital concepts in a democratic society: first, the notion that the electorate believes politicians hold office as a public trust and second, that politics is an honorable and commendable profession. Congress ought to make it unlawful for any American youngster to view this scene on the ground that that it could destroy whatever is left of the civic virtue.[4]

Bob Roberts: Right-Wing Folk-Singer Exploits Fears and Plays a Mean Harmonica

The "mock" documentary *Bob Roberts* (1992), written and directed by Tim Robbins, presents an ideological critique of contemporary politics and ambitious "self-made" men who seek power at any cost. Bob Roberts is a millionaire right-wing ideologue from Pennsylvania who uses folk songs to express his ultraconservative views and who is seeking a U.S. Senate seat. With a harmonica around his neck, Roberts releases albums such as *The Freewheelin' Bob*

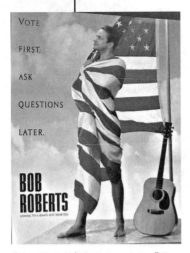

"Vote First. Ask Questions Later." Tim Robbins' biting satire *Bob Roberts* is a "mockumentary" of the 1990 U.S. Senate campaign of a Wall Street millionaire-turned conservative populist folksinger-turned opportunistic, ruthless politician.

Roberts, Times Changin' Back, and *Bob on Bob*—and sings songs such as "Drugs Stink" and "I Wanna Be Rich."[5] As is evident from these titles, Roberts throws the liberal, activist edges of the 1960s folk tradition on its head. Rather than strumming his guitar to promote racial justice or fight poverty and war, the senatorial candidate uses his music and campaign events to attack the poor and homeless, antiwar activists, hippies, and drugs. It is a media-savvy full frontal attack on 1960s idealism and liberalism, and Roberts' message draws young psychotic fans into his corner (including a young, hilarious Jack Black). As his campaign against liberal incumbent Sen. Brickley Paiste (Gore Vidal) heats up, Roberts smears him as a womanizer and an out-of-touch-big-government-liberal who wastes taxpayers' money on wasteful social welfare and antipoverty programs. When an industrious, activist reporter ties Roberts and close aides to illegal activity, Roberts fakes an assassination and has the reporter framed. In the raging narcissistic, right wing Roberts, Robbins is able to offer a scathing critique of the views, motives, and effects of conservative, populist politics in 1990s America. And it is a view that may have another day in theaters and the court of public opinion. In the fall of 2002, Robbins announced on ABC's morning talk show *The View* that a sequel to *Bob Roberts* was in the works. What would the folk-singing conservative be up to next? Why, a presidential run, of course.

The Simpsons' "Sideshow Bob Roberts"

So far-reaching was Robbins' hilarious send-up of an egomaniac conservative folk-singer, that an infamous 1994 *Simpsons* episode about a corrupt campaign was entitled "Sideshow Bob Roberts." In this installment of *The Simpsons,*

America's animated family: Homer, Marge, Bart, Lisa, and Maggie Simpson (with "Santa's Little Helper"). The longest-running sitcom of its kind in American television history, Matt Groening's *The Simpsons* has delighted millions with its unique mix of absurdity, razor-sharp wit, pop culture observations, and, especially, political commentary.

perennial nemesis Sideshow Bob (the voice of Kelsey Grammer), the incarcerated ex-sidekick to Springfield's star entertainer Krusty the Clown, gets out of prison in order to run against longtime incumbent Mayor "Diamond" Joe Quimby, a notorious wheeler-dealer and womanizer. Promoting Bob's release and mayoral candidacy is the blowhard Birch Barlow, a popular conservative radio personality

and prominent Republican. Longtime *Simpsons* viewers rec-
ognize the New England–accented "Quimby" as a facsimile
for "Kennedy," while Birch Barlow is clearly a prototype for
Republican radio king Rush Limbaugh. While Bob handily
defeats Quimby, it is later revealed—via a hilarious
Woodward-Bernstein Watergate parody complete with
"Deep Throat" and dark parking garages—that the former
Krusty sidekick stole the election with the help of massive
voter fraud. In "Sideshow Bob Roberts" we are treated to a
number of political and campaign references, from Rush
Limbaugh and the Kennedys to Watergate and *All The President's Men*. In addition, the episode's Quimby–Sideshow
Bob debate sequence cleverly echoes, in satirical fashion,
the 1988 presidential debate where CNN's Bernard Shaw
asked Democratic nominee Michael Dukakis if he would
support the death penalty if his wife, Kitty, was raped and
murdered. And, in further attention to the 1988 presidential
election between George Bush and Michael Dukakis, there
is a parody of Bush's "revolving door" prison ad.[6] In the
end, much like the conservative populist folksinger Bob
Roberts, Sideshow Bob will do anything to get elected. Like
Robbins' film, this installment of *The Simpsons* uses political satire and parody to get its point across. But unlike *Bob
Roberts,* "Sideshow Bob Roberts" does so in animated and
televised format.

The Simpsons
Monty Burns for Governor: "Two Cars in Every Garage and Three Eyes on Every Fish"

"Checkers," *Citizen Kane,* and much more are spoofed in
The Simpsons' gubernatorial campaign episode "Two Cars
in Every Garage and Three Eyes on Every Fish." This political tour-de-force from writers Sam Simon and John Swartz-
welder premiered on November 1, 1990, just days before
the 1990 midterm elections. In "Two Cars" Montgomery
Burns, filthy-rich overlord of the Springfield Nuclear Power
Plant, is fined millions by a government nuclear regulatory
commission for his unsafe, shoddy upkeep of his plant.

The state-imposed plant inspection is spurred when Bart Simpson catches a three-eyed fish (who Burns later dubs "Blinky") in a fishing pond adjacent to Burns' nuclear plant. Depressed at the money he will have to spend to improve his plant and be in sync with the code, Burns lashes out at government safety and environmental standards, and, after complaining to plant employee Homer Simpson (his notorious work station is "Sector 7-G"), about the government fines, he vows to run for governor against incumbent Mary Bailey. From there he can selfishly dismantle the state's nuclear power plant regulations. What follows is a sardonic take on the manipulation, management, and attack politics of modern campaigns.

Very much like *The Candidate,* Burns' campaign is completely managed, and he speaks whatever calculated populist drivel his handlers cook up. Unlike Bill McKay, however, Burns is neither young, attractive, nor idealistic in any way, shape or form. He is out to hoodwink and manipulate the public 100 percent, and his cynical mean-spirited attacks on Governor Bailey and his hilarious off-camera remarks denigrating middle-class citizens indicate just how little regard he has for the public. To cement the notion of over-handled candidates who use trickery and media manipulation, Burns' expensive campaign team consists of "speech writer, joke writer, spin doctor, make-up man, personal trainer, muckraker, character assassin, mudslinger, and garbologist."[7] Completely absent, of course, are policy advisors. When the frail, hunched, and elderly Burns reviews a campaign portrait that renders him a rugged, smiling, and larger-than-life Davy Crockett, he exclaims, "why are my teeth showing like that?" His campaign aide Danielson answers, "Because you're smiling." Burns then responds, "Ah. Excellent. This is exactly the kind of trickery I'm paying you for."[8]

In the grand tradition of prime-time political confessional-commercials, and in one of *The Simpsons'* many moments of unbridled hilarity coupled with penetrating political commentary, Mr. Burns and his campaign team cynically pull off their own shameless "Checkers." The issue of the three-eyed fish, a genetic mutation caused by the plant's pollution, must be neutralized. In an effort to put the contaminated waters and bizarre fish behind him in order to improve his image, Burns uses a paid political commercial to redefine the "Blinky" situation to his advantage. The fish is not a hideous mutation brought on by irresponsible pollution, claims Burns, but rather, a process of evolution:

MR. BURNS
I'm here to talk to you about my little friend here, Blinky. Many of you consider him a hideous mutation. Well nothing could be further from the truth. But don't take my word for it, let's ask an actor playing Charles Darwin what he thinks. . .

DARWIN
Hello, Mr. Burns.

BURNS
Oh, hello Charles. Be a good fellow and tell our viewers about your theory of natural selection.

DARWIN
Glad to, Mr. Burns. You see, every so often Mother Nature changes her animals, giving them bigger teeth, sharper claws, longer legs, or in this case, a third eye. And if these variations turn out to be an improvement, the new animals thrive and multiply and spread across the face of the earth.

BURNS
So you're saying this fish might have an advantage over other fish, that may in fact be a kind of super-fish.

DARWIN
I wouldn't mind having a third eye, would you?[9]

Burns' home run of image and chicanery over reason, splashed across Springfield's television screens (including the "Springfield Retirement Castle" where Grandpa Abe Simpson resides), immediately begins to push the nuclear plant owner up in the polls. How effective was the "Blinky" defense? Evidence that the Burns' stunt hits immediate political pay dirt is provided at the close of his commercial, when perennial patron of Moe's Tavern, Barney, exclaims, from his bar stool: "Wow! Super fish!" Then, without missing a beat, Moe the bartender spouts: "I wish government *would* get off my back!" Burns cynical populism was a smash hit with the gullible public. The political message, delivered with sidesplitting humor, is direct: backed by money, consultants, and television, politicians can manipulate the public. Even a super-rich, selfish hermit like the nuclear baron Burns can come across as a populist working to get government off our collective backs. And Mr. Burns' "government off our back" mantra has plenty of precedents in modern politics, perhaps most famously the 1980 presidential campaign of Republican Ronald Reagan. Throughout his successful run for the White House, Reagan effectively painted government, and its regulatory measures, as an unfair, intrusive force that overtaxed and stifled the entrepreneurial spirit.

But Burns was not done with molding his new man-of-the-people image. With his polls showing Burns deadlocked with Mary Bailey—Marge Simpson's choice for governor[10]—Burns' advisers plan a major publicity stunt. On the night before the election, he will have a staged dinner with an average middle-American family, The Simpsons, which will manufacture his credentials as a friend of the "little guy." Burns loves the idea and devilishly relishes the thought of using the media to fool the mindless sheep watching from home:

> Oh, I get your angle. Every Joe Meatball and Sally Housecoat in the God-forsaken state will see me hunkering down to chow with Eddie Punchclock. The media will have a field day![11]

In the end, however, Burns's campaign falters when Marge Simpson serves the gubernatorial candidate a three-eyed fish for dinner. Burns is unable to stomach the hideous fish, spitting it out rather than swallowing.

Bulworth: "Brace Yourself. This Politician Is about to Tell The Truth!"[12]

> Playful in tone but bravely radical in concept, ``Bulworth,'' a brilliant political satire by Warren Beatty, is one of the most surprising movies to come out of Hollywood in the past decade.

This is Beatty's premise: Imagine a politician who drops his phony, elect-me facade and decides to spill the blunt, unvarnished truth about race, class and economics.[13]

Warren Beatty, no stranger to the political scene, directed and co-wrote the political comedy-drama *Bulworth* (1998). Beatty plays California Senator Jay Billington Bulworth, who is up for reelection in the fall of 1996. Pictures of Rosa Parks, Angela Davis, Malcolm X, Bobby Kennedy, and George McGovern adorn the walls of his Senate office, but Bulworth is a fraud; he has long since abandoned their principles and progressive policies and has sold his soul to the highest bidder. He is now a moderate "New Democrat" in the mold of Bill Clinton, and speaks out against welfare, affirmative action, and government programs designed to fight poverty and make health care more accessible. He is in the pocket of big contributors, such as the health insurance industry, and uses his powerful committee position to kill legislation that would cost them profits. He spouts pious family values rhetoric while he has a severely strained and phony relationship with his wife (Christine Baranski).

Distressed at the pathetic fake he has become, Bulworth hires someone to kill him so that the insurance money can go to his daughter. However, this sense of impending death has a liberating effect on the depressed senator. Along the campaign trail he begins to rap throughout the Los Angeles area—from posh Beverly Hills fundraisers to impoverished South Central Los Angeles—about the insidious power of big business, media conglomerates, oil companies, and the insurance industry, among others. He chides Hollywood moguls for the steady stream of violent, dumb, and dirty films designed for maximum profitability. He meets and falls in love with an African American woman (Halle Berry) who reminds Bulworth of the devastation of urban centers due to the loss of good-paying manufacturing jobs. And, during an interview with a local reporter, the incumbent Senator promotes a concentrated worldwide plan of interra-

REEL CANDIDATES:
A BRIEF SAMPLING AND REVIEW

The Last Hurrah (1958): The Bright Side of Bosses, Machines, and Big City Politics
  Directed by John Ford; based on the novel by Edwin O'Connor; Spencer Tracy as Mayor Frank Skeffington; Jeffrey Hunter as Adam Caulfield (the mayor's nephew and a journalist).
  Summary: a nostalgic, romantic look at big city politics, party machines, and loyal constituencies and constituents; laments the move way from machines, bosses and strong parties toward vacuous, media-driven, reform candidates; takes a far different (i.e., significantly more positive) view of machines and political bosses than *Mr. Smith Goes to Washington* (1939).

The Candidate (1972): Lawyer-Turned-Politician Surrenders to Pollsters
  Directed by Michael Ritchie; written by Jeremy Larner (aide to Sen. Eugene McCarthy during his 1968 bid for the Democratic presidential nomination); Robert Redford asBill McKay; Peter Boyle as Marvin Lucas; (McKay campaign manager); Melvyn Douglas as John J. McKay (Bill McKay's father; former California Governor).
  Summary: U.S. Senate race in California ... Bill McKay (Redford) is a liberal antipoverty lawyer and son of a former California governor (Douglas) ... the age of media-driven, sloganeering, 30-second programmed candidates is in full swing, even when idealistic McKay runs for the Senate.

Bob Roberts (1992): Right-Wing Folk-Singer Seeks U.S. Senate Seat in Pennsylvania
  Written and directed by Tim Robbins; Tim Robbins as Bob Roberts; Gore Vidal as Senator Brickley Paiste (D-PA).
  Summary: A "mock documentary" of the fictional 1990 U.S. Senate candidacy (Pennsylvania) of Bob Roberts, a corrupt right-wing folk-singer, opportunist and millionaire ... filmed largely in Pittsburgh and Harrisburg, Pennsylvania ... Roberts' music and ascendancy to the U.S. Senate sticks a nail in the coffin of 1960s liberalism and idealism. In the proposed sequel to *Bob Roberts,* the Senator will seek the presidency.[16]

Bulworth (1998) : Despondent, Corrupt Senator Starts Telling the Truth
  Directed by Warren Beatty; written by Warren Beatty and Jeremy Pikser; Warren Beatty as Senator Bulworth; Halle Berry as Nina; Oliver Platt as Dennis Murphy (chief aide to the Senator).
  Summary: U.S. Senator Jay Billington Bulworth of California has become a sham—a greasy, money-grubbing, family-values fake "New Democrat" who has betrayed his ideals ... but his impending, self-imposed death fills him with a desire to break the rules and tell it like it is ... Bulworth raps (literally) about corporate power, big oil, the media, insurance companies, health care, poverty, race relations, campaign finance, and much more.

cial coupling to help make the world one race and, therefore, breakaway from the tethers of racism. In short, Senator Bulworth becomes, as one film critic observed, "a glee-
fully emancipated prankster who says exactly what he
thinks and doesn't give a damn about the consequences"[14]

The angry, politically charged, pull-no-punches script may
not have led to commercial success—the $30 million movie
brought in a gross of $26.5 million—but the critics paid at-
tention. *Bulworth* was nominated for an Academy Award, a
Golden Globe, and the Chicago Film Critics Association
Award for best screenplay. And Beatty, along with co-author
Jeremy Pikser, captured the Los Angeles Film Critics Association award (LAFCA) for best screenplay. Did the film have
any tangible effects on the political system and the issues
discussed in the upcoming 2000 presidential election?
Beatty, along with Donald Trump and professional wrestler-
turned Minnesota governor, Jesse Ventura, appeared on the
cover of major news magazines in the winter of 2000, presented as potential alternatives to the two-party system.
Beatty himself openly considered making a presidential bid
with the Green Party in 2000 in order to move the Democratic Party back to its more liberal grassroots and policy positions of the 1960s–1980s, an agenda clearly at the heart of
Bulworth. Ultimately, Beatty decided against such a bid for
the White House. While many may be uncomfortable with
or unmoved by the obscenity-laced critiques of the U.S. political system and the in-you-face progressive politics, several
critics lauded Beatty for presenting such a bold, unadulter-
ated dose of political satire. As one reviewer mused:

> Beatty directed, produced and co-wrote "Bulworth," and it's
> doubtful that any other Hollywood power could have put a story
> like this on the screen—or would want to. A shrewd political ob-
> server for decades, Beatty has fashioned a hilarious morality
> tale that delivers a surprisingly potent, angry message beneath
> the laughs.
>
> It's a fabulous, bold leap on Beatty's part, and you can feel
> how much the subject energizes him, just as the novelty of
> truth-telling invigorates his character and puts a goofy grin on
> Bulworth's face.

Hollywood rarely embraces political satire on this level—as if it were impolite and would make people uncomfortable—but Beatty's lampoon shows not only how much we need this kind of commentary, but also how entertaining it can be. Beatty also knows how much party politics have ignored racial injustice and uses humor to reopen the discussion.[15]

The Awful Truth: "Presidential Mosh Pit"

Another ideological critique of the state of politics, power, and campaigning from the left side of the political spectrum comes from writer-director Michael Moore. In a segment entitled "Presidential Mosh Pit" in season two of his television series *The Awful Truth,* the sarcastic guerrilla journalist declares that his program will offer an official endorsement to any presidential candidate of either party who will dive into his portable, traveling mosh pit. Why a mosh pit as the standard for choosing the next leader of the free world? Because, surmises Moore, so many of the 2000 presidential candidates are so close to each other ideologically and thus, the election and campaign process is a sham from the get-go. Along the primary campaign trail in Iowa, Moore asks nearly every candidate—from Democrat Bill Bradley to Republicans George W. Bush, Orrin Hatch and Steve Forbes—to dive into the traveling mosh pit of angry youth. Only one candidate, Republican Alan Keyes, agrees to go "in the pit," and Moore then "endorses" Keyes for president.

Real Candidates and Documentaries: Behind the Scenes, Uncovering the Good, Bad, and Ugly

A Perfect Candidate

One of the major concerns when using film to teach politics and provoke discussion and debate is to get students and citizens to get beyond—or at least temporarily throw aside—the cynical, oft-repeated mantra that all office-holders and candidates are vision-less, shameless, plotting scam artists devoted to winning at any cost, public interest be damned. Why? Because most citizens engaged in public service are performing valuable services and are passionate about bettering their communities and country. And then along comes the 1994 U.S. Senate race in Virginia, and it becomes harder to convince Americans of the nobility of public service and the legitimacy of their politicians! As educators and public servants attempt to present the view that most politicians are not shallow and superficial and we, as a society, must be vigilant participators in our political system, *A Perfect Candidate* (1996) stands as a nightmare of sorts.

R. J. Cutler and David Von Taylor's revealing documentary of the 1994 U.S. Senate race between incumbent Democrat Chuck Robb and Republican challenger Oliver North "has just about everything the modern political circus has to offer: negative advertising, demagoguery, flip-flopping on the issues, cynical manipulation of public opinion, shameless lying and an abject refusal to introduce real substance to an election campaign."[17] The film chronicles the twists, turns, drama, and dirty politics that transpire throughout the election, illustrating how candidates can deliberately contradict themselves and prove quite uninspiring. Viewers are treated to incumbent Sen. Robb's occasional obfuscation—and frequent awkwardness and incoherent mumbling—when *Washington Post* reporter Don Baker asks the candidate simple, straightforward questions. The film also documents the no-holds-barred, flame-throwing, attack politics of the nicotine-addicted Mark Goodin, Oliver North's campaign director and hatchet man. In the end, as audiences treat their recurring nausea and cynicism, Robb squeezes out a victory, one of the few major Democratic victories in an otherwise Republican year.[18] Summing up *A Perfect Candidate* and the 1994 Senate campaign, *Washington Post* critic Desson Howe asserted:

> If documentary filmmaking is about identifying the truth, no subject could be more invigorating, amusing and frustrating to

probe than American politics. . . . "A Perfect Candidate" is se-
renely damning in its indictment of political campaigns and, by
extension, America. Here's a choice, after all, between someone who admits to lying to Congress and someone who can't
admit to a hotel tryst with a Playboy model. In the words of a
frustrated voter, this election wasn't about which direction Virginia should go in, it was a choice between two diseases.[19]

At the same time, the film is hardly a disaster for those
who desire a more committed, engaged, educated populace. The hollowness and meanness of the 1994 Robb-
North race could—and should—inspire citizens to take an
active role in making sure voters have better, or at least
more inspirational and coherent, choices. *A Perfect Candidate* also does an excellent job of revealing Virginia's fascinating political culture. From the Shenandoah Valley to the
Atlantic coast, and from the cradle of the Confederacy to
the Northern Virginia, Washington, DC suburbs, the state
features an eclectic mix of cosmopolitan, rural, and evangelical Christian voters, and the film does an excellent job
of articulating the political, social, religious, and economic
currents that flow across the state and influence election
outcomes.

The War Room: Inside the Clinton Campaign

"They Changed the Way Campaigns Are Won."[20] D. A.
Pennebaker's and Chris Hegedus' *The War Room* (1993),
which chronicled Bill Clinton's 1992 bid for the White
House, captured the National Board of Review award for
best documentary.[21] The film follows the work of the Clinton campaign's inner-circle of strategists, pollsters, and
media consultants, with special attention given to the
rapid-fire response team of James Carville, George Stephanopoulos, and Paul Begala. Determined not to be another Michael Dukakis, the beleaguered 1988 Democratic nominee
who was lackadaisical in responding to George Bush's
charges of being soft on patriotism and crime enforcement,
the Clinton team hunkered down in its Little Rock "War
Room" and gave as good as it got. The documentary follows

the process of crafting response ads, managing the media, and shaping damage control, from the dark days of the New Hampshire primary to the emotional glow of victory on election night. In doing so, *The War Room* stands as one of the great documents of modern presidential campaign strategy.

Vote for Me: Politics in America

Offering an unflinching, and at times, uplifting look at American politics at all levels, the WETA-produced *Vote for Me: Politics in America* premiered on PBS stations nation-wide in October 1996. Part of PBS' "Democracy Project"—a "PBS initiative to stimulate citizen engagement in civic life and develop and provide viewers with innovative news and public affairs programming"[22]—the video was directed by award winning filmmakers Louis Alvarez, Andy Kolker, and Paul Stekler.[23] *Vote for Me* goes beyond the horse-race, polls-centered approach to politics and gets close to the action to reveal "how local culture and customs are reflected in our politics."[24] It does this from the New England breeze of Rhode Island, to the streets of Chicago, to the mountains of Asheville, North Carolina. The film shows the everyday aspects of campaigning and governing at the state, local, and national level, from fixing broken steps, ripping down posters, going door to door, helping shut-ins vote, kissing pigs, answering questions about guns and abortion, going to festivals, and dialing for cash. *Vote for Me* also features revealing interviews with Rep. Barney Frank (D-MA) and former three-term New York Governor Mario Cuomo, among others, who comment on the nature of campaigning and politics in America. The home page for "Vote for Me" articulates the unique approach of the documentary:

> VOTE FOR ME is not a high-school civics lesson. Politics, as one veteran campaigner puts it, is "show business for ugly people," and the series assembles a cast of political stars and wannabes as colorful and diverse as America itself. There's the mayor of a major city who kisses pigs at rallies, a profane media consultant

who makes Jack the Ripper look warm and fuzzy, a desperate gubernatorial challenger who organizes media events that unfold at 3 AM in a chicken-parts factory, and a novice Congressional candidate who woos voters with her dulcimer and gospel singing. . . .

The American political landscape that VOTE FOR ME discovers in its cross-country tour is a far cry from the angry, dour place we hear so much about on the Sunday political talk shows. It's a place where most voters care less about hot-button ideological positions than about which politician will repave their street and improve their quality of life. It's a place where the conventional wisdom about apathetic voters and irrelevant politicians is belied by the passion of thousands of volunteers of all ages, by the excitement of the half million state and local races that take place every two to four years, and by all the foibles and serendipity of the democratic process. . . .

Viewers of VOTE FOR ME will find themselves on the front lines of American politics as it is practiced day in and day out: eavesdropping on strategy sessions in hard-fought races, watching smooth talking lobbyists move in for the kill in the legislative feeding frenzy that is the Texas state legislature, and sharing the self-doubt and loneliness of life on the campaign trail with candidates who are driven to win.

From local precincts to the White House, it's not "insider politics," but politics as a mirror that unflinchingly and entertainingly shows who we are as a country and a people.[25]

Media Behavior and Candidate Access on the Campaign Trail

Journeys with George

The insightful, clever presidential campaign and media travelogue, *Journeys with George* (2002), premiered on HBO on Tuesday, November 5, 2002, on the night of the midterm elections of president George W. Bush.[26] The campaign-media diary documentary was directed and produced by Alexandra Pelosi, who shared writing duties with Aaron Lubarski. *Journeys* finds Pelosi, a network news producer for NBC—in her words, the "hired help behind the scenes"—on the planes, trains, and buses following George W. Bush's campaign. On her year-long journey, she files news stories, reports varying versions of his campaign's "message of the day," and works hard to gain substantive, unfiltered access to the candidate, a daunting task that is sometimes accomplished but frequently frustrated. In the early weeks of the campaign, members of the traveling press corps have little to no direct access to Bush; after his decisive loss to John McCain in the New Hampshire primary, however, his handlers change course somewhat, allowing the Republican frontrunner to mingle and associate with the traveling media in a more substantive manner . . . at least for a while.

While eating dreadful turkey sandwiches, catching intermittent shut-eye between photo ops, stump speeches, and rallies, and catching the flu, Pelosi does an excellent job of revealing the daily routines, professional and personal struggles, and petty jealousies of the traveling press corps assigned to a repetitive and, at times, grueling year-long campaign trek. Her witty, wry style shapes an approach that is neither heavy-handed nor frivolous, balancing humor and behind the scenes antics with a revealing exposé of campaign tactics and media behavior. In the process, *Journeys* offers valuable insight into the ebb and flow of presidential campaigns and media access, and in this respect, two dynamics and realities are especially noteworthy. First, while George W. Bush is an affable, personable fellow finding his stride as a campaigner, he becomes remarkably less approachable when Pelosi asks him about his execution of the death penalty in Texas. Indeed, after her capital punishment query, Pelosi finds herself temporarily "on the outs" with the Texas Governor, gaining no access for a spell. This leads to the second dynamic, or dilemma, revealed in Pelosi's documentary: How do members of the press perform their public duty—asking thorough, penetrating, public policy questions and disseminating useful political information—without alienating their subject, and thus, displeasing their employers who want access, stories, and the advertising revenue that goes along with it? Clearly there is enormous pressure to not offend the candidate and incur his wrath—or, in this case,

CAPTURING REAL CANDIDATES:
THE *"CINEMA VERITÉ"* DOCUMENTARY

Cinema Verité: in the political documentary world, a style and approach first pioneered by filmmakers Robert Drew and D.A. Pennebaker.[27] *This gritty, behind-the-scenes, insider's look at politics, without narration,* and usually featuring hand-held cameras, was first pioneered by Drew and Pennabaker and their crew in the film *Primary,* which chronicled the 1960 Democratic primary in Wisconsin between Senators John F. Kennedy (MA) and Hubert Humphrey (MN). It has become the preferred style for behind-the-scenes political documentaries, and has been used many times over the years to cover national and statewide political campaigns.

Listed below are some notable campaign documentaries in the Drew-Pennebaker *"cinema verité"* tradition:

Primary (1960)
    Directed by Robert Drew and Richard Leacock; sound by D. A. Pennabaker
    1960 Democratic Presidential Primary between U.S. Senators John F. Kennedy (Massachusetts) and Hubert H. Humphrey (Minnesota) ... gritty black and white footage, hand-held cameras.

Feed (1992)
    Directed by Kevin Rafferty and James Ridgeway
    1992 New Hampshire Presidential Primary ... features a less-than-flattering hodgepodge of tired and under-the-weather Democrats (Jerry Brown, Paul Tsongas, Bill Clinton, Bob Kerry) and Republicans (Pat Buchanan and George Bush).

The War Room (1994)
    Directed by Chris Hegedus and D. A. Pennabaker
    Nominated for an Academy Award for best documentary
    The 1992 Clinton presidential campaign, from the primaries through election night ... strategy and tactics ... Clinton aides James Carville, George Stephanopoulos, Paul Begala (strategists), Mandy Grunwald (media advisor), and Stan Greenberg (pollster) are featured prominently.

A Perfect Candidate (1996)
    Directed and produced by R. J. Cutler and David Van Taylor
    1994 U.S. Senate Race in Virginia between incumbent Chuck Robb (D) and Oliver North (R) ... Robb and the Democrats maintain a seat as the Democrats and Republicans offer a flurry of attack ads and obfuscation.

Vote for Me: Politics in America (1996, television, PBS)
http://www.pbs.org/weta/voteforme/home.htm.
    Directed by Louis Alvarez, Andy Kolker, Paul Stekler
    "All politics is local" ... As close to the action as it gets—a look at the non-spectator sport of politics at the street, festival, cook-out, bus, chicken factory, and lobby levels, all across the United States. Mayoral, gubernatorial, U.S. House, and Chicago alderman races, among others, are featured in detail. The PBS home page has several educational features, including a quiz and links that complement the two-part series.

Journeys with George (2002)
    Directed by Alexandra Pelosi and Aaron Lubarski
    NBC network news producer Alexandra Pelosi documents her one-year journey with George W. Bush on the planes and trains of the 2000 campaign trail. In the tradition of *cinema verité,* Pelosi offers a behind-the-scenes, insider's look at the politics of presidential campaigns and, especially, the politics of media coverage of a presidential candidate. But unlike classic *cinema verité, Journeys* features the director's narration.

silence and inaccessibility. Can members of the media serve two masters? What are you to do if your network or paper is displeased with a lack of access and applies pressure? This is a dynamic that Bush and his closest advisers—communications director Karen Hughes and campaign guru Karl Rove—understand and exploit. Yet this phenomenon is more far-reaching than any one campaign team's tactics. The Bush camp, however shrewd, certainly had no monopoly on using this delicate relationship of conflicting roles and dual masters to their advantage.

At the same, time, periodically keeping the press at bay and taking a bunker-type approach on the campaign trail away can sometimes backfire and have disastrous results. For example, many reporters who were not given access to the candidate reported that the Democratic nominee was distant and aloof, while characterizing George W. Bush as easygoing and congenial. As the *New York Times* reported during the 2000 campaign, "Bush 'not only slaps reporters' backs but also rubs the tops of their heads and, in a few instances, pinches their cheeks.'"[28] Most significantly, a few major media studies indicated that, as the campaign wore on, Gore received disproportionately negative press coverage.[29] As Jane Hall reported in the *Columbia Journalism Review,* after a brief period of positive coverage after his selection of Connecticut Senator Joe Lieberman in the summer of 2000, Gore received overwhelmingly negative treatment in the press. This dynamic is chronicled in a study funded, in part, by the Pew Charitable Trusts and executed by the Project for Excellence in Journalism:

> Examining 2,400 newspaper, TV, and Internet stories in five different weeks between February and June, researchers found that a whopping 76 percent of the coverage included one of two themes: that Gore lies and exaggerates or is marred by scandal. The most common theme about Bush, the study found, is that he is a "different kind of Republican."
>
> The survey (which included editorials and news stories) focused on *The Washington Post, The New York Times, The Boston Globe, The Atlanta Journal-Constitution, The Indianapolis Star,* the

San Francisco Chronicle, and *The Seattle Times.* It also included the evening newscasts of the major broadcast networks and talk shows such as *Hardball,* which alone accounted for 17 percent of the negative characterizations about scandal.[30]

Finally, the media-campaign journal *Journeys with George* implicitly revisits a lingering question that is hardly new to the American political landscape: Do marathon presidential campaigns, which frequently test stamina rather than intellect, and campaigning talent rather than governing skills, really serve the voters? Add to this mix the increasing tendency for the media to treat the entire election as a series of games and tactics rather than governing, and to focus on "character" at the expense of public policy, and we have a real pickle of a situation.[31] If you look close enough between the turkey sandwiches and chummy exchanges with George W. Bush, Alexandra Pelosi's easy-going campaign diary presents several vital dynamics and dilemmas that shape media coverage of presidential campaigns.[32]

Third Parties in the United States

Referred to as a "citizen response to major party failure" by prominent political scientists, third parties have a unique history within the American two-party system. Although they very rarely affect election outcomes, third parties serve a variety of vital functions in the U.S. political system. Third parties serve as policy advocates and as crucial safety valves for those unhappy with the political system and the choices presented by the major parties. Starting, joining, or voting for a third party is a concrete way of expressing discontent and, quite possibly, furthering a specific policy agenda or single issue. A number of major issues have been trumpeted by third parties over the years, from the abolition of slavery and prohibition, to women's suffrage, the eight-hour work week, the minimum wage, and an end to child labor.[33]

Yet there are many obstacles faced by third parties. The Electoral College, for example, with its winner-take-all

THIRD PARTIES IN THE UNITED STATES

Voting Your Conscience or Throwing Away Your Vote?
I'm on the Ballot (2000): A Film by Al Ward

Third Parties in the 2000 Presidential Election (Featured in *I'm on the Ballot*):
  Green Party: Ralph Nader
  Reform Party: Pat Buchanan
  Libertarian Party: Harry Browne
  Natural Law Party: John Hagelin
  Constitution Party: Howard Phillips
  Socialist Party: David McReynolds

After viewing *I'm on the Ballot,* consider these vital questions and issues.

Issues and Policy: Identify three or more issues and policy positions associated with each third party.

Obstacles to Third Parties: What are the major legal, political, and cultural obstacles faced by third parties?

Federal Matching Funds: What are "federal matching funds" and how do presidential candidates qualify for them?

The Commission on Presidential Debates: What percentage, in national polls, was required for inclusion in the 2000 presidential debates? Do you agree or disagree with this number? Which third parties, if any, do you believe should be included in presidential debates? Is the Commission on Presidential Candidates democratic? What are the alternatives? Should Congress pass legislation governing the structure of presidential debates?

Which Third Parties Are Closest to Your Views? With which of the third parties featured in the film do you most agree? Disagree? Why? Would you vote for a third party candidate? Who? Why?

Recent Performance: How did third parties fare in the most recent presidential elections? Which parties, if any, qualified for federal matching funds in those elections?

Influence: According to Ralph Nader and David McReynolds, what effect do third parties have on policy?

Revisiting the 2000 Gore-Bush Battle: Did Ralph Nader cost Al Gore the election? Why or why not? What do you think?

system of allocating electoral votes,[34] discourages third parties from entering the presidential fray. Consider the Electoral College performance of Ross Perot in 1992. The Texas billionaire and independent candidate received nearly 19 percent of the vote in the three-way race with Bill Clinton and George Bush, yet received no electoral votes. Moreover, state laws routinely make things difficult for third parties. The Democratic and Republican parties are automatically on the ballot across the country, but state laws mandate that third parties collect varying number of signatures to get on the ballot in each state. In some states, it is not difficult to collect the required signatures. In other states, however, such as Texas, it takes a Herculean effort and time and money that most people, Ross Perot aside, do not have. In fact, most third party bids for the White House must employ firms to go out and collect the signatures.

I'm on the Ballot

The aforementioned obstacles—as well as a host of others—are explored in detail in Al Ward's 2000 film *I'm on the Ballot*. Premiering on PBS stations around the country in the fall of 2000, the film offers a thorough review of the role of third parties in U.S. history, while focusing on the specific parties and candidates vying for attention in the 2000 presidential election. The Commission on Presidential Debates, lack of money (to receive federal matching funds, presidential candidates must first receive at least 5 percent of the vote nationwide), poor media coverage, and other legal and cultural constraints are examined in detail. In particular, Ward's work is to be commended for its review of third party achievements and policy influence, and for its in-depth and fair treatment of all of the major third parties in the 2000 presidential race. Candid interviews with the third-party candidates and some of their supporters allow for students and citizens to be exposed to alternative viewpoints—ranging from the left (Socialist, Green) to the right (Libertarian, Constitutional)—that often go uncovered in the mainstream media.

The Simpsons: "Treehouse of Horror VII: Citizen Kang"

Airing on October 27, 1996, just days prior to the 1996 presidential election between incumbent Democratic President Bill Clinton and Republican challenger Bob Dole,[35] *The Simpsons'* Halloween segment "Citizen Kang" critiques the two-party system and, to a lesser extent, the American voting public. In other words, it is critical of both! In this piece, the aliens Kang and Kodos come to earth and take over the bodies of Dole and Clinton. While they are aliens, the American voting public hardly notices the difference when the two speak. Apparently the vague pleasantries, banal generalities, and lack of substance spouted by the aliens Kang and Kodos (as Dole and Clinton) are what we are used to. Or, is such meaningless drivel what the public really wants? That is for us to decide. At one point, the aliens marvel at their ability to take over the bodies of Clinton and Dole and fool the public without much of an effort:

DOLE-KANG
Fooling these Earth voters is easier than expected.

CLINTON-KODOS
Yes, all they want to hear are bland pleasantries embellished by an occasional saxophone solo or infant kiss.[36]

Three specific exchanges especially accent the show's criticism of the two-party system. In the first scene, the Simpsons are watching the nightly news, chaired by longtime anchorman (and stock *Simpsons* character) Kent Brockman:

(The family watches Kent Brockman on TV.)

KENT BROCKMAN
Kent Brockman here, with "Campaign 96: America Flips a Coin." At an appearance this morning, Bill Clinton made some rather cryptic remarks, which aides attributed to an overly tight necktie. (The scene cuts to the news conference.)

CLINTON-KODOS
I am Clin-Ton. As overlord, all will kneel before me and obey my brutal commands.
End communication.

MARGE
Hmm, that's Slick Willie for you, always with the smooth talk.[37]

KENT BROCKMAN
Senator Dole, why should people vote for you instead of President Clinton?

DOLE-KANG
It makes no difference which one of us you vote for. Either way, your planet is doomed! Doomed!

BROCKMAN
Well, a refreshingly frank response there from Senator Bob Dole.

(Before a huge crowd at the Capitol Building, Homer reveals the candidates as space aliens.)

KODOS
It's true we are aliens. But what are you going to do about it? It's two-party system! You have to vote for one of us . . .

MAN IN CROWD
Well, I believe I'll vote for a third-party candidate.

KANG
Go ahead, throw your vote away! Ah-hah hah-hah-haaaah![38]

In classic *Simpsons* form, beneath the humor, satire, and Homer's antics, several biting critiques of American politics and the American electorate are presented. First, the "Treehouse of Horror" Halloween segment criticizes the lack of choice provided by a two-party system supported and enforced by law, culture, and socialization. The two major-party standard bearers are hardly off the hook in this regard, as the piece lampoons 1996 presidential candidates Bill Clinton and Bob Dole for providing little in terms of inspiration, choice, or specifics. Second, *The Simpsons* is also pointing a finger at the American public for its rather sloppy, apathetic, unsophisticated approach to politics. An implicit message here is that perhaps change *could* come if voters weren't so easily swayed (or hoodwinked) by candidate image, emotional appeals, infant kisses, and, as is the case in "Citizen Kang," miniature

American flags. A vigilant and erudite populace is needed to make a difference and force the candidates and parties to speak in a legitimate, inspiring, and substantive "non-alien" language.

Using the documentary form and animated humor, *I'm on the Ballot* and *The Simpsons* alien sketch "Citizen Kang" provide ample political facts and food for thought. What are the obstacles faced by third parties in the United States? Is voting for a third party "throwing your vote away"? Or, is casting your vote for someone outside the two-party system an act of conscience and political courage that will significantly affect politics? Are there negative consequences of third party participation? What do the results of recent presidential elections tell us? What third parties have garnered enough votes to influence the public debate on issues otherwise not brought to the table by the two parties? These questions, and many more, come to light after viewing the aforementioned programs. For the health of our political system, and to better understand the process, direction, and effect of our campaigns and elections, they are certainly questions worth pondering.

CHAPTER 7

War

Introduction

War—and the prevention of war—is the most serious and demanding duty of any country. The primary duty of any country is the survival and protection of its population. Thus, war is, and has been, a primary concern of international leaders. As time has progressed, preventing war has been seen as both noble and necessary. Nevertheless, given the enormous implications, war stories are both compelling and relevant.

This chapter briefly explores how films have portrayed war over the past ninety years. Before examining these films, the chapter will discuss a few concepts that are important in

understanding international relations theory in general: the
security dilemma, anarchy, and the theoretical divide
between realists and pluralists in international relations theory. The chapter then explores how film has portrayed war
during the twentieth century—specifically, war as being
necessary and war as being destructive. Next, the chapter
will examine the change the introduction of nuclear weapons has brought to films. Finally, the chapter will end with
the post-Cold War emphasis on ethnic conflict.

Concepts

Understanding war in modern world politics depends on
an understanding of key concepts. As discussed else-
where, a fundamental characteristic of the international
system has been the notion of *sovereignty*. The international system understands that each state has the right to
decide its own internal matters without interference from
the outside. Sovereignty has been understood as virtual
political independence, but in reality the term is more of
concept that implies equality and freedom from meddling
in domestic politics from outside actors. One could argue
that this is the most important characteristic of the modern state. At the same time, another important characteristic of the international system is *anarchy*: the absence of
higher authority in the international system. In an anarchi-
cal system, there is no entity that can enforce rules or
laws; each state must look after its own interests. Note
that this does not mean that the system is in chaos; actually the system is fairly orderly. Yet, if a state decides to
step outside the agreed behavior of states, there is nothing
to stop its actions, except maybe the coordinated actions
of other states.

For scholars, the likelihood war or peace is going to exist
in international politics depends upon how one views the
security dilemma and how likely the dilemma can be solved.
The security dilemma can be defined as the situation where
one state feels so insecure that it builds its military defenses

in order to address its insecurity. Because the international system is anarchic, meaning that the state has to rely on itself to defend its own interest, the state often sees this as its only option. The state's neighbors, seeing this increase in defenses, respond to this increase in arms by doing likewise. Because of these actions, the security of the first state is once again diminished. In the end, the state feels even more insecure than when it started.

One way of demonstrating the security dilemma is to reduce it to the story of two individuals. Suppose John and Lisa live in a town where there is no police or any authority that can adjudicate disputes. They live in a state of anarchy; each person is responsible for his or her own security. Suppose, too, that John feels exposed to the general threats of the community in which he lives. John may take measures to make himself feel more secure. For example, John may build a high brick wall around his house to deter intruders or anyone that may cause him harm. Lisa, looking towards John's house, might look upon the wall with some suspicion. Lisa could ask herself, "What is John doing that needs to be hidden from the rest of the us?" Lisa's suspicion might be enough that she decides to build a tower to be able to look over the brick wall in order to make sure that John is not up to anything that might endanger herself or her family. If Lisa builds such a tower, then John's worst suspicions have been seemingly confirmed: someone is directly answering his escalation with one of his or her own. One can imagine a situation where John and Lisa engage in an "arms race" simply because initially one of them feared that they were insecure.

While this may be a simplified understanding of the security dilemma, it at least lets us get a handle on motivation and construction. History has seen several examples of what appears to be a security dilemma. Prior to the First World War, Germany decided that the best way to become a major power was to make itself a predominant naval power. The move to create a substantial navy provoked a response from Great Britain to increase its naval capabilities. Both countries engaged in an arms race. Similarly, during the early years of the Cold War, there was an insistence that the United States have more missiles that the Soviet Union in order to ensure its own security. U.S. presidential candidates, especially John Kennedy in 1960, warned of the dangerous consequences of a real or perceived "missile gap" with the Soviet Union. During this period, each superpower's increase in the size of its nuclear arsenal or new missile technology led to a similar reaction from the other.

The Rabbit of Seville

Examples of the security dilemma and an ensuing arms race are found throughout the animated shorts of the Warner Brothers Studio. One of the most accessible of the cartoons is *The Rabbit of Seville* (1950). Since the cartoon is only seven and a half minutes long, enjoy the entire cartoon first. *The Rabbit of Seville* is a parody of Rossini's opera *Il Barbiere di Siviglia,* and captures some of the sense of humor that was present at the Termite Terrace throughout the 1930s, 1940s and 1950s. The premise, if you can call what occurs in the cartoon a premise, has Bugs Bunny being chased onto a stage being readied for a performance of *The Barber of Seville* by Bugs' arch-nemesis, the hunter, Elmer Fudd. What follows is an imaginative reworking of the opera to reflect the ongoing battles between Bugs and Elmer.

The second time through the cartoon pay particular attention to the sequence that begins about six and a half minutes into the film. The scene begins with Bugs applying hair tonic and fertilizer to Elmer's bald head. At first Elmer is excited as what is seemingly hair sprouts from his head, but then becomes quite upset as poppies begin to emerge from the spouts. Bugs runs away from the scene as Elmer chases him with a hatchet. Bugs responds by running off screen to retrieve an axe, with which he begins to chase Elmer, Elmer responds by running off screen to retrieve a pistol to resume the chase. The scene continues with upgrades to weaponry through rifles and various sizes of cannons until Bugs brings Elmer flowers, candy and an engagement ring. The scene culminates (along with the film) in a "marriage" of Bugs and Elmer (in a wedding dress), after which Bugs drops Elmer from a dizzying height onto a huge wedding cake scripted with "Marriage of Figaro."

What we see about six minutes into the cartoon is a threat to the well-being of Bugs. After Bugs has planted a patch of poppies on Elmer's head, Elmer begins to threaten Bugs with a hatchet. Bugs, fearing for his safety, counters with an axe and so on until the scene culminates in the wedding proposal. Of course, the cartoon does not end like we expect the security dilemma to end in the international community. Instead of ending in a marriage proposal, most of the time we expect two states engaged in the security dilemma to find some method of settling their dispute or to go to war.

It's a Mad Mad Mad Mad World

Note that the reason that the security dilemma is vexing is because the participants, that is, the states, are participating in an international system that is in anarchy. There is no higher power or authority that can enforce the rules and laws of the system. Hence, states are on their own in protecting their interests. One of the best examples of how anarchy operates can be demonstrated in the film *It's a Mad Mad Mad Mad World* (1963). The three hour and eight minute film includes almost every imaginable comedian of the era, including Milton Berle, Jonathan Winters, the Three Stooges, and several unbilled cameos. Because the film is so long, and some of the comedy sequences are funny but not pertinent to the political discussion, it is sufficient to limit the discussion to the first half an hour or so.

The film opens up with a car driving recklessly and dangerously passing cars in the California desert. On one particularly bad turn, the reckless car cannot make the turn and runs off the road over a small cliff and down a ravine. The car is badly damaged and the occupant, Smiler Grogan (played by Jimmy Durante), is thrown from the car and lies dying in the sun. Four cars stop to view the crash scene and the five men from the cars go down to the crash scene to see if they can render assistance. They quickly realize that Smiler is in bad shape, but he is still alive, and barely conscious. Smiler tells the men that he was on the way to pick up $350,000, stolen money that he insists he has paid for every day of his life. He knows that he is not going to make it, but someone should enjoy the money. Smiler says that he is giving it to them and that it is buried in Santa Rosita Park under a big "W." Before Smiler dies he tells them not to tell the police because they had been after him to give it to them. Smiler dies and the police show up shortly thereafter. Each of the men denies that Smiler has told them anything about the money.

The men return to the top of the hill where they have parked their cars, each expressing doubt about the story Smiler has told him. They each return to their cars and begin to weigh in their minds the occupants in the other cars as to whether they can trust them. The four cars contain a varying number of passengers:

> Vehicle #1—driven by J. Russell Finch (Milton Berle), who went to the scene of the accident, traveling with his wife and mother-in-law
>
> Vehicle #2—driven by Melville Crump (Sid Caesar), who went to the scene of the accident, traveling with his wife.
>
> Vehicle #3—car driven by Benji Benjamin (Buddy Hackett) and passenger Dingy Bell (Mickey Rooney), both of whom went to the scene of the accident.
>
> Vehicle #4—truck driven by Lennie Pike (Jonathan Winters), who went to the scene of the accident and is traveling alone.

The cars travel at a slow rate of speed at first, but then J. Russell Finch starts to speed up and the others quickly follow. Lennie Pike slows down his truck and finally stops, feigning bad tires, but soon finds that the others have stopped to see what he is doing. The eight people get together to try to come to a reasonable solution of how to get the money and how to divide it up. Dingy weighs in that they will have to come to a solution that makes sure that no one has an advantage over the others.

The group begins to engage in a long negotiation over how the money should be divided up, even though they are 200 miles away from it. They each understand that they have to keep an eye on each other and that there has to be a way to divide the money fairly. The first plan is to divide the money into four equal shares, a share for each vehicle. Benji and Dingy raise objections because although they share a car, both of them went to the scene of the accident and heard the last words of Smiler. The next plan is to divide the money into five equal shares, one share for each person who went to the scene of the accident. Yet, this plan is also objected to by Finch's mother-in-law because there were eight people who witnessed the accident. Lennie argues though that only five people went to Smiler's rescue and only four vehicles. Eventually, Melville Crump devises a plan to create 25 shares, 8 shares for each persons, 4 shares for each vehicle, 5 shares for each person who went to the accident, and 8 shares for each person in each vehicle.

Lennie notes that he would receive one share for being a part of the group, one share for his truck, one share for going to the accident, and one share for being a member of a vehicle. This would mean a total of four of the twenty-five shares available. Ultimately this would mean that he would not get as much as anyone else in the group. Slowly the group comes to the conclusion that there was only one way to decide about the money, every person for him- or herself. What ensues for the rest of the film is an incredible chase film, which has been imitated several times, but rarely lives up to the original. Along the way, each person makes side deals with others, increasing the number of people who are in pursuit of the money under the big W. In the end, the money goes to none of the pursuers and each winds up in the hospital with various ailments from the chaotic climactic scene.

It's a Mad Mad Mad Mad World represents how the international system appears to some. Notice that none of the actors can trust anyone in their pursuit of the prize. Temporary alliances may appear, but ultimately these alliances fall apart when individuals have interests that differ. Scholars who come from a realist perspective will argue that this is the way the international system looks. Other scholars, such as liberals, will argue that anarchy does not have such dire consequences for world politics. Liberals will argue that other factors, including ethnic and religious differences, perceptions and misperceptions, and the amount of interdependence among states, determines the likelihood of cooperation, war and peace between states.

Discussion

The divide in the discipline is often expressed in the dynamic between the history of the international system as being one of peace punctuated by conflicts, as opposed to the view that the history of the international system is one of war punctuated with moments of peace. Central to this understanding is the idea that war is inevitable, or that war is preventable, if we know what the causes of war are. Some scholars argue that states must sometimes demonstrate their ability and resolve to protect themselves. States are insecure and therefore their insecurity will lead them to actions that will inevitably clash with other states. Traditionally, studies of war have focused on what factors make wars more likely. For example, John J. Mearsheimer has suggested that the collapse of the bipolar system at the end of the Cold War will mean major changes and instability for the international system and that a foreign policy strategy must be devised in order to consider what powers may come to the forefront.[1] The bipolar system was one where two major states, the United States and the Soviet Union, had the predominance of power in the system. With the stabilization of power between these two states, the international system remained fairly stable and therefore peaceful. The collapse of this system was likely to mean that there would be more instability and conflict in the future. Others scholars though cite other factors that might cause conflict. One of the notable scholars to make the claim that religious and ethnic differences would be factors in future conflict was Samuel Huntington who predicted that the future of the international system will be one marked by a "Clash of Civilizations."[2]

Pluralists often seek to explain what factors might cause wars to occur. Scholars have examined factors such as a leader's perception of the enemy, regime type, the amount of interdependence in the world, and other factors to explain war and peace in the international system. One of the most promising lines of research has been the effect of regime type on war and peace in international politics. Popularly known as democratic peace, scholars such as Bruce Russett and Michael W. Doyle have argued that democracies do not fight other democracies.[3] If, as people like Francis Fukuyama have speculated, there is a spread of democracy among states around the world, then there would be a corresponding spread of international peace as well.[4]

Why We Fight

The Nazis Strike

It is very difficult to portray the differences between a realist perspective and a pluralist perspective in a narrative film. Movies tend to be a personal medium that tells stories of individuals. Therefore, theoretical debates are often not suited to narrative films. On the other hand, non-narrative films can sometimes help in exploring why countries go to war. Frank Capra made a series of films during World War II on behalf of the United States government entitled *Why We Fight*. In the second film of the series, *The Nazis Strike* (1943), Capra explores German aggression as a method of fulfilling geopolitical aspirations. Capra juxtaposes the need for world domination as seen by the Nazi leadership with liberal notions of democratic values and fundamental freedoms.

In *The Nazis Strike,* the film seems to present two different reasons as to what led to German expansionism. First, the film presents the idea that Germany was expansionistic because of primordial reasons. This sense of being German meant that the population was militaristic and expansionistic. The opening sequence of the film asserts that German ambitions for world domination date back to 1863, and that while the symbols and leaders have changed, the German desire to rule the world has been constant for the last 75 years.

The second reason for German militarism and expansionism can be found in the ideology of the regime. The film points out that the Nazis were particularly impressed with the writings of Karl Haushoffer, who modified the geopolitical theories of H. J. Mackinder, to develop a conception and plan of world domination.[5] Haushoffer argued that the world was comprised of two commodities, labor and raw material. Land, which constituted only a quarter of the world's surface, was where all the natural resources were. Furthermore, he argued that the world's land masses could be divided up into two main territories, the West Hemisphere and the World Island. The World Island, composed of Asia, Europe and Africa, had the majority of the world's resources and seven-eighths of the world's population. Thus, a theory of world domination, employed by the Nazis, argued that if you conquered Eastern Europe, then you dominated the heartland of the World Island. If you conquered the heartland, then you dominated the World Island. If you conquered the World Island, then you dominated the world.

The film goes on to refute some of the arguments made by the Nazis. First, it points to a number of German-Americans who did not agree with the militarism of Germany. Second, it argues that democracy is inherently more peaceful and just than the ideology of National Socialism. Finally, the film argues that the only thing that the German command had to fear in the attempt to accomplish world domination was collective action. If, the film argues, states worked together, then the Nazis could never carry out their plans. The film attempts to juxtapose the ideas expressed by the Nazis with the ideas of liberal democracies in an attempt to demonstrate why democracies were more peaceful, and why war against the German regime was necessary.

What the film *The Nazis Strike,* as well as other films in the *Why We Fight Series,* explores is the motivation behind why World War II occurred. Obviously, the film is not an unbiased examination of pre-war politics in Europe, but rather a propagandistic justification and explanation of United States participation in the war. Still, we should not underestimate the reasoning and motivation of the United States government in its participation. One of the reasons for participation according to the film is the militarism of the German regime. The film clearly argues that there is a reluctance among democracies to go to war, and motivating a democratic population for war is more difficult because democratic regimes are held to a standard or truth and popular will. More subtly though is a notion that no country should be allowed to gain too much power in the international system. The argument for opposing German expansion is one of opposing the concentration of too much power in Central Europe.

Because it is difficult to portray theoretical debates in terms of narrative films, the next two sections examine war along different classifications. The following section uses film to explore the premise that war is sometimes necessary. The next section then examines films that suggest that wars are destructive and should be (and can be) avoided at all costs.

War Is Sometimes Necessary

Alexandr Nevsky

The Soviet film *Alexandr Nevsky* (1938) demonstrates the idea that war between Germans and Slavs is inevitable because the Germans (Teutonic Knights) are bent on religious conquest and militarism. The film was made on the eve of the Second World War when it seemed that war was not inevitable because of the Molotov-Ribbentrop Pact in 1939, where Germany and the Soviet Union secretly divide up Poland. However, the film seems to be prophetic as the Germans proved to be untrustworthy and attacked the Soviet Union in June 1941.

The film *Alexandr Nevsky* is based on actual events and is set in thirteenth-century Russia. The film opens with an attempt by the Mongols to recruit Nevsky as a general for their army. He has gained fame and respect based on his exploits in the war against the Swedes. Nevsky refuses the Mongols, citing patriotic reasons; mainly it is better to die than to leave your own land. Soon Nevsky hears of a new threat against Russian lands, this time coming from the Teutonic Knights of Germany, Nevsky tells his followers that Novgorod is essential for the freedom of the Russians.

In Novgorod, news of the approaching German force reaches the city. The city is divided over what should be done; some citizens want to fight for their freedom while others are less inclined to do so and would prefer to submit to German rule. Some in the crowd argue that the rich merchants are less inclined to defend Russia than are the poor, because the rich see profit as their homeland.

Meanwhile in Pskov, the German invasion force has destroyed the town. The knights burn alive the citizens who refuse to submit, even infants, saying that anyone who does not submit to the Church of Rome must be destroyed. The Russian peasants in he crowd argue back that Russia will never submit to Germany.

Back in Novgorod, all the citizens join Nevsky and his army after his impassioned plea to defend their homeland. The rich are persuaded to join the battle after hearing arguments that patriotism is more important than profit. Even women suit up in armor to join the fight against the Germans. On 5 April 1242, the climatic battle between the Teutonic Knights and the Russian forces under the command of Nevsky takes place in the Battle on Ice at Lake Chudskoe, just outside Novgorod. The battle ends when the Germans are lured onto the frozen lake and fall through because of their heavy armor.

Alexandr Nevsky alternates between excitement and tedium at times. Certainly the scenes in which the Germans are committing atrocities in Pskov and the battle on the ice leads to some very exciting sequences. At other times, though, the narrative of the film drags to an agonizing pace. This was reflected in domestic Soviet criticisms at the time.[6] Yet the vision presented by Eisenstein is unique and important. The film also resonated with the Soviet population as well since it was the most popular film during the Second World War. In the film, the knights are presented as almost inhuman and definitely sinister. Notice that the uniforms of the Teutonic Knights allow only for a slit for the eyes. Also there is an attempt to divide the population prior to the invasion of the city. All of this is allegorical to the situation in Europe in the late 1930s.

Casablanca

During World War II, American films often reflected a sense that sometimes war was necessary, because ultimately one had to defeat the opponent to ensure peace and democracy. Certainly, *Casablanca* (1943) falls into this category. On the surface, *Casablanca* is a love story, perhaps one of the greatest love stories of the American screen. But on a deeper level, the film is about the United States' place in the world and a commentary on American foreign policy. The film opens with how the city of Casablanca (in French Morocco) accommodated refugees. Refugees fleeing Europe take a long voyage from Marseilles to Tunisia, around the horn of Africa, to Casablanca where they look for an exit visa to get to Lisbon, and from Lisbon to the new world. Most of the action in the film takes place in the Rick's American Café, run by Rick Blaine (played by Humphrey Bogart). The film opens up with the latest news to hit Casablanca: two German couriers have been murdered and the local French administration, which is run by Vichy France, is "rounding up the usual suspects."

Ugarte, a broker of exit visas in Casablanca, asks Rick to hold two letters of transit, signed by General de Gaulle, for safekeeping. Ugarte's plan is to sell the letters of transit for a huge price and to use the money to leave Casablanca. Unknown to Ugarte or Rick, the local prefect of police, Captain Louis Renault, has arranged for the arrest of Ugarte at Rick's that night to impress visiting Nazi Major Heinrich Strasser who is to there to observe Renault's efficiency. Renault tells Rick of the impending arrest and says that it will do no good to warn him; however Rick says that he would not stick his neck out for any one. Renault tells Rick that it is a wise foreign policy.

Renault goes on to tell Rick that the two German couriers were carrying two letters of transit, and that those letters of transit are not to go to a new visitor to Casablanca—Victor Laszlo. Rick, uncharacteristically, is impressed that Victor Laszlo is coming to Casablanca. Laszlo, a Czechoslovakian national, has been the leader of the resistance in Prague and later in other parts of Europe. Although the Nazis arrested him, he later escaped from a concentration camp to continue his work. He had made his way to French Morocco in an effort to escape to America to continue his work. Renault is under orders to prevent him from ever leaving Casablanca. Rick and Renault make a 10,000-franc bet on his eventual fate, Rick saying that it will be interesting to see how he manages to secure a letter of transit. Renault assures him that he will be seeking two letters, since he is traveling with a woman. While Rick is skeptical that Laszlo will not leave without the woman, Renault asserts that if he didn't leave her behind in Lyon or Oran, then he will not leave her in Casablanca. Nevertheless, Rick asks why Renault thinks he would be interested in helping Laszlo escape. Renault points out two episodes from Rick's past: in 1935 he ran guns to the Ethiopians and in 1936 he fought in Spain on the side of the loyalists. Although Rick points out that he was well paid on both occasions, Renault points out that the winning side would have paid more.

After the arrest of Ugarte is staged at Rick's for the benefit of the Nazis, Major Stroesser asks to meet the owner of the nightclub. Rick greets the guest and asks to join the group. Major Stroesser inquires if he can ask Rick a few questions unofficially. Rick agrees, but then gives evasive answers that seem to highlight his neutrality on everything. When asked if he was one of those people who couldn't believe that the Germans were in his beloved Paris, he replies it's not necessarily his beloved Paris. "What about London?" "Ask me when you get there." "What about New York?" "Now there are certain sections I would advise you not to invade." After more banter, Rick rises from the table and tells the group that their business was politics, while his was running a saloon.

The complicating factor in the story is that the woman that is traveling with Laszlo is Ilsa, the love of Rick's life. When Rick fled Paris to avoid the Nazi invasion he was supposed to travel with Ilsa but she left him a note at the last moment saying that she could not join him. Arriving in Casablanca, Rick opened the café, but withdrew from the rest of the world, declaring his strict neutrality on all matters. Now that Isla has come to Casablanca, Rick is hurt and has feelings of betrayal. Ilsa explains that Victor Laszlo is and was her husband, even when she and Rick were together in Paris. Hearing rumors that Rick may be in possession of the letters of transit, Laszlo comes to ask for Rick's help in securing them in order to help millions of people who depend on his work, but Rick bitterly tells him that he is not interested in helping Laszlo, saying that he is not interested in politics; "the problems of the world are not my department." When Laszlo asks him why he has turned his back on the cause, Rick tells him to ask his wife.

The chorus of German soldiers singing "Die Wacht am Rhein" interrupts Rick and Laszlo's meeting. During the scene in which the Germans are singing, everyone in the nightclub looks downtrodden and hopeless, staring impassively at the Germans singing triumphantly. Laszlo leaves Rick's side and stands in front of the band and demands that they play the "Marseillaise." After Rick signals his approval the band begins playing the French national anthem, the entire club comes to their feet to join in the singing. In the emotional high point of the film, the Germans are eventually shouted down and forced to cease their singing, over the patriotic fervor of "La Marseillaise." The song ends with shouts of "Vive la France!" from several of the patrons. Major Stroesser tells Renault that allowing Laszlo to stay in Casablanca may be more dangerous than letting him go. Stroesser orders Renault to close the nightclub.

After the club is closed, Ilsa returns to the club in an attempt to persuade Rick to give the letters of transit to Laszlo. Ilsa explains to Rick that she had been married to Victor at a very young age, and they were married before she knew Rick. The Nazis had captured Victor and she received word that he was dead. But on the day Rick and Ilsa were to flee Paris, Ilsa received word that Victor was still alive and needed help. She tells Rick that she is still in love with him and wants to stay with him, but she is tired and he will have to do the thinking for everyone now. With Ilsa's confession of love, Rick's confidence in humanity is restored.

Rick conceives a plan to get Victor Laszlo out of Casablanca. He stages a meeting with Laszlo to hand over the letters of transit so that Renault can make an arrest. But Rick double-crosses Renault and turns the gun on him. Rick uses Renault as a hostage to get Laszlo to the airport and to bypass security. Renault manages to get a message to Major Stroesser, but Stroesser is late in getting to the airport. Rick has Renault fill out the letters of transit in the names of Mr. and Mrs. Victor Laszlo. Renault and Ilsa are stunned, thinking that the whole point of the charade was to have Laszlo out of Casablanca so that Rick and Ilsa can be together. But Rick explains to Ilsa that she is what keeps Laszlo going, she is just as important to the cause as he is because she is his strength. In the famous airport monologue, Rick goes on to tell her:

> Ilsa, I'm no good at being noble, but it doesn't take much to see that the problems of three little people don't amount to a hill of beans in this crazy world. Someday you'll understand that.

As Victor and Ilsa leave to go on the plane, Renault tells Rick that he will of course have to arrest him. With his gun still drawn, Rick tells him as soon as the plane leaves he can. Major Stroesser comes racing in just as the plane is taxiing down the runway and asks what is going on. Renault tells him that Victor Laszlo is on the plane. Stroesser tries to radio the tower to stop the plane, but Rick shoots him before he can get a message out. When the rest of the police force arrives, Renault tells them that Major Stroesser has been shot and that they should round up the usual suspects. Opening a bottle of water, Renault tells Rick that he has become a patriot; Rick says it seemed like the right time to do so. Renault notices the water is "Vichy water" and says that perhaps he is right. Renault throws the bottle of water into the trashcan and kicks the can. The movie ends with the famous scene of Humphrey Bogart (Rick) and Claude Rains (Renault) walking into the fog, discussing plans to join a Free French garrison in Brazzaville, and Rick saying, "Louis . . . this could be the beginning of a beautiful friendship."

Casablanca is a plea for American involvement in the war in Europe. The film establishes a line between what is right and those who are wrong. In the film Rick astutely stays completely neutral throughout the film despite hearing several stories of hardship and deprivation. Rick's customers and employees are compelled to come to him to explain their problems; however, Rick remains aloof and noncommittal. In many ways, despite his protestations, Rick is seen as someone who can provide hope if only he can be reached. Rick's actions are a reflection of American foreign policy prior to its entry into the world war. Even some of the nuances of American behavior can be seen. In the film, Rick helps a young Bulgarian couple to obtain enough money at the roulette wheel to purchase an exit visa by fixing the game. However, after the couple win he denies and underplays his involvement, saying they had a lucky break. This can be seen as a parallel to American behavior of tacitly supporting the allies prior to December 1941, but wanting to maintain a façade of neutrality.

SINGING IN RICK'S CAFÉ

In Rick's Café, the German officers are having a good time and singing patriotic songs. This scene causes great anguish and despondency among the other patrons of the café. It is at this point that Victor Laszlo tries to rally the spirits of the patrons against German domination. The two songs that are sung are of note here: The Germans are singing, "Die Wacht am Rhein," while Laszlo and the patrons counter with the French national anthem, "La Marseillaise."

   Both songs have patriotic meanings; and both are dependent on war images. Compare the translation of both songs.

"Die Wacht am Rhein"
(The Watch on the Rhine)

A call flies like thunder
Like clanging of swords and noise of waves
To the Rhine, to the Rhine, to the German Rhine
Who will be the guardian of the stream?
Beloved Fatherland, you may be calm
Firm and loyal stands the watch on the Rhine

Through hundreds of thousands it flashes
And all eyes are flashing light
The German youth, pious and strong
Protects the holy borderland
Beloved Fatherland, you may be calm
Firm and loyal stands the watch on the Rhine

He looks up, where the sky is blue
Where Father Arminius looks down
And he pledges with proud desire to fight
"Ya, Rhein, will remain German as my chest!"
Beloved Fatherland, you may be calm
Firm and loyal stands the watch on the Rhine
"And though my heart breaks in death
You will not become a (Frenchman)
As rich as you are of water
Germany is of heroes' blood"
Beloved Fatherland, you may be calm
Firm and loyal stands the watch on the Rhine

"As long as there is one drop of blood left
And one fist draws the sword
And one arm cocks the gun
No Frenchman will step on your shore"
Beloved Fatherland, you may be calm
Firm and loyal stands the watch on the Rhine
The pledge resounds, the wave rolls,
The flags are flying in the wind
On the Rhine, on the Rhine, on the German Rhine
We will all be guardians
Beloved Fatherland, you may be calm
Firm and loyal stands the watch on the Rhine

"La Marseillaise"
(The Song of the Marseillaise)

Ye sons of France, awake to glory!
Hark! Hark! the people bid you rise!
Your children, wives, and grandsires hoary
Behold their tears and hear their cries!

Shall hateful tyrants, mischief breeding,
With hireling hosts a ruffian band
Affright and desolate the land
While peace and liberty lie bleeding?

To arms, to arms, ye brave!
The avenging sword unsheathe!
March on, march on, all hearts resolved
On liberty or death.

Oh liberty can man resign thee,
Once having felt thy generous flame?
Can dungeons, bolts, and bars confine thee?
Or whips thy noble spirit tame?

Too long the world has wept bewailing
That falsehood's dagger tyrants wield;
But freedom is our sword and shield
And all their arts are unavailing.

Lifeboat

Alfred Hitchcock's contribution to the war effort during the Second World War followed many of the same ideas. In *Lifeboat* (1944), one of the overriding themes is that there is a need for cooperation in order to defeat the enemy. The beginning of *Lifeboat* has a small group of people escaping a sinking ship after a German submarine has torpedoed it. One by one, people come to or are rescued by the lifeboat. The list of passengers include Constance (Connie) Porter, a socialite reporter who seems more interested in covering the shipwreck than in rescuing people; Gus Smith, a sailor who has a badly injured leg; John Hodiak, an engineer who has leftist leanings; Stanley Garrett, a radio operator; Alice MacKenzie, a nurse; Charles Rittenhouse, a very wealthy businessman; Joe Spencer, an African-American ship steward; Mrs. Higgins, a woman who has just lost her baby; and Willy, a German sailor, who it turns out was the captain of the submarine that had sunk the ship.

During the first part of the film the lifeboat is marked by people being generally polite, but suspicious of each other. The group does not know what to do with the German passenger. There is a strong sentiment to throw him over, while others want to offer him sanctuary and comfort that the German submarine did not show them. Eventually, the group allows him to stay. But they continue to be suspicious of him and relations are strained because Connie is the only one who speaks German. Their next immediate concern is what to do with the Mrs. Higgins, who is clutching the body of her dead baby. She understands that the baby is dead, but is very distraught. While Mrs. Higgins is sleeping, the rest of the passengers perform a burial at sea for the baby. When Mrs. Higgins awakes, she asks for the baby. The group tells her that the baby has died, and she attempts suicide by jumping overboard. They tie Mrs. Higgins to a chair in attempt to prevent her from harming herself, but while they are sleeping she slips overboard.

With everyone settled, the group has to decide where

they should go and how to get there. The lifeboat has a sail but the compass has been smashed. The group agrees the best course of action is to head toward Bermuda, which was to the southeast of where the boat sank. Hodiak asks Garrett which way he thinks the southeast is and Garrett tells him, but Willy disagrees saying, through Connie's translation, the southeast is a different way. Willy insists that southeast is the way that he is pointing and seems assured of himself, while Garrett is less sure. Nevertheless, the group, led by Hodiak, chooses to follow Garrett's direction.

The next problem the group has to face is what to do about Gus' leg. Alice notice that gangrene has set in and unless they get help immediately Gus will die. The only option for Gus is amputation, which Willy, the German officer, surmising the conversation agrees with. Willy volunteers to perform the procedure since he was a surgeon prior to the war. With the procedure performed Gus is left to recover and the rest of the survivors are left to settle in for a long wait until they reach Bermuda or are rescued by a passing ship.

Unbeknownst to the rest of the passengers, Willy in fact speaks English and he has a compass. Willy is monitoring the conversation of the other members of the lifeboat and he is deliberately leading the boat into German shipping lanes. As Gus is recovering from his injury, the lifeboat is beset by a storm that tests the mettle of the passengers. During the storm, the mast of the boat is destroyed and the food provisions and fresh water are lost. The passengers settle in for a long wait without food or water.

As time passes, the passengers grow tired, weak, and thirsty. Gus becomes delusional, spending a great deal of time imagining that he is home dancing with this girlfriend. Only Willy is seemingly surviving the ordeal intact. Willy takes over the oars and has begun to row in the direction of the shipping lanes. While the others are sleeping, Gus sees Willy take a drink of water from a flask. Gus in a delusional state begs for water, however, eventually Willy pushes Gus overboard and rows away. The rest of the passengers wake

HITCHCOCK GOES TO WAR

In addition to the World War II-era classic *Lifeboat* discussed in this chapter, legendary British director Alfred Hitchcock (1899–1980) made several other films that directly or indirectly examined the climate, chaos, and consequences of war.

Whether it involved international espionage during the height of the Cold War (*Torn Curtain and Topaz*) or the outset of World War II (*Foreign Correspondent*), the hunt for Nazis at the close of World War II (*Notorious*), or the plight of innocents caught in the middle of assassinations and international intrigue (to some degree, all of the following films), it is clear that the renowned "master of suspense" also used his creative vision to explore war-time situations.

The following Hitchcock films feature plots that transpire in the midst of "hot" and "cold" wars:

Foreign Correspondent (1940)	World War II
Saboteur (1942)	World War II
Lifeboat (1944)	World War II
Notorious (1946)	World War II
North By Northwest (1956)	Cold War
Torn Curtain (1966)	Cold War
Topaz (1969)	Cold War

up and realize that Gus is gone. They confront Willy and accuse him of holding out on them. He admits that Gus has found him out and he had to kill him to protect himself. Willy also admits to having a flask of water and food tablets, but allows the flask to break rather than sharing with the others. The rest of the passengers turn on Willy and beat him and throw him overboard.

With Willy gone, the boat has no direction. Tensions rise between the passengers. Hunger and thirst begins to overtake the remaining survivors. Finally, Connie gives up her expensive bracelet as bait for fish. The bright bracelet in fact attracts a large fish, but as they begin to reel the fish in a German destroyer appears and begins heading for the life-

The Master of Suspense . . . or the Master of Wartime Intrigue?
In films such as *Lifeboat,* among others, legendary British director Alfred
Hitchcock addressed human behavior, dilemmas, and theories of international
politics directly related to war.

boat. The fish escapes, but the members of the lifeboat fear
that they will not. Just as the destroyer deploys rowboats to
retrieve the lifeboat, a British patrol boat appears on the ho-
rizon and begins shooting at the German ship. The German
boat is sunk, and the lifeboat picks up a German survivor.

They begin to tend to his needs, but Rittenhouse raises the question of whether they should be treating the German considering the trouble they had with Willy. The group generally decide that they should, but as the discussion progresses, the young German sailor pulls out a gun. Joe wrestles the gun away. The German asks if the group is not going to kill him, and Hodiak rhetorically asks, "what do you do with people like that?" As the film ends, rowboats from the British patrol boat are en route to pick up the occupants of the lifeboat.

Throughout the film the German captain seems to have the upper hand. Willy is stronger, more capable, and better prepared for the task at hand. Early in the film he is able to dispose of weaker members of the crew. The implication is that Willy has killed Mrs. Higgins, directly or indirectly, and the audience is aware that he has pushed Gus overboard. This seems to mirror politics in Europe. Germany is able to dispose of some of the allies' weaker friends, such as Austria and Czechoslovakia. The rest of the survivors seem resigned to spending the rest of the war in a concentration camp until they are aroused and begin to work together against Willy. While they work against Willy, though there are temptations to do so, ultimately they do not lose their humanity and treat the new German prisoner with respect. The film is ultimately a plea for not only cooperation between different economic classes to push aside their differences to work together, but also a plea for the different democracies to do the same.

World War II: Why War Is Sometimes Necessary

Each of the World War II films, *Alexandr Nevsky, Casablanca,* and *Lifeboat,* presents reasons why involvement in a war against Germany was necessary. Both *Nevsky* and *Casablanca* worry about a militaristic ideology, and all three tout the need for cooperation among those who opposed the

Nazis. Each film, though, examined different factors that might inhibit cooperation. In *Alexandr Nevsky,* cooperation is threatened by class differences. Initially, the merchant class of Novgorod is reluctant to join the resistance to the German because of a decline in their profits. Similarly, in *Lifeboat* there is an element of class struggle as well. Certainly there is resistance to leadership by Connie and Rittenhouse early in the film. However, the barriers to cooperation are a little more complex in *Lifeboat*. Evidence of a racial divide is evidenced by how the survivors treat Joe. Similarly, there is a distinction on how Gus is treated by the rest of the passengers. Finally, cooperation in *Casablanca* is difficult because of different reasons: in the love story, Rick's feelings of betrayal prevent him cooperating against the Germans. In the more allegorical story, it is only when the United States cooperated with the rest of the allies that the Germans can be defeated.

World War I: War Is Destructive

The First World War in film becomes synonymous with the idea of futility in war. One of the earliest commentaries on the futility of war was Thomas Ince's film *Civilization* (1916). The film uses a moralistic overtone to tell the story of Christ returning to earth to prevent a massive conflict that mirrors the First World War. Films throughout the 1920s expressed an abhorrence of war. Famous silent films such as *The Big Parade* (1925) and *Wings* (1927) expressed the idea that while some ideas were worth fighting for, the end result was the death of a number of innocents and a decline in moral stature. *The Big Parade* (1925) sends troops off to war with American patriotism and flag-waving jubilation. It spends nearly ninety minutes showing recruits being "trained" for battle, but then thrown into a situation for which the protagonists are never prepared.[7]

The Grand Illusion

Set during the First World War, *The Grand Illusion* (1937) becomes a plea against war and an acknowledgment of the changing politics in Europe. The story is set during World War I in 1916, prior to the entry of the United States into the war. Three French pilots are shot down over German territory, but before they are transferred to a prisoner of war camp, their German counterparts treat the French prisoners to a magnificent dinner. As the group of combatants talk they find out that each has ties to the other side: one of the French pilots has a cousin in Berlin, one of the German pilots worked in Lyon, and so on.

When the prisoners arrive at the prisoner of war camp they are quickly integrated in to the prisoner culture. Although there is some mistrust of Boeldieu, because of his aristocratic manners, he is eventually let into the plot where the prisoners plan an escape. He tells his fellow detainees that it is the duty of officers to try to escape. The prisoners all eat well, even better than their German guards, thanks to the packages sent to Rosenthal, whose family are bankers and Jewish.

The new prisoners find out that the escape plan is through a tunnel, which they have been digging for two months and should be completed in the next couple of weeks. Then each of the officers in the barracks will escape by way of the garden after curfew one night. One officer jokes that in a couple of weeks the war will be over. He is rebuked by others saying that such thinking is only wishful imagination.

Thanks to the packages from Rosenthal's family, the prisoners decide to put on a music production to pass the time. While rehearsals are going on word comes that the Germans have captured the town of Douaumont. This sparks a celebration of among Germans who sing, "Die Wacht am Rhein." During the production, word comes that the French has once again captured the town of Douaumont, which results in the French breaking into "Le Marseillaise." The town remains in the news as both sides fight and temporarily gain control over it. However, the news sends the prisoners on an emotional roller coaster, prompting Maréchal to the verge of a nervous breakdown shouting incomprehensibly at his German captors. One of the German guards asks another, "Why did he shout like that?" The reply is "The war is lasting too long."

On the verge of their escape attempt, the prisoners are transferred further into Germany. The story is resumed when Boeldieu, Maréchal, and Rosenthal are transferred to a new camp, where, after an accident in his airplane, von Rauffenstein is the officer in charge. The new prison is actually a fortified castle, which is reputed to be impregnable. Captain von Rauffenstein reads the dossier of the new prisoners and notes that Boeldieu has attempted to escape five times, Maréchal four times, and Rosenthal three times. The commander pays tribute to the patriotism of the three men, but warns that an attempt to escape will mean an enforcement of the French law, which insists that escaping prisoners are to be shot.

Boeldieu and von Rauffenstein renew their friendship and both men feel an affinity with one another because of their class status. Boeldieu visits the Captain often, and von Rauffenstein meticulously takes care of his geranium. He explains to Boeldieu that it is the only flower in the castle and that he takes care of it as his tribute to beauty. In their conversation von Rauffenstein argues that even though he does not know who will win the war, it will result in the end of families like the Boeldieus and von Rauffensteins. Captain Boeldieu says perhaps, but maybe there is no need for families like that any more. The German replies that he thinks that is a pity: democracy has brought the introduction of people like Maréchal and Rosenthal to politics and power in Europe.

Meanwhile, Maréchal and Rosenthal are making plans for escape from the castle. Maréchal tells Rosenthal that he would have never believed before the war that he would be comfortable with a Jew, but now he feels closer to Rosenthal than he does with Boeldieu. Both men agree that they respect Boeldieu and think him a good man, but his aristocratic manners put a distance between them. Rosenthal thinks that Jews have been mistreated in Europe because they have been depicted as greedy; in reality, according to

Rosenthal, greed was never a problem, because anyone coming to a Jew's house was well treated and fed: the problem was pride. Jehovah had given the Jews a prominent position in the world, and led Jews to feel superior. Maréchal gently rebukes him, saying that he has always been a good friend.

As a counterpoint to the gifts sent by the Rosenthal family to the prisoners, the Russians prisoners receive a package from the tsarina. When the crate arrives, the Russians gather up all the prisoners saying that it is time to repay the other prisoners for their kindness. The Russians want to make sure that they share the caviar with their fellow prisoners and drink vodka all night. When the crate is opened all that the prisoners find are books, mainly education books. The Russians are upset and begin burning the crate. The other prisoners leave the area and the German guard rush in to restore order. Boeldieu notices that commotion brings all the guards, and such a distraction might afford an opportunity for escape.

Boeldieu tells Rosenthal and Maréchal that he will stage a distraction so that they can use a rope that they have made to scale down the wall of the castle and escape. Both men protest that he should come with them, but he replies that they have more in common and would likely be more successful. Besides, given his position, he will be able to create a longer distraction. He says that he can give them five minutes. When the time comes, all the prisoners begin blowing on flutes that have come in a package; after the Germans confiscate them the prisoners begin banging pots and pans and other materials to make noise. As the Germans are quelling the disturbance, Boeldieu climbs to the tops of the castle still blowing his flute, and as the German guards chase him, Maréchal and Rosenthal make their escape over the wall. The German guards finally corner Boeldieu and von Rauffenstein pleads for him to come down. Boeldieu continues to stall in order to give the escapees as much time as possible for their flight. After pleading with him, von Rauffenstein is forced to shoot Boeldieu to end the standoff.

A short time later, von Rauffenstein is informed that Rosenthal and Maréchal have escaped. He realizes that Boeldieu has sacrificed himself so that the two could escape. He goes to Boeldieu's deathbed to ask for forgiveness. Boeldieu tells von Rauffenstein that he has nothing to apologize for—that he was doing his duty. The German captain tells him he was aiming for his leg, to which Boeldieu replies that the conditions were not optimal for such a shot. Boeldieu admits that he would have never suspected that a bullet in the stomach would have hurt so much. As he lies dying, von Rauffenstein laments that such a tragedy would have taken place. Boeldieu replies that for a man of the people, it is terrible to die in the war, "for you . . . and me . . . it was a good solution." After Boeldieu dies, von Rauffenstein cuts the only bloom from his geranium and lays it on the body of the dead Frenchman.

Meanwhile, Rosenthal and Maréchal make their way to the Swiss border, which lies two hundred miles from the castle. The two begin to fight and argue constantly. Rosenthal hurts his leg, their food is short, and the weather is cold and terrible. Maréchal considers leaving his Jewish friend behind at times, but cannot bring himself to do it. One night, they find an old house that appears to be abandoned; they decide to stay in the barn in order to keep warm and rest. They are discovered there by a woman who tells them she is alone. Elsa invites them into the house, and initially the two escapees are suspicious of them. However, after a German patrol comes by asking directions and she does not turn them in, they begin to trust Elsa more and more. Elsa tells them that her husband has died at Verdun and she has been left to fend for herself and daughter. The two French escapees spend time with the German woman, building their strength and allowing Rosenthal's foot to heal. The two help with chores around the house and both grow fond of Elsa's daughter. They spend Christmas with Elsa and her daughter and during this time Maréchal and Elsa begin to fall in love. Despite this, the two Frenchmen know they have to press on to the Switzerland. Maréchal vows that if he makes it to Switzerland, after the war he will come back for Elsa and take her back to France.

As the two near the border, they realize that it might be the most dangerous part of the journey. The two decide that if they come across a German patrol, then they will split up to make capture or pursuit more difficult. After their time with Elsa, the two have renewed and deepened their friendship. As they set off to make a run for the border, Maréchal turns to Rosenthal with a smile on his face, "Goodbye, dirty Jew." To which Rosenthal replies, "Goodbye, old nut." As the two try to make their way across the border in waist-deep snow, a German patrol does spot them. A soldier manages to get off one shot, but is stopped by a superior officer who tells them that the two are now in Switzerland. The film ends as the two continue to make their way deeper into Switzerland.

The Grand Illusion uses World War I as a warning of what might be coming. Again, factors that prevent cooperation between individuals are explored. Issues such as economic class, religion, and nationality are all explored as potential roadblocks to cooperation. While these factors are vexing over the course of the film, each is seemingly overcome. With *The Grand Illusion* the main focus is on the effects of the war on individuals. Even though the French prisoners of war are living in better conditions than their German captors, their confinement is ultimately dehumanizing and they are willing to do almost anything to escape. While nationality seems important, the soldiers on each side find they have more in common than they might otherwise suspect.

The Great Dictator

With war clouds gathering in the late 1930s, some films like *The Grand Illusion* continued to look back at the First World War and warn of the consequences. Another anti-war film of the era was Charles Chaplin's *The Great Dictator* (1940). Chaplin's first sound film revives his tramp-like character to make an impassioned plea for avoiding war. Although the

As the Jewish Barber, Chaplin and co-star Paulette Goddard hide from the storm troopers that are supposed to look like Nazis. Chaplin's characterization of the Nazi regime was criticized as not being helpful before the war because it made diplomacy more difficult. After the war, the film seems naïve in its failure to capture the horrors of the regime.

film is a sound film and dialogue is important, there are long sequences of pantomime that can take away from the momentum of the film. Nevertheless, the film is an important statement for democratic values prior to World War II.

The film opens with a prologue set during the First World War. Chaplin plays a Jewish barber who is assigned to the artillery division of the army of the mythical country Tomania. With the war going badly for Tomania, all troops, including the inept Chaplin, are sent to the front. The Tomanian forces are being overrun everywhere. Chaplin comes across a wounded pilot, Major Schultz, who is sure that is he can get his information to his superiors, that Tomania might still win the war. Chaplin gets Schultz to his airplane, and they escape the front lines. However, after some comedic incidents, the plane crashes. Schultz is grateful that the

CHAPLIN'S SPEECH TO CLOSE
THE GREAT DICTATOR

I'm sorry but I don't want to be an emperor. That's not my business. I don't want to rule or conquer anyone. I should like to help everyone if possible, Jew, Gentile, black men, white. We all want to help one another. Human beings are like that. We want to live by each other's happiness, not by each other's misery. We don't want to hate and despise one another. In this world there is room for everyone. And the good earth is rich and can provide for everyone. The way of life can be free and beautiful, but we have lost the way. Greed has poisoned men's souls; has barricaded the world with hate; has goose-stepped us into misery and bloodshed. We have developed speed, but we have shut ourselves in. Machinery that gives abundance has left us in want. Our knowledge has made us cynical; our cleverness, hard and unkind. We think too much and feel too little. More than machinery we need humanity. More than cleverness, we need kindness and gentleness. Without these qualities, life will be violent and all will be lost. The aeroplane and the radio have brought us closer together. The very nature of these things cries out for the goodness in man; cries out for universal brotherhood; for the unity of us all. Even now my voice is reaching millions throughout the world, millions of despairing men, women, and little children, victims of a system that makes men torture and imprison innocent people. To those who can hear me, I say, "Do not despair." The misery that has come upon us is but the passing of greed, the bitterness of men who fear the way of human progress. The hate of men will pass, and dictators die, and the power they took from the people will return to the people. And so long as men die, liberty will never perish. Soldiers! Don't give yourselves to these brutes who despise you, enslave you; who regiment your lives, tell you what to do, what to think and what to feel! Who drill you, diet you, treat you like cattle and use you as cannon fodder. Don't give yourselves to these unnatural men—machine men with machine minds and machine hearts! You are not machines! You are men! With the love of humanity in your hearts! Don't hate! Only the unloved hate; the unloved and the unnatural. Soldiers! Don't fight for slavery! Fight for liberty! In the seventeenth chapter of St. Luke, it is written that the kingdom of God is within man, not one man nor a group of men, but in all men! In you! You, the people, have the power, the power to create machines, the power to create happiness! You, the people, have the power to make this life free and beautiful, to make this life a wonderful adventure. Then in the name of democracy, let us use that power. Let us all unite. Let us fight for a new world, a decent world that will give men a chance to work, that will give youth a future and old age a security. By the promise of these things, brutes have risen to power. But they lie! They do not fulfill that promise. They never will! Dictators free themselves but they enslave the people. Now let us fight to free the world! To do away with national barriers! To do away with greed, with hate and intolerance! Let us fight for a world of reason, a world where science and progress will lead to the happiness of us all. Soldiers, in the name of democracy, let us unite!

Jewish barber has saved his life, but when the two are rescued they learn that the war is over—Tomania has lost.

In the intervening years, Tomania suffers from economic
depression, riots and the rise of a dictator, Adenoid Hynkel.
Hynkel (also played by Chaplin) is self-important, yet paranoid at the same time. His dictatorship, of the "double
cross," is based on megalomania and intimidation of the
population. Meanwhile, the Jewish barber has never really
recovered from his injuries suffered during the airplane
crash. While physically he is fine, he believes that he has
only been in the infirmary for a couple of weeks and that he
will return to his barbershop in the ghetto in a couple of
days, not realizing that two decades have past.

In an effort to distract the population from the economic
troubles at home, the Hynkel regime has sought to blame
the Jewish population. The effect in the ghetto is that the
population cowers under the control of the storm troopers,
and very few of the residents stand up to the regime. The
film moves back and forth between two stories: one centered in the ghetto, the other in the palace of Adenoid Hynkel. The Jewish barber leaves the infirmary and makes his
way back to the ghetto, completely confused by the shop
that has been empty for twenty years; he begins to clean it
up. After he takes down the boards that have covered the
shop windows, he finds that storm troopers have started
painting "JEW" across the glass; when he goes out to
protest, he gets in a scuffle with them. Chaplin manages to
elude the storm troopers for a while, with the help of another ghetto resident, Hannah. However, Chaplin is eventually caught by a group of storm troopers who start to hang
him from a lamppost. At that point, Major Schultz is making
his way through the ghetto and stops to see what is going
on. He recognizes the Jewish barber as the one who had
saved his life back in 1918. Schultz saves his life and orders
that the storm troopers leave the barber and his friend
alone.

Hynkel wants to set in motion his plans to rule the world.
His first move is to invade Osterlich; however he is warned

that he does not have adequate funds to do so. His chief of propaganda, Garbitsch, tells him that the best way to raise the money for an invasion is through a loan from one of the Jewish bankers. Hynkel decrees that while he is negotiating a loan, the Jews in the ghetto are not to be mistreated. During this time, life returns to some sense of normality in the ghetto. Some Jews are actually even willing to support Hynkel. However, after Hynkel is refused the loan because of the past treatment of Jews, he unleashes the storm troopers on the ghetto. When Schultz protests the treatment of Jews, he is arrested and sent to a concentration camp.

The speech announcing the crackdown on the ghetto sends reverberations through it. Panic grips Chaplin and Hannah because they know that they would be among the first targeted. When they arrive home, they find out that Schultz has escaped and is hiding in their apartment building. While the men concoct a plan to kill Hynkel, Hannah intervenes and explains to them that none of them are cut out to carry out such an attack. The storm troopers break into the apartment and begin searching for the Jewish barber and Schultz. While they temporarily escape, they are eventually caught and sent to a concentration camp. Hannah and the rest of the people in the apartment building escape as refugees to Osterlich.

While Hynkel makes plans for the invasion of Osterlich, he notices that the dictator of Bacteria, Napaloni, has massed his troops along the border of Osterlich. Hynkel is worried that Napaloni will invade Osterlich before he can. Hynkel invites Napaloni to Tomania for a conference to discuss the future. After each dictator tries to impress each other. Hynkel appears to be on the short end each time. They leaders finally agree that Hynkel will not invade Osterlich, while Napaloni will pull his troops back. Hynkel's plans are to double-cross Napaloni and invade Osterlich anyway.

Schultz and the Jewish barber steal officer uniforms and escape from the concentration camp; they begin to walk toward the Osterlich border. Meanwhile Tomanian troops are preparing to invade. The soldiers mistake the Jewish barber

THE TRAMP AND THE DICTATOR

Premiering at the Berlin International Film Festival in February 2002, the documentary *The Tramp and the Dictator* (2002) made its U.S. television debut on Turner Classic Movies in the fall of 2002.

The Tramp and the Dictator offers biographical sketches of Charlie Chaplin and Adolph Hitler and examines the politically charged atmosphere surrounding the filming, financing, and distribution of Chaplin's anti-Nazi (and anti-Fascist) masterpiece *The Great Dictator*. Featuring never-before-seen color home movie coverage of the filming of Chaplin's epic, this documentary reveals the pressures placed on Chaplin as well as Hitler's reaction to Chaplin's razor-sharp lampooning of *De Fuhrer*, nazism and fascism.

At once a landmark comedy and courageous political statement—recall that the film was written prior to Hitler's invasion of Poland and Britain's entry into World War II—*The Great Dictator's* immediate and long-term impact is examined in detail. Film aficionados, historians, and citizens alike will relish this insider's look into the creative process and political implications of Chaplin's classic.

The Tramp and the Dictator (UK, 2002):

Directed by: Kevin Brownlow and Michael Kloft
Written by: Kevin Brownlow and Christopher Bird
Narrated by: Kenneth Branagh
Runtime: Germany: 58 min (Berlin Film Festival) /
                    USA: 56min (Turner Classic Movies)

for Hynkel and think that he has rehabilitated Schultz. At the same time Hynkel, who is hiding waiting for the invasion to occur near the border, is mistaken as the Jewish barber and arrested. The Jewish barber and Schultz are taken across the border where the dictator is expected to speak on the expansion of the Tomanian Empire. Both men are taken to the stage, and Shultz tells the barber that in order to continue the ruse, he will have to speak. The barber responds that he cannot. Schultz tells him that, "you must . . . it's our only hope."

The Jewish barber rises, dressed as the dictator of Tomania, and addresses the crowd. The speech becomes Chaplin's penultimate comment on European politics of the late 1930s. In it, Chaplin calls for democracy and a struggle against fascism, but many argue that rather than being one of the characters in the movie, Chaplin becomes himself, in a last ditch effort to save the continent and the world from war.

Of course, in the real world Chaplin's plea goes unheeded. The film was unsuccessful at the box office, and later in his career Chaplin's loyalties were questioned. Eventually, Chaplin would leave the United States during the Communist scare of the 1950s and subsequently would be *persona non grata*. Chaplin would only be invited back to the United States for a special Academy Award in 1977.

The Great Dictator, like *The Grand Illusion,* examines the effect of war and militarism on the civilian population. The hospital where the Jewish barber spends twenty years is one of the minor scenes of the film, but it is a reminder of the effects of war on the general population. The film also comments on the use of part of the population as scapegoats. The people in the Jewish ghetto are tempted to support Hynkel once he lifts the restrictions on the Jews. Ultimately, it is Hynkel's military obsessions that require the population to sacrifice economically and also require a scapegoat to blame.

Vietnam: Revisiting the Anti-War Film

The American experience during the Vietnam War prompted a number of films and television shows on the subject. During the war itself, the United States experienced a number of protests and demonstrations against the war. The effects on the United States were profound: At its height, more than 500,000 American troops were fighting in the war; over 58,000 Americans would lose their lives; an estimated two and half million civilians lost their lives; and, confidence was shaken in the government of the United States among its citizens and the international community. Such a divisive conflict stirred up antiwar sentiments both in the United States and around the world, and was reflected in the films produced by Hollywood.

Antiwar films after the Vietnam War, such as *The Deer Hunter* (1978) and *Platoon* (1986) would revisit the theme of war and the impact on the population. The movie and television show *M*A*S*H* (1970; 1972–1983), and the films *Born on the Fourth of July* (1989), and *When We Were Soldiers* (2002) examine the effects of the Vietnam War on the population as well. Although *M*A*S*H* was set in the Korean War, it was clearly an indictment of American involvement in the Vietnam War. *Born on the Fourth of July,* which told the story of veteran Ron Kovic, who was paralyzed in the war, and *When We Were Soldiers,* which told the personal stories of the soldiers who fought the first major engagement of the war, both examined the personal impact that Vietnam had on individuals. Kovic's experiences in Vietnam led him to become an outspoken opponent of not only the Vietnam War, but U.S. military intervention in other parts of the world as well. The devastating impact of the Vietnam War on the United States and Vietnam—from soldiers and families to lovers and innocent civilians—is a theme that has been at the heart of several films by *Born on the Fourth of July* director Oliver Stone (See Oliver Stone and *Vietnam* box on the following page).

Nuclear War

The divide between war as necessary and war as destructive begins to break down with the advent of nuclear weaponry in 1945. The prospects of mass devastation or even the elimination of human life from earth greatly changes the calculus of using war to achieve an end. While people like von Clausewitz suggested that war is an extension of politics,[8] nuclear weapons changed the equation. The possession of nuclear weapons by both sides means that there is little difference between winning and losing.

Films reflected the growing awareness of the destructive potential of nuclear weaponry. Early on, films in the

OLIVER STONE AND *VIETNAM*: THE DEVASTATING EFFECTS OF WAR

Prolific, political, opinionated, and controversial, the Yale and New York University-educated director-*auteur* Oliver Stone (1946-) has produced a stunning body of work that considers the domestic and foreign origins and implications of America's war in Vietnam.

Awarded the Bronze Star for Valor and the Purple Heart for his service in Vietnam, Stone has devoted significant screen time to examining his—and others'—lingering questions about U.S. military intervention in Southeast Asia (1947–1975). From the rice paddies, platoons and helicopters to presidencies and elections, from political and psychological dimensions to matters of the heart, a series of Stone films consider how America's involvement in Vietnam has adversely affected individual states, international relations, lovers, families, the media, presidents, and the U.S. body politic:

Platoon (1986)	*Born on the Fourth of July* (1989)
JFK (1991)	*Heaven and Earth* (1993)
Nixon (1995)	

Commenting on his style, artistic vision, and the destruction brought on by war, Stone has offered this observation:

> I consider my films first and foremost to be dramas about individuals in personal struggles and I consider myself to be a dramatist before I am a political filmmaker. I'm interested in alternative points of view. I think ultimately the problems of the planet are universal and that nationalism is a very destructive force.... They say I'm unsubtle. But we need above all, a theatre that wakes us up: nerves and heart
>
> Nationalism and patriotism are the two most evil forces that I know of in this century or in any century and cause more wars and more death and more destruction to the soul and to human life than anything else.*

In 2003, Stone entered the world of documentary filmmaking, releasing a movie of his meeting with Fidel Castro, *Commandante*. Sure to stir even more debate and discussion about his politics and U.S. policy toward the island nation, *Commandante* premiered at the Sundance film festival in January 2003 and was scheduled to debut on HBO several months later.

*See: http://us.imdb.com/Bio?Stone,%20Oliver

sci-fi genre did not take the destructive power as a necessary threat, but instead used the weapons as a force to conduct good, or its aftermath to create new heroes. Take, for example, the 1955 film *King Dinosaur*. In the not-too-distant future, explorers from earth travel to the newly discovered Planet Nova. There they find an almost Eden-like world inhabited by various animals (through the use of stock footage), some of which are friendly to the humans, like a pet lemur, and others are not, like an alligator. The humans travel to an island where they find a group of dinosaurs, including a Tyrannosaurus Rex, inhabiting the island. After "harrowing" experiences, the explorers escape the island leaving a nuclear device to destroy it. One of the characters comments, "It was the only thing to do." Of course this is another opportunity to use stock footage, this time of an atomic bomb test. The eventual premise of the film is that explorers from earth find a planet inhabited by animals, including dinosaurs, and blow it up, never mind the potential interest in scientific research or the moral implications of being a visitor to another planet and destroying life. The film views nuclear weaponry as just another tool to further the needs and desires of humans.

Films of the genre did present other views of nuclear weapons, but were not as serious as later films. Films of the sci-fi genre during the early part of the nuclear age warned of the impact of nuclear radiation. However, none of these films could really be taken seriously. In *Them!* (1954), radiation causes ants to be mutated into giant ants; in *The Beginning of the End* (1957), radiation caused grasshoppers to grow to an enormous size; and in *Godzilla* (1956), nuclear tests causes the awakening of an ancient monster, that goes on a rampage in downtown Tokyo.

On the Beach

Despite the fun and frivolity of these films, the subject of nuclear war and nuclear weaponry took on more serious dimensions as the Cold War progressed. During the 1940s

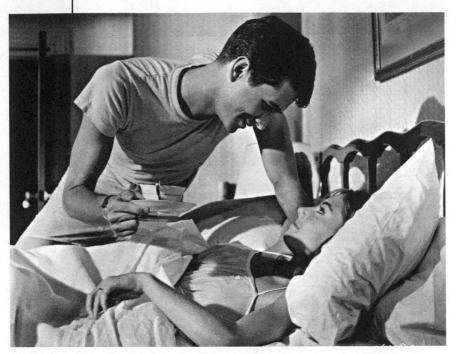

On the Beach: Young love interrupted—as radiation begins to poison the atmosphere in Australia, people begin to succumb to its effect. Difficult choices have to be made by the survivors of the war, this couple must decide if they should euthanize their newborn knowing that it may outlive them and die from radiation sickness or starvation.

and 1950s, the United States government produced a number of films that touted the benefits of nuclear weaponry. The films often downplayed the effects of radiation on the human body. Also, the films often showed U.S. government officials exhorting the potential peaceful uses of nuclear weapons as a reason for test detonations. These short subjects seem naïve and antiquated by today's standards. However, they served as the primary source of information about nuclear weapons and power for an entire generation of Americans before the dawn of television.

An early, but important exploration of the effects of a potential nuclear war was the 1959 film *On the Beach.* Based on the novel of the same name by Nevil Shute, the story is set in the aftermath of a nuclear war in 1964. An American submarine surfaces in Australia to find apparently what are the last people alive on earth.

On the Beach depicts the horrors of a potential nuclear war, without showing any violence or destruction. Through the course of the film normal Australians go through their lives waiting for death from radiation poisoning. While people desperately look for love, satisfaction and meaning in their final days, the overriding theme of the film seems to be the wastefulness of war in a nuclear age. The end of the film is a shot of a cautionary banner from a religious revival, that has a second meaning for the audience, "There is still time." The difficulty of war in a nuclear age is that it is unlikely that any one could survive a total war to make a film afterwards.

Nuclear War in Other Films

Other films in this genre capture the paranoia about nuclear war as well as the potential devastating effects of nuclear war very well. The Missiles of October (1974) explores the struggle in the Kennedy administration in trying to avoid nuclear war during the Cuban Missile Crisis of 1962. Adapted from Robert Kennedy's book Thirteen Days, the film reflects the struggle within the administration to understand and respond to the crisis. The Missiles of October depicts the problems of securing and understanding information during a crisis situation. While there was initial support for a military strike to destroy the missiles among administration officials, the realization that those strikes may trigger a nuclear response from the Soviet Union dampened the appeal of that course of action.

The events of October 1962 were revisited in the popular 2000 film Thirteen Days, which incorporated a great deal of information about the events that was declassified following the end of the Cold War. Starring Kevin Costner as Special Assistant to the President, Kenny O'Donnell, Bruce Greenwood as President John F. Kennedy, and Steven Culp as Attorney General Robert F. Kennedy, *Thirteen Days* provides a mostly accurate account of the Kennedy Administration's extensive (and secret) deliberations over how to respond to Soviet missiles in Cuba. In the process, we learn of the views of key EXCOM players, including Dean Acheson, Adlai Stevenson, Robert McNamara, McGeorge Bundy, Maxwell Taylor, and Curtis LeMay. The film also does an exemplary job of detailing JFK, RFK, and Khruschev's back-channel negotiations, diplomatic overtures, and political and strategic concessions used to defuse the crisis. Yet, the film was not without its critics. One concern articulated by some historians and students of politics was that the film substantially overplayed the significance of Kennedy aide Kenny O'Donnell, who, alongside JFK and RFK, is clearly the star of the film. Another criticism lodged by some was that the hawks in the military brass—namely Curtis LeMay—were portrayed in an overly negative light. Lastly, another complaint concerned the fact that O'Donnell's son Kevin, an Earthlink millionaire, was an investor in the company of *Thirteen Days* producer Armyan Bernstein, thus raising the issue of conflict of interest and the inflation of Kenny O'Donnell's role in the film and the real life crisis.[9] These legitimate complaints aside, however, the film is refreshingly accurate in its depiction of most of the aspects of the military, political, and diplomatic history of the Cuban Missile Crisis. In addition, it is worth noting the several worthwhile features are contained in the DVD release of *Thirteen Days*. Among the indispensable items for those who are interested in the Cuban Missile Crisis are a timeline of key events, biographies of the political and military players in the real-life drama ("Historical Figures Biographical Gallery"), and an excellent documentary film, *Roots of the Cuban Missile Crisis,* which provides valuable, essential political and historical context by covering U.S.-Soviet relations from WWII through 1962. And, it does so in slightly under an hour.

The events of October 1962 drew the United States and the Soviet Union probably as close as they ever came to a nuclear confrontation. The prospect had a sobering effect on policy-makers and citizens alike. One could almost say that a preoccupation and paranoia began to creep into the minds of many concerning the potential effects of a nuclear war. Films like *Dr. Strangelove* (1964) and *Fail-Safe* (1964) continued an examination of the preoccupation with paranoia and eminent destruction. *Dr. Strangelove, or How I Learned to Stop Worrying and Love the Bomb* (the official satirical and long-winded title), Stanley Kubrick's classic dark comedy, uses absurdity to laugh our collective way through an accidental nuclear Armageddon. The director employs hilariously demented, selfish, and frequently sex-crazed presidents, generals, and nuclear physicists to drive home his argument that the arms race and nuclear deterrence theory was the height of irrationality. The overall message is clear: the dominant theory of nuclear deterrence, MAD (Mutually Assured Destruction)—which was based on human rationality and assumed that states would not strike first because world destruction was assured when the other state responded with its own nuclear attack—was itself "mad." Those in charge of nuclear weapons in *Dr. Strangelove* are hardly rational actors.

Kubrick's landmark movie tells the story of General Jack D. Ripper (Sterling Hayden), commander of the Strategic Air Command, who launches a first strike on the Soviet Union. Ripper believes that the Soviets are responsible for his sexual dysfunction, and also sees the fluoridation of water as a vast communist conspiracy. He takes it upon himself to give the order to attack the Soviets, bypassing the President of the United States and the seemingly established chain of command. Along the way, a number of characters sweeten the plot with their belligerence, bullheadedness, and testosterone, among them General "Buck" Turgidson (George C. Scott) and Major T.J. "King" Kong (Slim Pickens). Other key political actors in the film determining the fate of mankind are just plain dimwitted (Keenan Wynn as Colonel "Bat" Guano) or just too darn calm, egg-headed, or intellectual, given the tense circumstances (Peter Sellers as both U.S. President Merkin Muffley

DEALING WITH DOOMSDAY: THE MILITARY, NUCLEAR WAR AND *DR. STRANGELOVE*

After viewing *Dr. Strangelove*, consider these essential questions that connect Cold War politics, nuclear deterrence theory, and Stanley Kubrick's landmark film:

Cite at least four major political developments/events from 1917–1962 that caused distrust and frayed relations between the US and the USSR.

What is "MAD"?

Cite the major players in "The War Room" and at Burpelson Air Force base, and identify the real life political-military figures who inspired the character Dr. Strangelove.

Citing specific examples from the movie, how do you believe Stanley Kubrick's film directly reflects "popular uneasiness about science and technology, as well as growing fears of an arms race escalating out of control?"*

What is *Dr. Strangelove's* view of realism, nuclear deterrence, and the rationality of our top military leaders?

What other film from 1964 deals with a nuclear Armageddon—and in what fundamental ways (i.e., in style and substance) does it differ from *Dr. Strangelove?*

*Paul Boyer, "Dr. Strangelove," in *Past Imperfect: History According to the Movies,* Mark C. Carnes, ed. (New York: Owl Books, 1996), 266–269.

and British Group Captain Lionel Mandrake). Dr. Strangelove (Peter Sellers, in his *third* role in the film!) is a nuclear physicist and former Nazi who now advises the Pentagon on U.S. nuclear policy.

The character "Dr. Strangelove" represents a clear connection between history and Hollywood, as the character is a composite of three vital players in Cold War politics and nuclear deterrence: Henry Kissinger, Edward Teller, and Wehrner von Braun.[10] Kissinger, author of the realist-driven treatises *Nuclear Weapons and Foreign Policy* (1957) and *The Necessity for Choice* (1961), among others, was Richard Nixon's top foreign policy adviser, and one of the chief architects of U.S. nuclear strategy from the late 1950s through the1970s, serving as Nixon's National Security Adviser and, later, as Secretary of State in the Ford administration. Teller oversaw the development and testing of the first hydrogen bomb in 1952 at the University of California's Lawrence Livermore Radiation Laboratory, and used his clout to push for the unimpeded expansion of the United States' nuclear arsenal. In addition, he fiercely opposed the Limited Nuclear Test Ban Treaty of 1963. Von Braun was a rocket technician for Hitler's Nazi regime and later worked for the U.S., where he was eventually stationed in Huntsville, Alabama, "directing more than one hundred German scientists and engineers with whom he had worked in Hitler's day."[11] But that is not the end of the real world political parallels of the film. The bizarre, impotent, and paranoid Gen. Ripper is patterned after the renowned hawk and one-time head of the Strategic Air Command, Curtis LeMay. During the Cuban Missile Crisis in October 1962, LeMay promoted a preemptive air strike against the missile sites followed by a full-scale invasion. Running as George Wallace's vice presidential nominee on the American Independent Party ticket in 1968, LeMay suggested that he would "bomb North Vietnam back to the Stone Age" if elected.[12]

The topic—and conclusion—of the film may be the senseless annihilation of the world at the hands of delusional, irrational men, but Kubrick's sardonic take on Cold War superpower strategies provides a way to both critique the dominant theories shaping foreign policy and laugh at the absurdity of the irrational human condition. As great mushroom clouds encompass the globe after Slim Pickens' Major "King" Kong guides and rides (yes, rides) a nuclear missile to its final destination, we hear Vera Lynn's sugary, comforting crooning of the standard "We'll Meet Again"—"a 1939 song indelibly associated with England's heroic stand during World War II."[13] *Dr. Strangelove* is both a political statement *and* a way to laugh through the omnipresent fear and madness of a nuclear doomsday . . . what more could one possibly hope for in a film?

POWER BROKER, PEACEMAKER, OR ... WAR CRIMINAL?

The Trials of Henry Kissinger

The Trials of Henry Kissinger (2002), directed by Eugene Jarecki, written by Alex Gibney, and based on the book *The Trial of Henry Kissinger* by journalist Christopher Hitchens, offers a major reassessment of the legacy of Richard Nixon National Security Adviser and Gerald Ford's Secretary of State, Henry Kissinger.

Utilizing interviews from international law experts, Kissinger critics, and CIA operatives, declassified documents, archival footage, and evidence from historical record, *Trials* offers a damning appraisal of Kissinger's actions, suggesting that the lauded scholar, power-broker, businessman, and Nobel Laureate might also be, at worst, a war criminal, or at best, a duplicitous, selfish, cynical politico who knowingly carried out unsavory actions and assassinations in direct violation of U.S. and international law.

Specifically, *Trials* reviews Kissinger's behavior during the 1968 Paris peace talks between the U.S., North Vietnam, and South Vietnam, and examines his roles in the "secret" bombing of Cambodia, the U.S.-engineered coup of Chile's popularly elected socialist president, Salvador Allende; and Indonesia's military incursion into East Timor.

Fail Safe, on the other hand, is a much more serious examination of a potential unintentional nuclear war. While both *Fail Safe* and *Dr. Strangelove* are based on the same nuclear war novel—Peter George's *Two Hours to Doom* (published in Britain under the author's pseudonym Peter Bryant)—and deal with inadvertent nuclear holocaust, their similarities end there.[14] In the film, through a series of computer and human errors, as well as miscalculations, the United States mistakenly launches a nuclear attack against the Soviet Union. Before the situation can be rectified, the bombers on their way to Moscow have crossed the fail-safe line and cannot be called back. The Soviets, of course, have no choice but to retaliate, even if they are convinced that the attack is a mistake. Moral questions abound, but one of the most poignant is, can you trade New York for Moscow? In the end, the two sides cannot solve the problem, and each is forced into attempting to destroy the other side.

Despite the effectiveness of both *Dr. Strangelove* and *Fail Safe,* when it comes to depicting the overwhelming horror of nuclear war, these commercial films pale in comparison to a British film made about the same time. The film *The War Game* (1965) describes the effects of a nuclear attack on a typical English town. So devastating and disturbing were the scenes in the film that the film was never shown on television as it was meant to be, and played on a limited number of screens. The film, running a mere forty-five minutes, is shot as if it is a documentary. It draws on the experiences of Hiroshima and Nagasaki, as places that were destroyed by nuclear weapons, and also cities like Dresden and Hamburg, which suffered from severe firebombing, to project what an attack on Britain would look like. In describing the probable aftermath of a nuclear attack, the filmmakers do not pull away from some of the most gruesome events. Children are shown with burnt retinas, firefighters are pulled into burning structures by the 100-mile per hour winds of a firestorm, individuals with severe burns who have no chance of recovery are shot rather than allowed to suffer without medicine, and food riots break out among the survivors. In the end, *The War Game* is perhaps one of the most memorable and frightening films ever made. The film does not shy away from raising question about the public's ignorance, nor does it dress up the potential horrors of a nuclear war to allay the fears of a middle-class audience.

As the anti-nuclear movement gained momentum in the 1980s, the motion picture industry reflected the sentiment. A subtler commentary on nuclear weaponry is found in the documentary film *Atomic Café* (1982). This film used archival footage juxtaposed with American propaganda films and newsreels with no commentary to chronicle the history and development of nuclear weaponry in the 1940s and 1950s. The film begins with the first four nuclear detonations of atomic bombs: the Trinity Test in New Mexico, the bombings of Hiroshima and Nagasaki, Japan, and the test at Bikini Atoll in the South Pacific. U.S. Army information films describe the test at Bikini Atoll as a test to determine the effects of the weapon. The inhabitants of Bikini Atoll were relocated from the island by the United States government, and the film "records" the meeting at which the move is discussed. The scene however, uses the actual footage to reveal that the meeting was staged for the cameras.

Later, the film examines the dangers of radiation after a detonation. U.S. government films assure soldiers that the radiation after a blast is of minimal danger and that it is perfectly safe to conduct maneuvers in the wake of an atomic blast. The audience sees soldiers talking about getting a mouth full of dust as the concussion shock washes over their bunkers. The residents of a small town in Utah receive a dose of radiation as wind directions change after a test. The residents are told to stay inside for one hour and the danger will pass. The point of the film and newsreels is to downplay the risk of radiation. However the next scene shows the effect of radiation on pigs exposed to a blast. Pigs are deformed, burned, and suffer from debilitating deformities. Taken as a whole, the film compiled in *Atomic Café* paint a picture of ignorance among the mass population about the effect of nuclear weapons and serves as a cautionary tale about relying solely on governmental information about issues that have an important impact on society.

The most famous of the films during this period was the TV movie, "The Day After" (1983). The film hypothetically explored the effects of a nuclear attack on Lawrence, Kansas. Unfortunately, the message of the films seems to get lost in some of the sentimental contrivances of the story. The British counterpart to "The Day After" was "Threads" (1986). "Threads" examined the long-term effects of an attack on a Northern English town. The film follows generations following the war and emphasizes the environmental impact and genetic mutations that are a result of radiation. Other films during the period, such as *War Games* (1983) and *When the Wind Blows* (1986), reflected similar concerns. While this type of film reached a climax in the mid-1980s, the elevation of Mikhail Gorbachev to the General-Secretary of the Communist Party of the Soviet Union dramatically changed world politics. The end of the Cold War greatly reduced the attention that the potential of a nuclear war received.

Civil and Ethnic Conflicts

As some scholars have pointed out, war between major powers since the Second World War have virtually ceased. In fact, no wars between major powers have occurred since 1945. Interstate wars are seemingly on the decline as well. Of the 185 wars that occurred between 1946 and 1999, only about a quarter were interstate wars.[15] What has been on the rise is the number of civil conflicts, often times centered on ethnic, religious or racial politics. The civil conflicts during the late 20th century proved to be complicated and in some cases particularly brutal. Ethnic conflicts between Hutus and Tutsis in Rwanda during the spring of 1994 cost an estimated 800,000 to 1,000,000 persons their lives. Countries such as Angola and Guatemala experienced civil conflicts that lasted for decades. While these types of conflict are not new, their predomination of the international system puts strains on mechanisms and institutions that were designed to prevent interstate conflicts rather than intrastate conflicts.

Before the Rain

During the 1990s the United States conducted two air campaigns in an effort to have some effect on the wars in Bosnia and Kosovo. The effects of ethnic strife and the problems of the intermixing of ethnic groups, which are cast as ancient rivalries, remain a problem in that region. The film, *Before the Rain* (1994), is told in circular dramatic form, so that the audience comes into the story and is taken around the narrative, which in this film begins and ends in Macedonia. The film also takes us through London as well, and brings us back to the original point in the story. The impression is that the director, Milcho Manchevski, is making a statement that ethnic conflict transcends time and place and affects individuals not even directly related to the conflict. The film is dramatic and, at times, disturbing.

The story is told in three chapters, the first being called "Words." It opens at an Orthodox monastery in Macedonia where a young priest who has taken a vow of silence finds a young Albanian Muslim girl hiding in his quarters. He feeds the girl, but cannot understand her because he does not understand Bosnian, and to complicate communication, he does not speak at all. Soon men from the surrounding village, tracking the girl who they accuse of murdering a man in the village, come to search for her. They search the monastery, do not immediately find her, but still believe her to be hiding within the walls. The men take up positions around the monastery so that the girl cannot leave without their knowledge. Meanwhile that night, the fathers enter the young priest's quarters to find the girl in his quarters. They order the priest to leave, so after the villagers get drunk and fall asleep, the couple departs in the middle of the night. The young priest tells her in Macedonian that his uncle is a famous photographer in London, and that they can live there. Before long, though, the couple is intercepted by the girl's extended family, who beats her for cavorting with Macedonian men and being a whore. They berate her for escalating the tensions between the Albanian and Macedonians, and send the young priest away. But the girl starts to follow him; as she runs after the young Macedonian, her brother opens fire with his machine gun. The young priest holds her as she dies.

The second chapter, "Faces," takes place in London and opens in a photography studio where Anne is surrounded by several photographs, including pictures of the young priest and girl as she is dying in Macedonia. She later meets her lover, the Pulitzer–prize winning photographer Aleksandar, who tells her that he is quitting journalistic photography because he was forced to kill while working in Bosnia. Aleksandar asks Anne to return with him to his hometown in Macedonia, where he believes that ethnic hatred and violence has not yet begun. He hopes to return home to forget the things that he has seen. Anne says that she cannot go with him at that moment and says she might follow later. Aleksandar takes this as a sign that she does not want to be with him and he leaves for his home. Meanwhile, Anne has dinner with her estranged husband, Nick, that night to tell him that she is pregnant and that she wants a divorce. As the conversation proceeds, the camera and customers have their attention fixed on a growing argument between a Muslim waiter and a Serbian customer. The customer is asked to leave and the innocent waiter is fired for having caused a scene (it is at this point that there are some sly references to the situation in Northern Ireland as well). Minutes later, the customer returns with a gun to kill the Muslim and to indiscriminately shoot people in the restaurant. After the gunman leaves, Anne finds the body of Nick in a pool of blood. The clear implication here is that the ethnic conflict in the former Yugoslavia has implications outside of the former Yugoslavia.

The third chapter, "Pictures," follows Aleksandar back to his village in Macedonia. On the way home a soldier on the bus questions him about returning home and tells him that he is mistaken to think that ethnic conflict has not reached Macedonia. When Aleksandar arrives in his village he is confronted by a youth who is carrying an automatic weapon. Aleksandar's training as a war photojournalist allows him to disarm the youth after proving he too is a Macedonian. The villagers are initially suspicious of him, but as he frequents his extended family he comes to gain the respect of the villagers. Aleksandar makes a visit to the Muslim Albanian village to renew acquaintance with his old sweetheart Hana, who is recently widowed. He finds the lines between the two villages severely drawn and as he enters the Albanian village gunmen stop him while word is sent to Hana's family of his wish to visit. He has tea with Hana's father who describes the problems between the two sides; Hana barely acknowledges Aleksandar in the house and her son is openly hostile towards him. Aleksandar returns to his village more depressed and we find out how his camera killed a person in Bosnia. Early one morning Hana comes to him and says that her daughter is missing and is being held by some Macedonian men in the village. Hana asks Aleksandar to intervene. Apparently Hana's daughter has been used for sexual gratification by some of the Macedonian men and she has killed one of her attackers, Aleksandar's cousin Zdrave. Aleksandar frees the girl, but as they are moving away Aleksandar's extended family gun him down. The film ends with Hana's daughter running into the monastery, the scene that opened the film.

Ethnic Conflict

Many of the films about the wars in the former Yugoslavia have employed a circular storytelling style, similar to *Before the Rain,* to describe the violence in the Balkans. In addition to *Before the Rain,* a film from Serbia, *Cabaret Balkan* (*Bure Baruta—The Powder Keg*) (1998), uses a similar method. In this very disturbing film, the narrative of the film relies on the ramblings of a cabaret performer to link the stories together. The performer discusses how those who live outside of the Balkans look down on those who live in the Balkans, while commenting on the absurdity of life and the beauty of death. The depiction of life in Belgrade on a winter night in the mid-1990s has all of the characters on edge and ready to explode, as depicted in the film's original title, *The Powder Keg*. A taxi driver transports people to meet their fate, death and chaos. A Muslim teenager hits a professional Serbs' cherished VW and the Serb goes on a violent tirade. He tracks the teenager down to his house and takes his revenge out on his father's apartment. A boxer murders his best friend after his friend confesses that he has had an affair with the boxer's wife. The taxi driver encounters the policeman he had beaten so badly that the policeman could barely function. The taxi driver had beaten the policeman because the policeman had pulled him out of a car when he was making love to his girlfriend and beaten him so badly that he became sterile. The only comedy in the film is black, and the film exudes a negative and dark energy.

The film *Bloody Sunday* (2002) examines the events of January 30, 1972 in Derry, Northern Ireland, which would come to be known as "Bloody Sunday." On that day, Catholic protestors gathered to protest the new British policy of detaining Roman Catholics in the province of Northern Ireland without trial. Before the day was over, there was a confrontation between some of the marchers and British paratroopers. The confrontation resulted in 13 marchers being killed and 14 in the hospital (one would die later). Although no British soldiers were killed, an official inquiry later stated that the soldiers had returned the fire of the protestors. The event became a galvanizing episode in the conflict between Catholics and Protestants in Northern Ireland.

The film examines the events of that day in a documentary style. The camera appears to be at the scene, moving within the crowd and capturing the events as they actually happen. To that extent, some of the camera angles are non-conventional and not all the conversations are heard clearly, as if the audience were a part of the event. One of the unfortunate parts of the film is that it does not provide a context to the violence; instead it focuses on the event of those twenty-four hours. However, it is an excellent examination of how sectarian violence comes about.[16]

Ethnic conflict is something that is not usually found in American narrative films. Films like *Billy Jack* (1971) and *Do the Right Thing* (1989) deal with race and ethnicity in a sense, but do not get at the heart of what communities locked in hatred and violence mean when genocide is attempted. One American film that does deal with the wars in former Yugoslavia is *Welcome to Sarajevo* (1997), which deals with the horrors of the war in Bosnia, much in the same way *Before the Rain* deals with the complexity of ethnic relations in Macedonia. However, overall American films that deal with genocide are limited to films such as *Holocaust* (1978) and *Schindler's List* (1993). Yet, dealing with ethnic conflict in places like Rwanda and the former Yugoslavia has been somewhat limited in the American cinema.

Terrorism

The horrific events of September 11, 2001 may demonstrate a new level of unconventional political violence. In an event that has had a transforming effect on American society, the brutality and random violence that is associated with terrorism was brought home to American soil. Four jet planes were hijacked: two of them were flown into the World Trade Center in New York City, destroying the seemingly invincible tower of steel and international commerce; one was smashed into the nerve center of the American defense establishment, the Pentagon; and another, also en route to Washington, D.C., crashed near Somerset, Pennsylvania, just outside of Pittsburgh. Roughly 3,000 people lost their lives. Of course this was not the first time a major terrorist bombing had occurred on American soil: On April 19, 1995 the Alfred P. Murrah Federal Building in Oklahoma City was destroyed by a truck bomb, killing 168 people. Timothy McVeigh, a Gulf War veteran and associate of the Michigan Militia, was ultimately convicted of the crime. Terry Nichols, an associate of McVeigh's, was also connected to the terrorist attack and convicted. That attack was a case of domestic terrorism, but the events of September 11, 2001 represent a case of international terrorism. Regardless of the distinction between domestic and international terrorism, the results are the same: innocents are killed and in the aftermath of the event, questions are raised about the nature of society and the strategies used to prevent such cataclysmic acts.

Terrorism is in no way a new phenomenon. Some authors have claimed that as far back as the first century, terrorism has been used to create a situation where no one felt safe.[17] It has not been in the too distant past that some may have even considered terrorism an acceptable form of polit-

ical violence. Even President Ronald Reagan in 1981 in discussing the Contras of Nicaragua argued, "One man's terrorist is another man's freedom fighter."[18] The problem is
some acts that are seen as "justified," can be seen by those
who are the target as terrorism.[19]

Even popular American films have championed the
cause of rebels and saboteurs. The original *Star Wars* trilogy,
comprised of *Star Wars* (1977), *The Empire Strikes Back*
(1980), and *The Return of the Jedi* (1983), is one of the most
famous and popular series in the history of the movies. In
the trilogy, the audience roots for the exploits of Luke Sky-
walker, Princess Leia, and Hans Solo in their fight against
the imperial government and its number one henchman,
Darth Vader. To be sure, the Imperial government does not
hold the moral high ground in the story—in fact, early on
the government destroys the entire planet of Alderaan. Yet,
the trio, along with their allies, uses sabotage, ambush, and
surprise attacks to try to wrest the power of the galaxy away
from the imperial government. Interesting historical parallels can be drawn between them and freedom fighters in
the past. There is no question that most would prefer the
ideals of many freedom fighters over oppressive governments. There seems to be general agreement among people
as to what constitutes terrorism and what constitutes legitimate resistance. However, how does one definitively draw
the line between the two? Scholars have had just as difficult
a time defining terrorism as have policymakers, but one
definition that many people have accepted is by George
Rosie, who defines terrorism as violence intended to have a
target group meet the political demands of the group (or
people) who commit the terrorist act.[20]

The Twilight Zone: "The Monsters Are Due on Maple Street"

The goal of terrorism is not necessarily to kill enough people
to gain a political end, but to use death and violence to scare
(or terrorize) the target population into an action. Hence the
effectiveness of terrorism is found in the ability to get people

to do things with as little action as possible. What this means is that the battle with terrorists often portrayed in such movies as *Invasion U.S.A.* (1985) and *Air Force One* (1997), does not capture the psychological pressure target populations feel. This psychological pressure can lead societies to begin to question the society's core values.

Perhaps one of the best depictions of how fear and terror leads a community to reassess the basic notions of society is contained in one of the most famous episodes of the classic television program, "The Twilight Zone." In the half hour drama, "The Monsters Are Due on Maple Street," the story opens up on Maple Street on a late-afternoon Saturday. The scene on Maple Street mirrors the perceived stereotypes of Americana at the time; people are washing their cars and mowing the grass, while children are playing baseball. Suddenly something passes over the sky and grabs the attention of everyone on the street. The camera remains focused on the street and the reactions of the residents. Thus, the audience cannot evaluate for itself what has flown over in the sky. The viewer relies on the interpretations of the people on Maple Street for the rest of the story.

The initial assumption of the residents is that the object was a meteor. However, if it was a meteor, then it was one with special property. After it passes over, most of the conveniences of modern life cease to work. Various residents report that electricity, telephones, radios, automobiles, and lawnmowers have stopped working. This causes great consternation among the residents, because while they understand the electricity of telephones may have been knocked out, it seems to make no sense that the automobiles or portable radios would stop working as well. One resident, Pete van Horn goes over to Floral Street to see if he can find out anything.

Meanwhile, the residents gather to decide what should be done. Steve (Claude Akins) emerges as a leader and he suggests that he and Charlie walk downtown to see if the police know what was going on. Before they can leave, Steve and Charlie are warned by one of the teenagers not to go: in every story that he has ever read, the monsters who come from outer space want the people to stay where they are. Initially people are dismissive of the teenager's story, but when he starts telling them how the monsters always send a few in advance to pose as humans to prepare the way for an invasion, the residents of Maple Street begin to eye each other suspiciously. No one is allowed to leave the area except the people that were sent down ahead.

Les, who has not come out to see the meteor, comes out to get in his car but it does not start. He comes toward the group, but then Les' car starts on its own, and people begin to suspect Les. Les is considered a real oddball, because he spends some nights in his yard looking up at the star (as if he is waiting for someone). He claims that he has insomnia. Night falls and people are still suspicious of Les, but suspicions shift as people find out that Steve uses a ham radio (questions of who he is talking to is raised).

As the residents trade suspicions and accusations, a shadowy figure begins walking up Maple Street toward the residents. Someone yells, "It's the monster!" Charlie grabs a gun and shoots the figure, which falls to ground. The residents run down to get a good look at the monster only to find that Charlie has shot Pete van Horn, who had gone over to Floral Street to see if they had any power there. Charlie is accused by the group, which is fast becoming a mob, of preventing Pete from telling the residents what was going on or warning them who the monster was. Mayhem ensues. The final scenes of the show have the residents fighting and killing one another. As the camera pans up from a Maple Street littered with bodies and debris, the camera has in the foreground two figures standing on a hillside overlooking the rioting:

FIGURE 1

Understand the procedure now? Just stop a few of their machines, and radios, and telephone, or lawn mowers . . . Throw them into darkness for a few hours and then sit back and watch the pattern.

FIGURE 2
And this pattern is always the same?

FIGURE 1
With few variations, they pick the most dangerous enemy they can find, and it's themselves. All we need do is sit back and watch.

FIGURE 2
Then I take it this place, this Maple Street, is not unique?

FIGURE 1
By no means. Their world is full of Maple Streets. And we'll go from one to another and let them destroy themselves.

One of the hallmarks of *The Twilight Zone* was the commentary offered at the end of the program by the show's creator, Rod Sterling. Sterling, who was also the author of this particular episode, offered the following commentary:

> The tools of conquest do not necessarily come from bomb and explosives and fallout. There are weapons that are simply thoughts, attitudes, prejudices to be found only in the minds of men. For the record, prejudices can kill, and suspicion can destroy, and the thoughtless, frightened search for a scapegoat has a fallout all of its own . . . for the children and the children yet unborn. And the pity of it is that these things cannot be confined to the Twilight Zone.

Perhaps one of the casualties of any society that has suffered a terrorist attack is its self-confidence. The task is to resist the temptation of undermining the fundamental values of a society. It is a difficult task, but part of surviving and persevering through a terrorist attack is to maintain one's way of life and one's values.

The Sum of All Fears

In the aftermath of the September 11 attacks, some films that were in production in Hollywood at the time seemed all the more poignant. *The Sum of All Fears* (2002), based upon the 1991 novel by Tom Clancy, fell into this category. Following the exploits of Clancy hero Jack Ryan (played by Ben Affleck), the story examines the possibility of a terrorist attack using nuclear weapons on the homeland of the United States. The plot of the movie, which has been widely criticized as impossible,[21] has the United States and Russia duped into confronting each other in a nuclear war by a neo-fascist terrorist. The premise is that a re-emergent fascist state in Europe would survive after the two superpowers take each other out. The mysterious fascist, played by Alan Bates, is able to acquire a nuclear weapon after it had been found in a forgotten Israeli jet crash from the Yom Kippur War in 1973. This is another point of contention, because most analysts doubt whether Israel would have left a missing nuclear weapon buried in the sand for thirty years

The important aspect of this film is the possibility of having a nuclear weapon smuggled into the United States. While Israeli bombs may not be buried in the sands of the deserts of the Middle East, there is evidence to suggest that some nuclear warheads from the arsenal of the former Soviet Union may be missing. The plot of *The Sum of All Fears* relies on Cold War fears and stereotypes to fuel the story. However, what should be considered is the possibility that a nuclear, biological, or chemical weapon can be smuggled into any country, even the United States, virtually undetected and detonated with very little, if any, warning.

Conclusion

Foreign and domestic films, from dramas and documentaries to cartoons to comedies, reveal a number of vital concepts and theories in international relations, among them: sovereignty, anarchy, the security dilemma, realism, and liberalism. In addition to shedding light on these fundamental ideas, the movies reviewed in this chapter illustrate how different wars in different times shape our view of the nature and effect of war itself. How war has been portrayed over the last ninety years is, in part, a reflection of international politics and realities of specific eras. For example, films that had the First World War as the major subject usually portrayed war as senseless and destructive. On the other hand, films about World War II focused on just causes and how cooperation could be achieved. The introduction of nuclear weaponry also changed how war was portrayed. In the nuclear age, just causes seemed to take a back seat to questions of survival. In addition, with other wars—such as America's foray into Vietnam—film continued to look at the devastating consequences of war, focusing on the plight of civilians caught in the crossfire. With the passing of the Cold War the attention of the cinema, particularly the European cinema, turned toward ethnic conflicts. In the wake of the terrorist attacks of September 11, 2001, American cinema will surely turn toward more films about terrorism and unconventional political violence as filmmakers and citizens alike continue to grapple with the causes, consequences, and morality of war.

CHAPTER 8

Special Topics

The Interplay between International and Domestic Politics

One of the chief goals of *Seeing the Bigger Picture* has been to show how film can be used to explain political concepts and shed light on political institutions and debates in the U.S. and around the globe. We believe that film and television can provide us with ample food for thought, questions to answer, and dilemmas to solve. On this journey through politics and film it is impossible to adequately discuss every salient topic and relevant film. Therefore, in this final chapter, "Special Topics," we will briefly touch upon some of the other domestic and international dynamics that warrant our attention and that have been explored in film and television. In that endeavor, we now present a small sampling of films (and suggested discussion questions and assignments) that examine the media, the environment, the death penalty, human rights, genocide, and colonialism.

The Media: Private Profit or Public Interest? *Network* and *All the President's Men*

Network (1976)

> Ladies and gentleman, I would like at this moment to announce that I will be retiring in two weeks' time because of poor ratings . . . and since this show is the only thing I had going for me in my life, I have decided to kill myself. I'm going to blow my brains out right on this program a week from today. So tune in next Tuesday. That'll give the public relations people a week to promote the show. That ought to get a hell of a rating, a fifty share easy.[1]
>
> — Howard Beale, UBS anchorman and "Mad Prophet of the Airwaves" (*Network,* 1976)

Sidney Lumet's classic tale of television gone mad (and we mean, *really, really* mad!), *Network* (1976), chronicles the descent of responsible, enlightened television journalism into the revolting, obnoxious swamp of entertainment, titillation, violence, ratings, and greed.[2] The deterioration of a once-venerated institution has been triggered—and accelerated—by the mergers of giant multinational corporations hell-bent on maximizing profits, no matter the cost to civility, truth, and public discourse. Whatever will increase ratings and generate advertising dollars—whether it's ranting lunatics, live terrorism, or palm readers—is what will go on the air.

Paddy Chayefsky's prophetic screenplay, winner of the 1976 Academy Award, brilliantly satirizes the brave new world of international mega-corporate television and those that make it tick. In *Network,* the chief villains who turn the

FAYE WILLIAM PETER ROBERT
DUNAWAY HOLDEN FINCH DUVALL NETWORK

It's a Mad, Mad, Mad, Mad Media World! Robert Duvall (back row, left) and William Holden (back row, center) are among the stars in *Network* (1976), Sidney Lumet's cautionary tale of corporate interests, ratings, and profits run amok.

news division of UBS (United Broadcasting System) upside down in the hunt for a ratings winner and deeper profits are UBS Vice President of Programming, Diana Christensen (Faye Dunaway) and Frank Hackett, UBS Executive Senior Vice President/Chairman of the Board (Robert Duvall). And although he has become emotionally unhinged and now spends his time ranting and raving—and telling everyone to put their head out the window and yell "I'm as mad as hell, and I'm not going to take it anymore!"—former UBS anchorman Howard Beale is somewhat of a hero here, as, even in his state of dementia, he understands the inordinate power of television in this modern age. In his new role as "Mad Prophet of the Airwaves" on his own show—*The Howard Beale Show*—Beale articulates the danger of relying on television for reality, deeper truths, and meaning:

There is a whole and entire generation right now who never knew anything that didn't come out of this tube. This tube is the gospel. This tube is the ultimate revelation. This tube can make or break presidents, popes, and prime ministers. This tube is the most awesome goddam force in the whole godless world! And woe is us if it ever falls in the hands of the wrong people. . . .

and when the twelfth largest company in the world controls the most awesome goddam propaganda force in the whole godless world, who knows what shit will be peddled for truth on this tube? So listen to me! Television is not the truth! Television is a goddamned amusement park. Television is a circus, a carnival, a traveling troupe of acrobats and story-tellers, singers and dancers, jugglers, sideshow freaks, lion-tamers and football players. We're in the boredom-killing business! If you want truth go to God, go to your guru, go to yourself because that's the only place you'll ever find any real truth. But man, you're never going to get any truth from us. We'll tell you anything you want to hear. We lie like hell![3]

Chayefsky's over-the-top, in-your-face critique of the brave new world of television ratings obsession, profit maximization, media monopolies, and the mega-multinational conglomerate Wizards of Oz behind the curtain directing the show, presents us with a sobering and depressing dilemma in a political system such as ours. To be informed, enlightened citizens and voters, we must rely on a vigilant, responsible media with some sense of the public interest to give us the tools to participate and make thoughtful decisions. But what if the media has little to no interest in the public interest? What if the quest for private profits substantially outweighs any concern for the accuracy or the health of the republic? In a world of *Survivor, Joe Millionaire, COPS, World's Most Dangerous Animals,* and entertaining, competitive, and often superficial "shout shows" on cable news networks that all too often pass for deliberative political discussions, how do we further the public interest and inform, rather than merely entertain, our citizenry? In the final analysis, the hyperactive, unhinged Howard Beale of *Network* just may be right. But an "amusement park" is hardly a solid foundation on which to build an informed, engaged citizenry and a robust democracy.

All the President's Men (1976)

As an alternative to *Network*, *All the President's Men* presents a much more flattering depiction of the media. Made in the same year as *Network*, *All the President's Men* chronicles *Washington Post* reporters Carl Bernstein (Dustin Hoffman) and Bob Woodward (Robert Redford) as they uncover the political scandal known as Watergate. The film follows their investigative reporting exploits from the break-in at the Democratic National Committee Headquarters at the Watergate office building in June 1972, and the arrest of the burglars, to the eventual resignation of President Richard Nixon in August 1974. The contrast between the two films' portrayal of the media could not be more dramatic. While *Network* depicts the media as increasingly controlled by dominant, ruthless corporations unconcerned with truth or the public interest, *All the President's Men* presents dogged reporters who are overly concerned with arriving at the truth and getting verification of their story. Indeed, on more than one occasion, the crusty, sage editor of the *Post*, Ben Bradlee (Jason Robards), hounds "Woodstein" (his nickname for Woodward and Bernstein) for more sources and refuses to run some of their Watergate articles. Bradlee demands multiple sources, as he does not want the veracity of his paper to be challenged. As he tells his ace reporters, *"There's nothing at stake here except the Constitution and the Presidency of the United States."* Simply put, this is serious, serious business, and since the media can have an awesome effect on pubic opinion and political institutions, the press *must* go the extra mile for accuracy.

In contrast to the heroic portrayal of Woodward and Bernstein—and the institution of the press in general—the film portrays the government, politicians, and political players in a very dark and shadowy light. For example, the pressroom at the *Post* is perpetually bathed in brightness,

The media and the public interest: Bob Woodward (Robert Redford) and Carl Bernstein (Dustin Hoffman) are *Washington Post* reporters hot on the trail of the Watergate scandal in *All the President's Men* (1976).

whereas the corridors of power and national monuments in Washington, D.C. are almost always shot in the dark. Thus, the government is frequently presented as an ominous institution where no one can be trusted and the depth of corruption is unimaginable. In contrast, the reporters are saviors, shedding light on corruption and exposing the illegal chicanery and dirty tricks at the heart of Watergate.[4] Here we see responsible media clearly acting in the public interest—a far cry from the irresponsible cutthroat greed and corporate madness of *Network*.

Environment

It has only been in the last generation that mainstream public attention has recognized the issue of the environment. In the 1970s it was common for motorists to simply throw

COMPARING MEDIA FILMS: *NETWORK* & *ALL THE PRESIDENT'S MEN* . . . THE ESSENTIALS

Network (1976)
Nominated for the Academy Award for best picture
Directed by Sidney Lumet **nominated, best director**
Written by Paddy Chayefsky ** BEST SCREENPLAY**

Starring: William Holden as Max Schumacher, UBS President of News Division **nominated, best actor**; Peter Finch as Howard Beale, News anchorman **BEST ACTOR**; Faye Dunaway as Diana Christensen, UBS Vice President of Programming **BEST ACTRESS**; Robert Duvall as Frank Hackett, UBS Executive Senior Vice President/Chairman of the Board; Ned Beatty as Arthur Jensen, Owner UBS **nominated, best supporting actor**

All the President's Men (1976)
Nominated for the Academy Award for best picture
Won Academy Awards for BEST SOUND; BEST ART DIRECTION/SET DECORATION
Directed by Alan J. Pakula **nominated, best director**
Written by William Goldman **BEST ADAPTED SCREENPLAY**
Based on the book *All the President's Men* by Carl Bernstein and Bob Woodward
Starring: Robert Redford as Bob Woodward; Dustin Hoffman as Carl Bernstein; Jason Robards as Ben Bradlee, Executive Editor of *Washington Post* **BEST SUPPORTING ACTOR**; Jack Warden as Harry M. Rosenfeld, Metro Editor of *Washington Post;* Hal Holbrook as Deep Throat

Suggested Reading:

Bob Woodward and Carl Bernstein, *All the President's Men;* Bob Woodward and Carl Bernstein, *The Final Days*

Related Films:

For a psychological profile of Nixon, from childhood through Watergate, see Oliver Stone's controversial presidential psychohistory *Nixon* (1995) . . . Anthony Hopkins portrays President Nixon.

For a comedic, over-the-top, and purposely absurd retelling of Watergate — from the point of view of innocent teens Kirstin Dunst and Michelle Williams — see Dan Hedaya as Richard Nixon in *Dick* (1999).

TWO VIEWS OF THE MEDIA: COMPARING *NETWORK* AND *ALL THE PRESIDENT'S MEN*

Watch *Network* (1976) and *All the President's Men* (1976). Then, taking each film one at a time, consider the following questions:

- What are the key issues, dilemmas, and political events at the heart of each film? Who are the heroes and villains, and why? In answering these questions, be sure to also cite the key characters and the actors in each film.

- Compare and contrast the portrayal of the media in the two films, using specific scenes, quotes, etc., to illustrate the positive and negative aspects of print and television media. With which portrayal of the media do you most agree and why?

- According to *Network,* what are the consequences of media mergers and the struggle for profit in corporate America? What are the consequences for public interest, civility, and the body politic?

- Look at a couple of articles from the *Columbia Journalism Review* web site below, connect the issues raised in *Network* to the state of media mergers and ownership today. Were *Network's* criticisms of the modern corporate media accurate? If yes, how? If no, why not? Lastly, cite the relevance of the 1996 Telecommunications Act to the issues raised in *Network.* (Consult the web and the CJR for information on the 1996 act.)
http://www.cjr.org/
http://www.cjr.org/year/98/4/moneylust.asp

- What are some of the criticisms that have been raised about *All the President's Men*?

- After viewing the film, where do you stand on such criticisms?

their trash out the window when finished. Public awareness began to be raised primarily over the beauty and aesthetics of the environment. This concern led to one of the most famous and effective public service announcements (PSA) ever broadcast on American television. In a spot entitled "Crying Indian" a Native American, portrayed by Iron Eyes Cody, paddles up a polluted stream, past smoke stacks

...ne on Earth has a ...al temperature is at ...that life on Earth is ...and vegetable, his col- ...ssed wafers that serve as ...s on Earth order the project's ...Perhaps in another commen- ...panions in an effort to disguise his ...east one of the forests. He sends a ...eriors that he has had problems and ...n the forest. The implication is that he ...o make it look as if his ship has been de- ...he denotation destroys the ships. He ma- ...Once he has saved a forest, Lowell has diffi- ...to the solitude of a spaceship with no other ...ard. His only companions are two robots, re- ...wey and Dewey (Louie was destroyed during his ...his loneliness leads him to neglect caring for the for- ...t begins to die. Meanwhile, search ships begin con- ...Lowell for a rescue. Ultimately, Lowell realizes that he ...realizes that the lack of light has caused the problems in ...sacrifice himself if the forest is to survive without him. ...e forest, and he instructs Hewey how to care for the forest. ...Lowell then disengages his ship and detonates nuclear weap- ...ons to destroy himself.

In some ways the film is very dated. Folk singer Joan Baez's song in the middle of the film singing "Earth... between my toes and a flower in my hair / That's what... wearing when we laid among the ferns," will s... some snickers among modern audiences... ning is still a cautionary tale calling the... to the need for biodiversity. Bruce... prevent the extinction of eve... sets up an interesting co... guments about sa... around having...

that trees are no longer necessary. Every
job, there is plenty of food, and the glob
a constant 75 degrees. Lowell retorts
bland; while he enjoys fresh fruits
leagues are content to eat preproce
their subsistence.

Lowell mutinies when official
termination and destruction.
tary, the ships are destroyed
ends up killing his two com
attempts to preserve at
message out to his sup
cannot disconnect fro
will be killed when th
neuvers the ships
stroyed as well.
culty adjusting
humans abo
named Hew
mutiny). H
est and i
tacting
must
He
th

have
the prob

Silent Running

Films of the late 1960s a
mental issues, but did so in a
mes without the complexity of th
at at least attempted to make a
the problems is *Silent Running* (1
pletely in outer space. Several shi
et Saturn, loaded with what is le
st, Freeman Lowell, played by
e preservation of these envi-
anions and co-workers,
mmitted; in fact,
ject, arguing

efit, or provide a certain quality of life. *Silent Running* takes these issues off the table for us. Marty Barker argues in the film that people on Earth all have a job, everyone has more than enough food, the planet is comfortable, and there is plenty of food. There is another way of looking at the construction of this problem as well. By protecting the environment some argue that environmental concerns come at the expense of jobs and development. The film isolates those concerns and asks us if trees, fresh food, and beauty are reasons enough to protect the environment? Are we so concerned with progress and technology, in other words, that we are willing to jettison the things that the forest provides the population?

Soylent Green (1973)

Another film made around the same time addresses the problem of overpopulation and pollution. Starring Charlton Heston and Edward G. Robinson (in his final role), *Soylent Green* (1973) examines the life of a police detective (Heston) in a future New York that has a population of 40 million people. Set in the year 2022, one of the key features of the film is the constant examination of how overpopulation affects the lives of the individuals in the film. One of the key points is that overpopulation has created an upper class that is far removed from the plight of everyday people. Life in this future has people living on stairwells in apartment buildings, cars that are immobilized in the streets with people who live in them, and near-riots at food distribution centers. The Soylent Corporation, the seemingly sole provider of processed food, has a new product that meets the desires of most people—soylent green. Soylent green is so popular that the state is forced to ration it to the population.

Against this background, detective Robert Thorn is sent to investigate the murder, or assassination, of a leading executive of the Soylent Corporation, William Simonson. When Thorn arrives at the apartment he is overwhelmed by the opulence in which Simonson lives. During the investigation, Thorn "helps himself" to a number of items, including fresh meat, apples, and whiskey. He also questions the various people associated with Simonson, including Shirl, a concubine who is "a part of the furniture" in the apartment, and the bodyguard Tab Fielding (played by Chuck Connors), both of whom were out of the building at the time of the murder.

Thorn returns to his own apartment, which he shares with Sol Roth (Edward G. Robinson), and his booty of goods. Sol does research on behalf of Thorn and uses his extensive library to help his work; he remembers a time when the Earth was still beautiful and food was still plentiful. He marvels over the loot Thorn brings home, among which is a book detailing the activities of the Soylent Corporation, a very rare book that very few people have access to.

Thorn's investigation leads to the fact that Simonson had been attending church. Thorn goes to see the priest, Father Paul, who has heard Simonson's confession and is devastated by the information he had received from the confession. The church is completely overwhelmed with large numbers of people living in the church, most of whom are either listless or sick. Some sanctuary is provided to the people living there, but given the state of society it is not much better than the street. Overwhelmed by fatigue and bewilderment, Father Paul asks Thorn to come back later. Before Thorn can return though, Tab Fielding, the former bodyguard of Simonson, murders Father Paul.

Meanwhile, Sol uncovers the secret of the Soylent Corporation, and rather than facing the consequences of the news, Sol elects to be euthanized. Before he dies, Thorn manages to reach Sol, who reveals the great cover-up that has led to so much anguish. Soylent green is made out of people. With the decline of food stocks and the oceans dying, the Soylent Corporation is forced to rely on dead people to help feed the rest of the population.

The warnings of *Soylent Green* are very interesting, especially in a more globalized world: unchecked pollution and population growth have the capability of making an

meat, apples, and whiskey. He also questions the various people associated with Simonson, including Shirl, a concubine who is "a part of the furniture" in the apartment, and the bodyguard Tab Fielding (played by Chuck Connors), both of whom were out of the building at the time of the murder.

Thorn returns to his own apartment, which he shares with Sol Roth (Edward G. Robinson), and his booty of goods. Sol does research on behalf of Thorn and uses his extensive library to help his work; he remembers a time when the Earth was still beautiful and food was still plentiful. He marvels over the loot Thorn brings home, among which is a book detailing the activities of the Soylent Corporation, a very rare book that very few people have access to.

Thorn's investigation leads to the fact that Simonson had been attending church. Thorn goes to see the priest, Father Paul, who has heard Simonson's confession and is devastated by the information he had received from the confession. The church is completely overwhelmed with large numbers of people living in the church, most of whom are either listless or sick. Some sanctuary is provided to the people living there, but given the state of society it is not much better than the street. Overwhelmed by fatigue and bewilderment, Father Paul asks Thorn to come back later. Before Thorn can return though, Tab Fielding, the former bodyguard of Simonson, murders Father Paul.

Meanwhile, Sol uncovers the secret of the Soylent Corporation, and rather than facing the consequences of the news, Sol elects to be euthanized. Before he dies, Thorn manages to reach Sol, who reveals the great cover-up that has led to so much anguish. Soylent green is made out of people. With the decline of food stocks and the oceans dying, the Soylent Corporation is forced to rely on dead people to help feed the rest of the population.

The warnings of *Soylent Green* are very interesting, especially in a more globalized world: unchecked pollution and population growth have the capability of making an

efit, or provide a certain quality of life. *Silent Running* takes these issues off the table for us. Marty Barker argues in the film that people on Earth all have a job, everyone has more than enough food, the planet is comfortable, and there is plenty of food. There is another way of looking at the construction of this problem as well. By protecting the environment some argue that environmental concerns come at the expense of jobs and development. The film isolates those concerns and asks us if trees, fresh food, and beauty are reasons enough to protect the environment? Are we so concerned with progress and technology, in other words, that we are willing to jettison the things that the forest provides the population?

Soylent Green (1973)

Another film made around the same time addresses the problem of overpopulation and pollution. Starring Charlton Heston and Edward G. Robinson (in his final role), *Soylent Green* (1973) examines the life of a police detective (Heston) in a future New York that has a population of 40 million people. Set in the year 2022, one of the key features of the film is the constant examination of how overpopulation affects the lives of the individuals in the film. One of the key points is that overpopulation has created an upper class that is far removed from the plight of everyday people. Life in this future has people living on stairwells in apartment buildings, cars that are immobilized in the streets with people who live in them, and near-riots at food distribution centers. The Soylent Corporation, the seemingly sole provider of processed food, has a new product that meets the desires of most people—soylent green. Soylent green is so popular that the state is forced to ration it to the population.

Against this background, detective Robert Thorn is sent to investigate the murder, or assassination, of a leading executive of the Soylent Corporation, William Simonson. When Thorn arrives at the apartment he is overwhelmed by the opulence in which Simonson lives. During the investigation, Thorn "helps himself" to a number of items, including fresh

pouring out polluted air, and watches as cars on an inter-state throw trash out their windows. As the Native American turns towards the camera, he has a single tear running down his face. A voice over tells the viewer, "People start pollution . . . people can stop it." This PSA probably remains one of the most memorable in American television history, even the Simpsons, almost a quarter of a century later, par-odied the spot.[5]

Of course environmental concerns are more complex than just simply litter. In the times since the beginning of the modern environmental movement, issues have spread to discuss overpopulation, industrial waste, concern about nuclear power, and nature preservation. One of the great problems in dealing with such issues is that they tend to be interrelated. One of the best ways to deal with high popula-tion growth is by encouraging industrial development. In-creasing industrial development, though, also increases the output of industrial pollution. Also, an increasing population requires more land, both for people to live on and for the growing of food to feed an ever-increasing population. Be-cause of the complex interaction between these environ-mental and development issues, narrative feature films have had a difficult time in portraying stories that cover all the problems associated with these issues.

Silent Running (1972)

Films of the late 1960s and early 1970s did address environ-mental issues, but did so in a heavy-handed way and often times without the complexity of the issues that are due. One film that at least attempted to make allusions to the com-plexity of the problems is *Silent Running* (1972). The film takes place completely in outer space. Several ships are in orbit around the planet Saturn, loaded with what is left of Earth's trees. One scientist, Freeman Lowell, played by Bruce Dern, is committed to the preservation of these envi-ronmental assets. Lowell's two companions and co-workers, John Keenan and Marty Barker, are less committed; in fact, Keenan and Barker are contemptuous of the project, arguing that trees are no longer necessary. Everyone on Earth has a job, there is plenty of food, and the global temperature is at a constant 75 degrees. Lowell retorts that life on Earth is bland; while he enjoys fresh fruits and vegetable, his colleagues are content to eat preprocessed wafers that serve as their subsistence.

Lowell mutinies when officials on Earth order the project's termination and destruction. Perhaps in another commentary, the ships are destroyed with nuclear weapons. Lowell ends up killing his two companions in an effort to disguise his attempts to preserve at least one of the forests. He sends a message out to his superiors that he has had problems and cannot disconnect from the forest. The implication is that he will be killed when the denotation destroys the ships. He maneuvers the ships to make it look as if his ship has been destroyed as well. Once he has saved a forest, Lowell has difficulty adjusting to the solitude of a spaceship with no other humans aboard. His only companions are two robots, renamed Hewey and Dewey (Louie was destroyed during his mutiny). His loneliness leads him to neglect caring for the forest and it begins to die. Meanwhile, search ships begin contacting Lowell for a rescue. Ultimately, Lowell realizes that he must sacrifice himself if the forest is to survive without him. He realizes that the lack of light has caused the problems in the forest, and he instructs Hewey how to care for the forest. Lowell then disengages his ship and detonates nuclear weapons to destroy himself.

In some ways the film is very dated. Folk singer Joan Baez's song in the middle of the film singing "Earth between my toes and a flower in my hair / That's what I was wearing when we laid among the ferns," will surely draw some snickers among modern audiences. Yet, *Silent Running* is still a cautionary tale calling the audience's attention to the need for biodiversity. Bruce Dern's character wants to prevent the extinction of everything in the forest. The film sets up an interesting conundrum for the audience. Most arguments about saving the environment are constructed around having enough food, or some kind of economic ben-

enormous impact on society. Not only will this impact be in terms of massive degradation for substantial numbers of people and a quality of life in developed countries that is highly undesirable, but also that it creates a widening gap between haves and have-nots and may ultimately lead to the commoditification of humans.

Soylent Green was based on the novel *Make Room! Make Room!* by Harry Harrison.[6] Many people are surprised that Charlton Heston, perhaps better known for his outspoken conservative politics and his presidency of the National Rifle Association in later years, would be committed to a film with such a message. Heston is said to have loved the novel and wanted to bring an adaptation to the screen. He also starred in the 1969 film *The Planet of the Apes,* which was ultimately about the dangers of nuclear weapons. However, what this may illustrate is that concern for environmental policies need not be confined to one side of the political spectrum.

Erin Brockovich (2000)

Perhaps one of the changes in films that deal with the environment since the early 1970s is that more attention has begun to be focused on specific issues rather than all-encompassing epics. An oft-repeated theme is the role of regular citizens and stressed-out lawyers faced with impossible odds while seeking recompense from irresponsible corporations. With a tagline, "She brought a small town to its feet and a huge corporation to its knees," box office smash *Erin Brockovich* (2000), starring Julia Roberts, is an example of this genre. The film, based on a true story, follows the crusading efforts of a down-on-her-luck single mother of three, Erin Brockovich, who battles a behemoth California power company, Pacific Gas & Electric, over their environmental malfeasance. PG&E is accused of polluting the ground water in Hinckley, California.

Working for her crusty-but-lovable lawyer, Ed Masry (Albert Finney), Brockovich begins to learn of the contamination of the small town's water supply, and the debilitating effects it has had on local working class residents. When necessary, Brockovich uses her physical attributes, particularly her cleavage, combined with shrewd maneuvers and creative investigative work to demonstrate that PG&E was guilty of dumping the lethal toxic waste hexavalent chromium into Hinckley's water supply. Through her tenacious investigative work and the support of Masry, Brockovich helps secure a $333 million settlement for the families (and the law firm), a sizable dividend in one of the largest class-action lawsuits in American history. In the end, justice was served; contrary to what many would have believed, the small town lawyer and Brockovich won and PG&E was held accountable for polluting the environment.

The overwhelming success of *Erin Brockovich* proved that, backed by the star power of Julia Roberts, skillful marketing, and some cinematic clichés, most notably a significant romantic subplot, political films can perform very well at the box office. Clearly, many explicitly political films do not—or cannot—offer the budget, entertainment amenities, or eye candy of an *Erin Brockovich*. Though some critics found the David vs. Goliath tale of environmental justice to be a "loose and funny Norma Rae," and praised the script for getting "to the engrossing bare bones of Erin's search for justice"[7]—others sneered at the over-the-top cleavage shots, skimpy clothing and formulaic romantic plot that ran alongside the battle against corporate polluters. One prominent film critic, for example, characterized the screenplay as having the "depth and insight of a cable-TV docudrama."[8] Nonetheless, Roberts' sassy performance and revealing outfits, combined with a compelling tale of pollution and corporate abuse, helped *Erin Brockovich* gross over $125 million in the U.S. and an additional $258 million around the world.[9] In addition to earning Julia Roberts an Oscar for Best Actress, *Erin Brockovich* garnered Academy Award nominations for Albert Finney (Best Supporting Actor) and Steven Soderbergh (Director), and also competed for Best Picture.

A Civil Action (1998)

Another film based on a similar situation is the 1998 film *A Civil Action*. Adapted from the 1995 National Book Critics Circle Award–winning nonfiction novel by Jonathan Harr, and directed by Steven Zaillian, the film was released on Christmas Day, 1998 and featured previous Oscar nominees Robert Duvall, John Travolta, and William H. Macy. James Gandolofini, one year before hitting the mega-big time as New Jersey "family man" Tony Soprano in HBO's cultural phenomenon *The Sopranos,* also added his acting chops to the cinematic effort.

In *A Civil Action*—which is based on real life events outlined in meticulous detail in the bestseller by Harr—the scene of the crime is not working-class California but working-class Woburn, Massachusetts. And while *Erin Brockovich* features a ragtag amateur sleuth–single mom as a crusader, the righteous cause in *A Civil Action* is taken up by a wealthy, hotshot, high-profile personal injury lawyer named Jan Schlichtmann (Travolta). What environmental malady struck the citizens of this Boston suburb? In Woburn, over a period of 14 years, twelve children have died from leukemia linked to tap water contaminated by toxic chemicals. Investigations soon indicate that a major well near factories was contaminated by the industrial solvent trichloroethylene (TCE), which the Environmental Protection Agency (EPA) suggests is a carcinogen. Is the TCE to blame for the leukemia? Should the corporations who allegedly polluted the well with TCE be held liable for the illness, death, and environmental clean-up?

In 1981, eight families, with the help of attorney Schlichtmann and his small firm, sue the corporate powers—W.R. Grace and Beatrice Foods—in a case known as *Anne Anderson, et al. vs. W. R. Grace & Co., et al.* The hardnosed, erudite Jerome Facher (Robert Duvall) provides the chief legal representation for W.R. Grace, and proves to be a master tactician and superior legal mind that skillfully defends his corporate clients. Schlichtmann and his firm go into enormous debt to finance their investigation, which endures a number of legal obstacles and setbacks.

In the end, *A Civil Action* is a sober, well-paced film that does not offer a clichéd, good vs. evil, fist-pumping courtroom climax resulting in neither a slam-dunk for the grieving Woburn families nor a financial windfall for Schlictmann. There is no immediate multi-million dollar settlement for the families nor Schlictmann's law film. Rather, justice eventually comes down the road in the form of environmental cleanup after EPA action against the corporations, and Schlictmann does not gain back all of the millions lost after years of litigation. As the film's tagline notes, "justice has its price." It is also worth noting that the David in this Goliathic struggle, Schlictmann, is hardly a stock hero, driven by a sincere passion for justice and a clean environment. It is very clear at the outset that he is a Porsche-driving ambulance chaser who relies on major settlements to fund his fledgling firm and expensive suits.

What transpires in *A Civil Action,* therefore, are really three major dynamics: one, the potentially devastating effects of pollution on the health and well being of regular, hardworking, and often powerless, citizens; two, a careful review of the twists, turns, challenges, and injustices of civil litigation; and three, a spiritual awakening for Schlictmann. Along the way, the cynical Schlictmann, who loses money, his car, his firm, and nearly his sanity, gains a sense of right and wrong. It is through his lengthy investigation that the EPA gains the appropriate information to take action to clean up the mess in Woburn. Schlictmann, in the meantime, has since devoted his efforts to other noble causes, including an environmental justice case in New Jersey.

Yet, unlike the more far more formulaic, sexy, and predicable *Erin Brockovich, A Civil Action* did not perform very well at the box office—at least by modern Hollywood's standards. Despite the bona fide star-power of *A Civil Action,* which also included John Lithgow, Sydney Pollack, and Kathleen Quinlan, and a fair amount of critical praise, the

U.S. gross for *A Civil Action* was a paltry $56.7 million. Apparently not all true tales of injustice and dirty water—and Davids vs. Goliaths—are equal in the mind of American consumers.

Conclusions: Environment

Awareness of the problems of pollution, environmental degradation, and conservation has been raised in the minds of a large portion of the population over the last generation. In the early 1990s, Turner Broadcasting network even broadcasted a half-hour animation series about a group of five teenagers who battle to save the planet called "Captain Planet and the Planeteers." However, the environment remains a difficult problem to represent on the screen. The sheer scale and complexity of the problems associated with it makes it difficult to address. What are the lines between the need for economic development and the need to protect the environment? In a broader sense, can the environment afford any significant development from the Third World? If it cannot, can people in the developed world in good conscience say that the planet cannot afford the development of the Third World?

What the films in this section demonstrate is that the problems associated with environmental degradation have only begun to scratch the surface of the problems. The difficulty in discussing the interrelatedness of these issues is probably not well suited for the screen. At the same time, films such as *Erin Brockovich* and *A Civil Action* remind us that failure to address some issues might lead us to a catastrophic society such as depicted in *Soylent Green* and *Silent Running*.

The Death Penalty

One of the most vexing and intellectually challenging debates in American society today is the necessity, legality, and morality of the death penalty. There is a long history, in many societies, of executing people who have committed the most heinous of crimes. Many are quite familiar with the notion of "an eye for an eye, a life for a life." However, for years voices have been raised over the issue of death penalty in a civilized society. Does society have the right to kill? Should society, as a whole, stoop to the level of those who committed the crime? Are there proper safeguards to insure the fairness of the trial and the quality of the lawyers? Does the administration of the death penalty constitute "cruel and unusual" punishment? Passionate voices on both sides of the issue attempt to answer these questions as they raise other intriguing and difficult issues.

In 1972, in the case of *Furman v. Georgia,* the United States Supreme Court struck down state death penalties, finding the application of capital punishment to be "arbitrary and capricious." Specifically, the Court struck down the Georgia and Texas death penalty procedures, and set aside *all* death sentences imposed under existing state and federal law. However, in 1976, with the Court's decision in *Gregg v. Georgia,* the death penalty was reinstated after new measures were adopted by states to guarantee proper legal procedures. From 1976 until 1988, there was no federal death penalty until Congress adopted similar measures. Since that time, however, the federal government has continually expanded its death penalty jurisdiction, making a number of criminal offenses federal crimes punishable by death. The federal government has also pursued the death penalty in a number of cases, perhaps most notably the 1995 Oklahoma City bombing. The U.S. government sought and achieved the death sentence for Timothy McVeigh, the man convicted of killing 168 people in the bombing of the Alfred P. Murrah Federal Building.

What makes the death penalty all the more difficult is the finality of the punishment. If an innocent person is convicted of a crime and sentenced to jail, then that person's freedom could be reinstated. However, if an innocent person is convicted of a crime and sentenced to death, then that person's life cannot be reinstated. Questions such as these prompted

DEBATING THE DEATH PENALTY IN THE UNITED STATES

The Death Penalty in the United States—Film and Television

The Thin Blue Line (1988)—directed by Errol Morris; documentary; setting: Texas
Dead Man Walking (1995)—directed by Tim Robbins; commercial film; setting: Louisiana
The Execution of Wanda Jean (2002)—directed by Liz Garbus; documentary; setting: Oklahoma
The Awful Truth (television, 2002): "Sibling Rivalry"; setting: Texas and Florida

After viewing these films, consider these questions for discussion and debate:

Does the death penalty constitute cruel and unusual punishment?
Is the death penalty a deterrent?
Should the United States execute the mentally retarded?
Should the United States execute juveniles?
What do U.S. law and international law have to say about capital punishment?

Supreme Court Decisions

Legal Information Institute at Cornell University (Cornell University's Archive of Supreme Court Decisions): http://supct.law.cornell.edu/supct/

Pro-Death Penalty Web Resources

Pro-Death Penalty.Com: http://www.prodeathpenalty.com/
The Death Penalty—A Defence: http:// w1.155.telia.com/~u15509119/ny_sida_1.htm (Swedish author David Anderson defends the death penalty.)
WW Death Penalty Links: http://www.clark
   prosecutor.org/html/death/death.htm (Steven D. Stewart, Prosecuting Attorney of Clark County, Indiana, and advocate of the death penalty, provides over 1,000 links to articles and statistics concerning capital punishment in the United States)

Anti-Death Penalty Web Resources

Amnesty International
   "The Death Penalty in the United States of America"
   http://www.amnestyusa.org/rightsforall/dp/index.html
Death Penalty Information Center http://www.deathpenaltyinfo.org/dpicmr.html (Provides state-by-state information on executions, a history of the death penalty; and looks at issues such as mental retardation, race, innocence, and deterrence)

Human Rights Watch
"The Death Penalty in the United States of America": http://www.hrw.org/campaigns/deathpenalty/
"Beyond Reason: The Death Penalty and Offenders with Mental Retardation": http://www.hrw.org/reports/2001/ustat/
The Justice Project: Campaign for Criminal Justice Reform: (www.CJReform.org)
"A Broken System: Error Rates in Capital Cases, 1973–1995" (James S. Lineman, Simon H. Rifling Professor of Law, Columbia University School of Law; Jeffrey Fagan, Professor, Joseph Mailman School of Public Health, Visiting Professor, Columbia University School of Law; Valerie West, Doctoral Candidate, Department of Sociology, New York University): http://justice.policy.net/jpreport/

A SAMPLING OF PROMINENT SUPREME COURT DEATH PENALTY CASES

Furman v. Georgia (1972)

The Court held that the imposition of the death penalty is a discretionary process not guided by legislatively defined standards, and as such, is a violation of the Eighth and Fourteenth Amendments. The Court struck down the Georgia and Texas death penalty procedures, and set aside *all* death sentences imposed under existing state and federal law.

Gregg v. Georgia (1976)

The Court upheld new state death penalty statues; at the same time it held that a constitutional violation could be established if a plaintiff demonstrated a "pattern of arbitrary and capricious sentencing."

McCleskey v. Kemp (1987)

The Court rejects a Fourteenth Amendment Equal Protection Clause challenge to Georgia capital sentencing laws and procedures, despite a statistical study—the Baldus Study—which "revealed significant disparities in the imposition of the death sentence based on the race of the victim."

Thomson v. Oklahoma (1988)

The Court held that the implementation of a death sentence on a person who is 15 years old at the time of the offense was outside the parameters of "evolving standards of decency" at home and, especially, abroad. In his dissent, Justice Scalia posits that the international standards evoked by the majority were irrelevant when interpreting the U.S. Constitution.

Stanford v. Kentucky (1989)

The Court ruled constitutional the execution of Kevin Stanford, who was 17 years old at the time he committed murder.

Atkins v. Virginia (2002)

The Court held that executions of mentally retarded criminals are "cruel and unusual punishments" prohibited by the Eighth Amendment.

Ring v. Arizona (2002)

The Court held that, based on the Sixth Amendment's guarantee of a fair, impartial jury trial, a jury, not a judge, must determine whether a capital defendant gets the death penalty. The ruling invalidates the death penalty procedures in Arizona and four other states.

Governor George Ryan to suspend the use of the death penalty in Illinois in the year 2000. Between the years 1977 and
2000, Illinois executed 12 people on death row. Using new
DNA techniques and prompted by the investigation of a
Northwestern University professor and his students, Illinois
later freed 13 people on death row, finding them innocent
of the crimes they committed. Governor Ryan was stunned
that more people had been exonerated than had been executed from death row, and concluded that the system was
flawed.[10] As Ryan left office in January 2003, he commuted
the death sentences of everyone on death row in Illinois.

The debate over the death penalty is certainly not limited
to the United States. Concern about the death penalty takes
on a worldwide dimension. Advocates for the abolition of
the death penalty call on countries that impose *Sharia* law
to rethink their punishments. For countries that aspire to
become part of the European Union, they must first, among
other things, abolish the death penalty. What do you think
about the legality, necessity, and morality of the death penalty? What recent films have addressed the myriad issues
that surround the death penalty? Listed in the boxes on the
previous pages are death penalty-related films and web
sites that address many of the debates surrounding this
highly controversial and emotional issue. In addition, the
boxes provide a review of seminal Supreme Court cases
that deal with the administration of the death penalty in the
United States. After viewing the documentaries and commercial films listed in the box—all of which are based on
real death penalty cases in Texas, Oklahoma, and Louisiana—consider the questions, consequences, and dilemmas posed by the administration of the death penalty. Do
these films alter or reinforce your previously held view of
the death penalty? Why or why not?

Human Rights

Generally, the portrayal of human rights violations is particularly effective on film. First, a discussion of human rights

violation lends itself to film because it is dramatic. Second, human rights violations also leave a record that is visual, particularly when that violation is something like torture or genocide. Whatever the case, there are a plethora of films that explore the topic of human rights. However, our discussion here is limited to emphasizing the vital human rights concerns raised by a small but representative sampling of films in the human rights genre.

The idea of sovereignty suggests that the internal decision-making process or politics of a country is not the concern of other states. Because the principle of sovereignty has been a particularly relevant force in the international system since the Treaty of Westphalia in 1648, human rights have not typically been a concern of states prior to the Second World War. That is not to say that there were not considerations domestically. In fact, several films in the United State dealt with human rights violations as a justification for entering World War I. In *Hearts of the World* (1918), famed silent-film director D. W. Griffith depicts a French town occupied by the German where torture is commonplace. A highly propagandized film, *Kaiser, the Beast of Berlin* (1918), focused on the alleged depravities of the German regime during the war. Even Mary Pickford, America's sweetheart, in *The Little American* (1917) is the target of an attempted rape by Germans.

The slaughter of six million Jews and several million others during the Second World War prompted the international community to take up the discussion of human rights in international forums. The newly formed United Nations in 1948 adopted two instruments that attempted to address the subject of human rights. The first was a resolution designed as a guide for the formulation of human rights conventions in the future. Former First Lady—and outspoken advocate for human rights at home and abroad, Eleanor Roosevelt—chaired the UN committee charged with drafting a worldwide declaration of human rights. Known as the Universal Declaration of Human Rights, the document laid out thirty articles that delineated what constitutes fundamental human rights in the international community. Among its thirty articles, the Universal Declaration calls for guaranteeing all individuals vital human rights, including "the right to life, liberty and the security of person," freedom from slavery, protection from discrimination, the prevention of torture or "cruel, inhuman or degrading treatment or punishment," and other basic social, political, and economic rights.

A second document adopted by the United Nations in 1948 that more directly confronts some of the problems arising from the Second World War is the Convention on the Prevention and Punishment of the Crime of Genocide. This is an attempt to prevent and punish one of the most pernicious problems of the twentieth century. Genocide is defined in the Convention as the attempt "to destroy, in whole or in part, a national, ethnical, racial or religious group." Looking back on the events in Europe during the 1930s and 1940s, the international community was outraged at the attempts of the Nazi regime to eradicate particularly Jews, but also Gypsies and homosexuals as well. As horrific as what was to become known as "The Holocaust" was, it was neither the

This advertisement from the *Chicago Tribune* for *Kaiser, The Beast of Berlin* (1918) demonstrates how the enemy was perceived during the First World War. Notice that the advertisement makes reference to the private life of the Kaiser, referred to as "the mad dog of Europe." While the advertisement purportedly gives equal weight in the debate over human rights violations, those who might favor the German position in the war are quoted as saying that "the Kaiser's morals are good." However, the intentions of the film are clear: the German government is considered to be one that is committing atrocities.

first, nor last time the complete destruction of a group was attempted. We are familiar with some of the most egregious cases, but other examples often tend to be underreported.

Missing

Most people in Europe and North America are far removed from a world where human rights violations occur on a regular basis. Perhaps some of the most interesting and dramatic stories that can be told are when people faced with terror and torture live in fear of severe human rights violations. One of the best films for capturing this nightmare is *Missing* (1982). Starring Jack Lemmon, the film is based on the real-life experiences of Ed Horman, whose son disappeared after a military coup in Chile. Ed's son, Charles, was a writer and political activist, living and working in Chile with his wife Beth. During the September 1973 *coup d'etat* of General Augusto Pinochet, Charles Horman was picked up, taken to a soccer stadium along with other students, writers and activists, and was beaten, tortured, and finally executed the week following the coup.

In the film, Ed Horman flies to Chile at the behest of his daughter-in-law, Beth, to help search for Charles. Ed's political leanings are the opposite of his son's. He is a conservative who believes that any American involvement in Chile is justified. His first assumption is that Charles has done something wrong, and has been arrested by the police for some crime, but as the film progresses he begins to understand that his only crime was he might have known about the coup in advance. Reports also indicated that Charles had evidence of American, specifically CIA, involvement in the planning and carrying out of the coup. To that extent, Charles Horman knew too much for the new military regime.

Ed begins making the rounds to the police and American officials in Santiago. At each turn he is stonewalled, delayed and sent to other officials. Gradually, Ed comes to the realization that even the United States government is lying to him. When Charles' body is returned to the family, it was badly decomposed, making it difficult to tell whether or

HUMAN RIGHTS ORGANIZATIONS AND REFERENCES

There are several international human rights organizations around the world. We have chosen a few prominent advocacy organizations to highlight the advancement of international human rights around the world.

Non-Governmental Organizations (NGOs)

Amnesty International
http://www.amnesty.org
   Perhaps the most well known of the international human rights organizations, Amnesty is famous for getting citizens involved in letter writing campaigns to raise attention about the plight of the victims of human rights abuses. Amnesty International was founded in 1961 and today has over one million members. Currently, the organization operates in over 140 countries and is considered independent from any government, religious persuasion, or political ideology. Its fundamental driving force is the Universal Declaration of Human Rights, a document signed by every government in the world in 1948 which guarantees every human being basic political, social, and economic rights, regardless of race, religion, or the political system under which they live.

Human Rights Watch
http://www.hrw.org
   Another independent human rights organization is Human Rights Watch, which is based in New York but has offices around the world. Founded in 1978, HRW was originally founded to help monitor the Eastern European Governments compliance with the Helsinki Accords. The organization seeks to publish human rights abuses as a way to raise consciousness about severe international human rights violations.

Medecins Sans Frontieres
http://www.msf.org
   Actually less of a human rights organization and more of a humanitarian relief organization, "Doctors Without Borders" is a French-based organization that helps provide medical assistance to populations that are in danger. Operating in over 80 countries, MSF works to rebuild medical service, instigate vaccination programs, and to create clean water and food sanitation.

Information and Resources

   In addition to the organizations listed above you might want to consider consulting these Internet resources:

   Committee to Protect Journalists—http://www.cpj.org
   Freedom House—http://www.freedomhouse.org
   Human Rights Web Resources—http:// www.hrweb.org
   Lawyers Committee for Human Rights—http://www.lchr.org
   Physicians for Human Rights—http://www.phrusa.org
   UN High Commissioner for Human Rights—http://www.unhchr.ch
   United Nations Human Rights Page—http://www.un.org/rights/

not Charles had suffered from torture. Years later, after repeated efforts by many activists, the CIA released some
documents surrounding the death of Charles Horman. In
one document, dated August 1976, the State Department
admitted that American intelligence officials might have
played "an unfortunate part" in Charles Horman's death. [11]

Genocide

"Holocaust"

During the 1970s one of the most popular mediums in
American television was the mini-series. The first and most
famous of these mini-series was "Roots" (1977), based on
Alex Haley's novel. Another major mini-series was "Holocaust" (1978), [12] which followed the trials and tribulations of
each member of the Weiss family, who were Jewish, compared with the Dorf family, who were Germans, during the
Nazi regime in Germany. For four nights in April 1978,
Americans watched as the Weiss family was stripped of
their jobs, honor, citizenships, and eventually for most, their
lives. It is difficult to sum up the story of a film that took 475
minutes to screen on television, but the audience is educated in a general history of the major events of European
Jewry during the 1930s and 1940s.

At the same time as we see the plight of the Weiss family,
the audience is also asked to consider the plight of other
Germans who are not Jewish. Erik Dorf is an out-of-work
lawyer, who joins the SS to support his family. As the film
progresses, Erik becomes more and more aligned with the
movement and identifies with the objective of "saving
Western civilization from the Jews." Other Germans in the
story have difficult choices to make, as their lives are inter-
twined with the lives of Jews. In the end, the film forces the
audience into a dilemma: Given the same situation what
would we do? Options are rather limited and depressing. Ultimately people could have become the persecutors or the
persecuted.

Some television critics have complained that the story is too contrived at points. It is rather hard to imagine that such a small number of people were witnesses to so many events during the war, including the *kristallnacht,* the uprising in the Warsaw Ghetto, and the final solution at Auschwitz.[13] Even some Holocaust survivors (most notably Elie Wiesel) thought that by portraying a fictional family in the midst of such horrific events cheapened and diminished what had actually happened during those fateful years.[14]

Nevertheless, "Holocaust" was an important event in U.S. television history. The television show raised consciousness about the crimes of Nazi Germany and the effects of genocide. When the mini-series was shown in West Germany the following January the impact on public opinion was dramatic. The entertainment trade journal *Variety* reported that among teenagers in West Germany seven in ten reported that they had learned more by watching the mini-series than they had in all their studies of West German history.

The events of the Holocaust have been portrayed on film a number of times. Steven Spielberg's acclaimed film *Schindler's List* (1993) recounts the true story of the efforts of Oskar Schindler to save Jews in Poland. Spielberg would win the Academy Award for Best Picture and Best Director for this film, which many consider one of the best films of the 1990s. The film is at once moving and at the same time an in-depth exploration of humanity. Roberto Benigni co-wrote and directed the 1999 Academy Award winner for Best Foreign Language Film *Life Is Beautiful* (*La Vita è Bella*—1997). The film starts out as a comedy with Benigni playing a farcical Jewish man who falls in love. But as the film progresses, and Benigni raises his family, he is first deprived of his home, then sent to a concentration camp, and ultimately sacrifices himself to save his son. The Czech film, *Divided We Fall* (*Musíme si pomáhat*—2000), also uses some humor to address the seriousness of the holocaust. Set in Prague during the war, a childless couple hide the son of their former employer who is Jewish for the better part of the German occupation. The original title, which translates as, "we must help one another," explains the situation all the characters find themselves in. While each of these three films are excellent films and each adds a layer of understanding to the events of the holocaust, the mini-series "Holocaust," despite its drawback, continues to provide an overall picture of the enormity and the tragedy that was the holocaust.

The *Genocide Factor*

While the movies mentioned above do an excellent job of portraying the personal stories of people involved in the stories of human rights violations and genocide, to gain a better sense of the overall picture of genocide we should consider a documentary source. *The Genocide Factor* is a four-part documentary that traces the history of genocide from Biblical times all the way to the present time.[15] The film concludes that factors like the lack of democracy and hyper-nationalism contribute to the possibility that genocide might occur, but it leaves open the question of how an individual can torture, maim, and desecrate other human beings. The film, in graphic and uncomfortable detail, documents the effects of genocide in a number of different settings. Film and still photography of some of the most egregious events of crime against humanity are displayed.

While many Americans are cognizant of the attempt of the Nazis to eradicate the Jews, *The Genocide Factor* (2000) asks the audience to move beyond this incident and see the larger picture of the history of genocide. Included in the discussion of genocide is the Soviet-orchestrated famine in the Ukraine during the 1930s, the reign of terror in Cambodia under Pol Pot (see the 1984 film *The Killing Fields*), the Japanese invasion of Nanking, the 1923 massacre in Rosewood, Florida (which is also depicted in the 1997 film *Rosewood*), and the numerous wars in the Balkans and Sub-Saharan Africa during the 1990s. Particularly disturbing and moving are the scenes of Rwandan amputees holding their limbs. A story that was common to many survivors was that they witnessed their families brutally killed before their eyes.

There is no doubt that these scenes are difficult, at best, to watch. All of the films listed in this section are difficult to watch and comprehend on an emotional basis. However, as the filmmakers point out, if these events of horror are to be prevented from happening in the future, we, as engaged and informed citizens of the world, must be cognizant of what people are capable of doing to one another. In that effort, there are a number of international bodies determined to keep citizens informed and the past from repeating itself. In addition to international governmental organizations (IGOs) dedicated to monitoring the state of human rights across the globe—such as the United Nations Human Rights Commission—there are nongovernmental organizations (NGOs) that devote their efforts on behalf of human rights worldwide, among them, Amnesty International and Human Rights Watch. The good news is that the mission, history, and work of these groups can be readily accessed and digested within mere minutes: extensive information on these IGOs and NGOS—and the state of human rights around the world—be found on their home pages on the World Wide Web, just a mouse-click away.

Colonialism

One of the most pernicious problems in the modern world is the lack of development in many parts of the world. Poverty and lack of development can have many effects on the international system. Poverty can lead to disease, displacement, migration, and ultimately instability.

Some scholars point to the lingering effects of colonialism as a cause for the lack of development and poverty in Africa, Asia, and Latin America. According to some authors, colonialism helped to destroy the social, political, and cultural infrastructure of indigenous societies. In doing so, when the colonial power left, the territories and societies left behind were incapable of sustaining themselves in the international community. This section examines three films that deal with the lasting effects of colonial rule.

Several political scientists have chronicled the difficulties and disadvantages that colonialism placed on countries. Steven Krasner has argued that the conflict between North and South has become the defining aspect of the current international system.[16] Few students (and even academics) understand how the institution of colonialism undermined the political and economic development of many lesser-developed countries. The study of international political economy is particularly difficult for many people because of the complex nature of the subject. Here film can be used to help students understand the effects of colonialism, while at the same time understanding the day-to-day existence in a colonial frontier village.

While the effects of colonialism are debated in many political science quarters, concepts like the imposition of a Western social order over the existing indigenous order have ramifications in many states. Some have pointed out that in African colonies, after the slave trade was abolished, the primary reason for owning colonies was the acquisition of cheap raw materials.[17] The institution of colonialism was to change the existing social pattern of colonies from one in which the primary task of self-sufficiency was changed in order to meet the needs of European colonial power.

Black and White in Color

Black and White in Color, winner of the Academy Award for Best Foreign Language Film in 1977, is set primarily in the French colonial town of Port Coulais at the end of 1914. The film opens with German colonials from a nearby settlement in town buying provisions. The local French residents are a mixture of oddities, among them: two brothers, one a mental incompetent, the other shrewd and calculating, who along with his wife run the larger of the stores in the village; two priests, Fathers Simon and Jean de la Croix, who attempt to convert the local population to Christianity, while at the same time exchanging religious statues for wood cravings that can be exported for a substantial profit; and an army sergeant, Sergeant Bosselet, who is more interested in his sexual conquest of local girls than he is in his duties. Finally, the main protagonist of the film is geographer, Hubert Fresnoy, who, after receiving only marginal grades, is posted to Africa to observe and study. The local residents are severely behind in receiving the news, and when the mail finally arrives in January 1915, the French colonialists find themselves at war with Germany. Patriotism ensues and the residents, save the young geographer, cajole the sergeant into acting upon the news that war has come to France and Germany by attacking the local German garrison with local Africans.

While the sergeant wants more time to train the Africans, the local residents insist that he begin an attack immediately. With little preparation the French conscripts set off to attack the German village on the other side of the creek the following Sunday, rationalizing that the Germans would go to church. The other residents follow along to picnic while the battle ensues. As the French troops approach the German village, it becomes apparent that the Germans are waiting for them. Unbeknownst to Sergeant Bosselet or the others, the Germans have a machine gun, which they use to decimate the French troops. The white residents are startled by this change of events and begin to run back to their village, leaving behind their troops to die of blood loss and thirst in the heat of the sun. Only Bosselet and Fresnoy stay behind to administer to the wounded.

Fresnoy returns to the French village disgusted by the other residents and worried about a counterattack. He meets with the sergeant, who agrees to reorganize the French village in preparation for a German attack with Fresnoy in charge. The two meet with the other white members of the community, and after some negotiations, they agree to allow Fresnoy to organize the community and have Bosselet properly train a military force. Fresnoy sends his most competent rival to nearby St. Pierre for supplies and men. He orders the women of the village to make uniforms. He also takes into his possession the inventory data for the local store from which he catches the local merchants hoarding food for their own use. As Fresnoy's dictatorial powers grow, the French women become more and more attracted to him. However, Fresnoy takes a feisty local African girl as his lover and forces the French colonists to treat her as their equal.

When the convoy returns from St. Pierre, they bring guns and ammunition, however, they can spare no men. Fresnoy appeals to the local chief for men, but knowing of the misadventure of their incursion against the German garrison he is reluctant to turn over any of his own men. Fresnoy convinces the chief to assist in capturing one hundred men from neighboring tribes to help fight to defend the French village. When the results of these efforts are unsuccessful, by only bringing in a handful of sick and old men, Fresnoy returns to the chief to demand help. The chief tells him that he is unable to capture any men because the neighboring tribes are hiding, knowing their fate if they are captured. Fresnoy resorts to the torture of neighboring tribesmen in order to build up his forces to one hundred.

Sergeant Bosselet trains the newly captured men and sets them to marching drills. Priests are enlisted to help the men to learn French words, like "bayonet," "gun" and "ammunition." However, when no one is watching, they teach the slaves how to drop to their knees in prayer at the sign of the crucifix. In one of the funnier moments of the film, the fathers try to convince the African men that the white man's god is stronger than the black man's god. In order to demonstrate this they produce a bicycle, which none of the black men can ride, except for one the of the Fathers' assistants who they claim now believes in the white man's god.

Meanwhile, Fresnoy oversees the construction of a series of trenches to surround the village for protection. When the Germans finally do attack, the trenches prove to be a sturdy line of defense for the French; however, the result is a stalemate between the two sides. The Germans resort to propaganda in an attempt to break the will of the black French soldiers to no avail. The advent of the rainy season means that the French side suffers disease and discomfort similar to that suffered in the trenches in France. The stalemate is only broken by the arrival of English troops, lead by an Indian, who brings news that the Germans have lost the war and that the German colony was to be taken over by Her Majesty's Government. When Fresnoy finally meets his German counterpart, he admits that in school he was a socialist. To which the German replies, "So was I."

Perhaps one of the debatable points of *Black and White in Color* is the depiction of the intellectual Hubert. It is doubtful that had these events been real that the residents would have taken Hubert seriously. First his radicalism, his call to first argue for peace, then to become a brilliant author of strategies, then advocate racial equality seem a little unrealistic for 1914 French colonial Africa. However, rather than seeing the film as an accurate recreation of the events of 1914, we should assume that the filmmakers have created characters for the sake of arguments being placed in front of the audience.

At the same time, the film does give insight to the nature of the colonialism, and a demonstration of how colonialism was carried out. Note the willingness of the French leaders in Africa to mirror what was happening in Europe: the troops built trenches to protect themselves just as was depicted in the newspapers, and when the rainy season came African soldiers suffered similar afflictions as their counterparts in Europe. The attempt to transplant France to its African colonies should not be lost either take, for example, the inappropriateness of the African soldiers wearing combat boots in their training. While the film does not necessarily follow the historical events of French colonial Africa in 1914, it does create an overall picture of how the colonial experience affected both the French and the Africans.

Xala

In an era of increased globalization and debt among lesser-developed countries, movies made by Western institutions, most notably the World Bank and the International Monetary Fund, may be perceived as having a sinister effect.[18] Issues like conditionality and property rights are often cast in terms of holding on to power and wealth within a country. It is understood that these points are debatable: however it is essential to be able to understand both sides of this story in order to be able to critically think about the issue. Many Africans were to claim that, after the end of political colonialism, newly independent African states had no real power to move in the international system. African states remained tied to the same economic institutions because, although the political leadership had changed, those who owned businesses, land, and capital in African states remained in the hands of Europeans. If foreign interests did not own indigenous businesses, those Africans who owned local enterprises were so tied to foreign interests that foreign interests may as well have owned them.

African cinema has had few standouts in the eyes of the international community. An early standout was *Xala* (1975), a film made by Senegalese director Ousmane Sembene. The film tells the story of a local elite who takes a third wife in an effort to "appear" more traditional. The film is really an allegory for neocolonialism. The film opens with Senegal gaining its independence. The opening montage reveals how neocolonialism works in blunt terms. Black Senegalese, wearing traditional dress, come to the chamber of commerce and kick the whites out and take the busts of Napoleon out of the meeting rooms. The black Senegalese return to meet in the chamber of commerce wearing their European business suits. In the room, around the table, the blacks congratulate themselves. The whites reenter the room as "advisers." They offer briefcases of money to each of the members of the chamber. While the opening scene is explicit in terms of the political message it is delivering, it is nonetheless quite effective in demonstrating how some Africans felt about postcolonial politics.

The main protagonist in the film is Hadji Aboucader Beye, a wealthy businessman who, at the beginning of the film, is set to take a third wife to demonstrate his wealth and power. Hadji throws an elaborate party to celebrate his marriage, but must first collect his first two wives from their houses.

His first wife is a woman of tradition who represents traditional Africa; she dresses in traditional clothes and is strong,
but reserved, and refuses to be distracted by her husband's
dalliances. The second wife represents modern Africa; she
dresses in a short white dress, wears sunglasses, is brash
and somewhat crude. The second wife does not like her
older counterpart, but feels superior, given her youth to the
older wife. But now, with the introduction of a third wife, she
begins to feel unsettled. In conversation the two wives agree
that Hadji is taking a third wife to demonstrate his wealth
and virility, but it is a façade, and he can neither afford the
wife nor needs her. In many ways, the third wife represents
the lure of what could be: westernization, industrialization
and modernization. At the wedding, the second wife (modern Africa) explains to the first wife (traditional Africa) that
she is not her enemy; the new wife is.

Upon arriving at the wedding party, Hadji celebrates his
wedding by scattering coins to the crowd. While the poor of
Dakar scramble to get coins, a young boy and an older blind
man reach for some, but the polished black boot of a military guard steps on the coins and keeps them for himself. At
the wedding ceremony Hadji refuses to take part in a ceremony to ward off evil spirits saying that it is superstitious
and not modern. That night however, Hadji is unable to consummate his marriage with his third wife. He finds that
someone has placed a Xala (curse) on him.

As the film plays out, Hadji's place in the business community begins to decline as more and more people discover
his inability to consummate his marriage. His third marriage
collapses as the third wife's family forbids her to be associated with him. Hadji begins to be thought of as weak, and
the other members of the chamber of commerce start to
abandon him. The local bank stops lending him money, and
suppliers refuse to service his business. Soon Hadji loses
his business and his second wife abandons him. Losing
everything that he has worked for, Hadji is forced to move
in with his first wife. In desperation he tells her that she
might as well leave too; but she remains steadfast. Hadji

tries a number of solutions to rid himself of the curse but none seem to work. In the end the poor of Dakar, who accuse him of exploiting and ignoring them in order to gain his wealth and power, confront him. The movie ends with Hadji undergoing a humiliating ritual to rid himself of the xala.

Lumumba

Black and White in Color and *Xala* provide a very subdued picture of colonialism. While both offer condemnations of the institutions of colonization, the condemnation is somewhat muted and indirect. The film *Lumumba* (2000), on the other hand, delivers a stinging indictment of colonialism. The background to the film, which is based on actual events, is that the African continent was divided up among the European powers at a conference in 1885. The territory now known as the Democratic Republic of Congo (formerly known as Congo or Zaire) became the personal property of Belgian King Leopold II. Over the next three quarters of a century the Belgians extracted the natural resources of the country.[19] Patrice Lumumba represents a political prophet who according to the director is a figure whose story went a long way in explaining the plight of post-colonial Africa.[20]

As the film opens, Patrice Lumumba, the former prime minister of Congo, is being driven to the place of his execution. Once dead, the Belgian authorities are not satisfied with his death and have his body dug up, chopped into pieces, and burned. The story of Lumumba is thus told in flashback. Because Congo is governed so patronizingly very few citizens are educated well enough to be considered a threat to the leaders when independence comes. Patrice Lumumba himself is a self-educated man who has sold beer in the capitol early in his career. Later in the 1950s, he becomes the leader of the Congolese National Movement, a post that exposes him as a person of talent to the Belgians. Subsequently Lumumba is arrested, jailed and beaten. He is released just in time to travel to Brussels in 1960 for round-table talks on independence.

Lumumba eventually becomes prime minister upon

Congo's independence in 1960 at the age of 36. However, his term in office is very brief, lasting only two months. He is arrested and six months later he is executed.

Lumumba is forced from power for a number of reasons, but his uncompromising views and his propensity to confront problems rather than use diplomacy, helps hasten his demise. His old friend, Joseph Mobutu, replaces Lumumba. The film lays a good deal of the blame for Lumumba's fall at the hands of the Belgians, the Americans, and the United Nations. The United States insistence that it need clear allies in the Cold War necessitated, at least in the American eyes, someone more dependable. The tragedy is for all that Congo has suffered at the hands of the Belgians, it is once again denied an advocate in Lumumba by outside powers.

While clearly considered a hero, the film does not sanctify Lumumba. One gets the sense that had Patrice Lumumba been more tactful in his dealing with foreigners he may have served longer as prime minister and remained alive. However, our conception of heroes is usually defined in terms of their unwavering pursuit of their ideals. Lumumba's vision of a united Congo, proud and self-reliant, is an image that still garners support and admiration from around the world.

Colonialism: Conclusion

What *Black and White in Color, Xala,* and *Lumumba* bring to the audience is a depiction of Africa that is unsensationalized. In the past films, like the alleged documentary *Congorilla* (1932), the Edgar Bergen–Charley McCarthy vehicle *Africa Speaks—English* (1933), and the Abbott and Costello vehicle *Africa Screams* (1949), Africa is portrayed as a place of man-eating apes, wild rivers, jungles and cannibals. Even as films moved into the 1980s and 1990s, the depiction of Africa in films such as *Coming to America* (1988) and *Mighty Joe Young* (1998) projected American ideals on to what Africa was like more than anything based on reality. What two films, *Black and White in Color* and *Xala,* do is to present Africa as an exotic place, but one in which the inhabitants' wants and desires are not substantially different from our own. *Lumumba* depicts an Africa that has been stripped of its natural wealth, and in the aftermath of colonialism the continent is at the mercy of Cold War politics and the military dictatorships of a few men in power. These three films, all made outside of the United States, provide a much more realistic image of Africa than we are accustomed to seeing on film or the television screen. By presenting the continent and its inhabitants in a more realistic light, the result should be to consider the problems of the continent not as unfathomable problems of an extremely foreign culture with only the slightest similarities to ourselves, but as the problems of people that are not so different from people from other parts of the world.

Conclusion

As this chapter reveals, a wide array of domestic and foreign films exist that can provide us with the tools to define, question, and debate some of the great political dynamics and dilemmas that we face here at home and across the globe. Whether these documentaries, commercial films, or television clips and sketches seek to critique and explain the media, the environment, the death penalty, human rights, genocide, or colonialism, it is clear that the medium of film is ripe with possibilities for addressing some of the seminal political concepts and realities of our day. Indeed these are far-reaching issues that will influence international relations, our politics, and quality of life for decades to come. Furthermore, web sites and the work of NGOs also inform our examination of these vital domestic and global issues, offering additional context, data, and insight as we start down the path of "seeing the bigger picture." Roll the cameras, start the film, and get ready: the path toward greater citizenship and political awareness may very well be aided, at least in part, by considering the diverse perspectives presented on the big screen.

Filmography

4 Little Girls
  1997—United States
  Director: Spike Lee
  Documentary
  Subjects: civil rights, racism
  Sensitivities: violence, disturbing images of dead bodies

Abe Lincoln in Illinois
  1940—United States
  Director: John Cromwell
  Cast: Raymond Massey, Gene Lockhart, Ruth Gordon,
    Mary Howard, Minor Watson
  Subject: presidency

Absolute Power
  1997—United States
  Director: Clint Eastwood
  Cast: Clint Eastwood, Gene Hackman, Ed Harris,
    Laura Linney, Scott Glenn
  Subjects: presidency, elections
  Sensitivities: violence, sexual violence, language

Africa Screams
  1949—United States
  Director: Charles Barton
  Cast: Bud Abbott, Lou Costello, Clyde Beatty, Frank Buck,
    Max Baer
  Subject: Africa
  Sensitivities: racial stereotypes

Africa Speaks—English
  1933—United States
  Director: Ray Mack
  Cast: Edgar Bergen, Charlie McCarthy
  Subject: Africa
  Sensitivities: racial stereotypes

Air Force One
  1997—United States
  Director: Wolfgang Peterson
  Cast: Harrison Ford, Gary Oldman, Glenn Close,
    Wendy Crewson, Liesel Matthews
  Subjects: presidency, terrorism, foreign policy, Twenty-
    Fifth Amendment (presidential health & disability)
  Sensitivities: violence

Alexandr Nevsky
  1938—Soviet Union
  Director: Sergei M. Eisenstein and Dmitri Vasilyev
  Cast: Nikolai Cherkasov, Nikolai Okhlopkov,
    Andrei Abrikosov, Dmitri Orlov, Vasili Novikov
  Subjects: communism, war, rebellion
  Sensitivities: violence

All in the Family (television)
  1971–1979—United States
  Cast: Carroll O'Connor, Jean Stapleton, Rob Reiner,
    Sally Struthers, Mike Evans
  Subjects: race relations, war, Vietnam, gun control,
    homosexuality, abortion, rape, anti-Semitism
  Sensitivities: language, racial stereotypes

All the King's Men
  1949—United States
  Director: Robert Rossen
  Cast: Broderick Crawford, John Ireland,
    Mercedes McCambridge, John Derek
  Subjects: elections, democracy

All the President's Men
  1976—United States
  Director: Alan J. Pakula
  Cast: Dustin Hoffman, Robert Redford, Jack Warden,
    Martin Balsom, Hal Halbrook
  Subjects: presidency, Watergate, media, corruption

Amadeus
  1984—United States
  Director: Miles Forman
  Cast: F. Murray Abraham, Tom Hulce, Elizabeth Berridge,
    Simon Callow, Roy Dotrice
  Subjects: individual liberties

American Dream
  1990—United States / United Kingdom
  Director: Barbara Kopple
  Documentary
  Subject: labor struggle
  Sensitivities: mild violence, language

The American President
  1995—United States
  Director: Rob Reiner

Cast: Michael Douglas, Annette Bening, Martin Sheen,
   Michael J. Fox, Anna Deavere Smith
Subject: presidency, elections, media

American Standoff
   2002—United States
   Director: Kristi Jacobson
   Documentary
   Subject: labor struggles
   Sensitivities: language

Amistad
   1997—United States
   Director: Steven Spielberg
   Cast: Morgan Freeman, Nigel Hawthorne, Anthony
      Hopkins, Djimon Hounsou, Matthew McConaughey
   Subjects: presidency, slavery
   Sensitivities: violence

Armageddon
   1998—United States
   Director: Michael Bay
   Cast: Bruce Willis, Billy Bob Thornton, Ben Affleck,
      Liv Tyler, Will Patton
   Subjects: presidency, nuclear weapons

Atomic Café
   1982—United States
   Director: Jayne Loader and Kevin Rafferty
   Documentary
   Subject: nuclear war

The Awful Truth (television)
   1999–2000—United Kingdom / United States
   Director: Michael Moore
   Cast: Karen Duffy, V. Emerson, Lucianne Goldberg,
      Ben Hamper, Jay Martel
   Subjects: civil rights, racism, labor struggles, death
      penalty, campaigns, elections, abortion

Before the Rain
  1994—Macedonia / France/ United Kingdom
  Director: Milcho Manchevski
  Cast: Katrin Cartlidge, Rade Serbedzija, Gregoire Colin,
    Labina Mitevska, Jay Villiers
  Subjects: ethnic conflicts, war
  Sensitivities: violence, violence against animals, nudity,
    language

The Beginning of the End
  1957—United States
  Director: Bert I. Gordon
  Cast: Peter Graves, Peggie Castle, Morris Ankrum,
    Than Wyenn, Thomas Browne Henry
  Subjects: nuclear weapons

The Best Man
  1964—United States
  Director: Franklin J. Schaffner
  Cast: Henry Fonda, Cliff Robertson, Edie Adams,
    Margaret Leighton, Shelley Berman
  Subjects: presidency, campaigns, elections, homosexuality,
    civil rights

Big Jim McLain
  1952—United States
  Director: Edward Ludwig
  Cast: John Wayne, Nancy Olson, James Arness,
    Alan Napier, Veda Ann Borg
  Subjects: communism, red scare

The Big One
  1997—United States / United Kingdom
  Director: Michael Moore
  Documentary
  Subjects: labor struggle, globalization, capitalism,
    campaigns, elections

The Big Parade
  1925—United States

Director: King Vidor
Cast: John Gilbert, Renee Adoree, Hobart Bosworth,
    Claire McDowell, Claire Adams
Subject: war
Sensitivities: mild violence

Billy Jack
1971—United States
Director: Tom Laughlin
Cast: Tom Laughlin, Delores Taylor, Clark Howart,
    Victor Izay, Julie Webb
Subjects: ethnic conflict, racism
Sensitivities: mild violence

The Birth of a Nation
1915—United States
Director: D. W. Griffith
Cast: Lillian Gish, Mae Marsh, Henry B. Wathall,
    Miriam Cooper, Mary Alden
Subjects: democracy, civil rights, racism, war
Sensitivities: attempted rape, suicide, racial stereotypes

Black and White in Color
Noir et Blancs en Couleur
    1976—Côte d'Ivoire / West Germany / Switzerland /
    France
Director: Jean-Jaques Annaud
Cast: Jean Carmet, Jean Dufilho, Catharine Rouvel,
    Jaques Speisser, Maurice Barrier
Subjects: colonialism, war, race relations
Sensitivities: violence, nudity

Blacklist: Hollywood on Trial
1996—United States
Documentary
Subjects: communism, red scare

Bloody Sunday
2002—United Kingdom / Ireland
Director: Paul Greengrass

Cast: James Nasbitt, Allan Gildea, Gerard Crossan,
   Mary Moulds, Carmel McCallion
Subject: Ethnic conflict
Sensitivities: language, violence

Bob Roberts
   1992—United States / United Kingdom
   Director: Tim Robbins
   Cast: Tim Robbins, Giancarlo Esposito, Alan Rickman,
      Ray Wise, Brian Murray
   Subjects: campaigns, corruption, media

Born on the Fourth of July
   1989—United States
   Director: Oliver Stone
   Cast: Tom Cruise, Bryan Larkin, Raymond J. Barry,
      Caroline Kava, Josh Evans
   Subjects: war, human rights
   Sensitivities: sex, language, violence

Bowling for Columbine
   2002—Canada / United States
   Director: Michael Moore
   Documentary
   Subjects: gun control, media, war, social and economic
      justice
   Sensitivities: violence

Bulworth
   1998—United States
   Director: Warren Beatty
   Cast: Sean Astin, Warren Beatty, Graham Beckel,
      Halle Berry, Don Cheadle
   Subjects: presidency, elections, corruption, media,
      race relations
   Sensitivities: language, sex, obscenity

By Word of Mouse
   1954—United States
   Director: Friz Freleng

Subject: capitalism

Cabaret Balkan
Bure Baruta
  1998—Yugoslavia / Macedonia / France / Greece / Turkey
  Director: Goran Paskaljevic
  Cast: Mira Banjac Ivan Bekjarev, Aleksander Bercek,
    Vajislav Brajovic, Azra Cengic
  Subjects: ethnic conflict, war
  Sensitivities: violence, sexual content, nudity, language,
    sexual attack

Canadian Bacon
  1994—United States
  Director: Michael Moore
  Cast: John Candy, Alan Alda, Rhea Perlman, Kevin Pollak,
    Rip Torn
  Subjects: presidency, foreign policy, war

The Candidate
  1972—United States
  Director: Michael Ritchie
  Cast: Robert Redford, Peter Boyle, Melvyn Douglas,
    Don Porter, Allen Garfield
  Subjects: campaigns, elections, media

Captain Planet and the Planeteers (television)
  1990—United States
  Cast: David Coburn, LeVar Burton, Joey Dedio, Kath Souci,
    Janice Kawaye, Whoopi Goldberg
  Subject: environment

Casablanca
  1943—United States
  Director: Michael Curtiz
  Cast: Humphrey Bogart, Ingrid Bergman, Paul Henreid,
    Claude Rains, Conrad Veidt
  Subjects: war, democracy, fascism

The Celluloid Closet
  1995—United States / United Kingdom / France / Germany

Director: Rob Epstein and Jeffrey Friedman
Documentary
Subjects: homosexuality, social justice, censorship
Sensitivities: brief nudity, violence, sexual content

Citizen Ruth
1996—United States
Director: Alexander Payne
Cast: Laura Dern, Swoosie Kurtz, Kurtwood Smith,
    Mary Kay Place, Kelly Preston
Subject: abortion
Sensitivities: violence, sex, language

A Civil Action
1998—United States
Director: Steven Zaillian
Cast: John Travolta, Robert Duvall, Tony Shalhoub,
    William H. Macy, Zeljko Ivanek
Subjects: environment, legal system

Civilization
1916—United States
Director: Reginald Barker and Thomas H. Ince
Cast: Howard C. Hickman, Enid Marky, Lola May,
    Kate Bruce, J. Frank Burk
Subject: war

Clear and Present Danger
1994—United States
Director: Philip Noyce
Cast: Harrison Ford, Willem Dafoe, Anne Archer,
    Joaquim de Almeida, Henry Czerny
Subjects: presidency, terrorism, national security,
    corruption, murder
Sensitivities: violence

Coming to America
1988—United States
Director: John Landis
Cast: Eddie Murphy, Arsenio Hall, James Earl Jones,
    John Amos, Madge Sinclair

Subject: Africa
Sensitivities: nudity, language

Confessions of a Nazi Spy
  1939—United States
  Director: Anatole Livak
  Cast: Edward G. Robinson, Francis Lederere,
    George Sanders, Paul Lukas, Henry O'Neill
  Subject: fascism

Congorilla
  1932—United States
  Directors: Martin E. Johnson and Osa Johnson
  Documentary
  Subject: Africa
  Sensitivities: nudity

Contender, The
  2000—France / United States
  Director: Rod Lurie
  Cast: Gary Oldman, Joan Allen, Jeff Bridges,
    Christian Slater, Sam Elliott
  Subjects: presidency, campaigns, election, women's rights
  Sensitivities: sexual situations

Cradle Will Rock
  1999—United States
  Director: Tim Robbins
  Cast: Hank Azaria, Ruben Blades, John Cusack,
    Joan Cusack, Cary Elwes
  Subjects: democracy, red scare, new deal politics, communism

Crisis: Behind a Presidential Commitment
  1963—United States
  Director: Robert Drew
  Documentary
  Subjects: racism, civil rights, presidency, federalism

Crossfire
  1947—United States
  Director: Edward Dmytryk

Cast: Robert Young, Robert Mitchum, Robert Ryan,
  Gloria Grahame, Paul Kelly
Subjects: anti-Semitism, social justice

The Cup
Phörpa
  1999—Bhutan / Australia
  Director: Khyentse Norbu
  Cast: Orguen Tobyal, Neten Chokling, Jampang Lodro,
    Lama Chonjor, Godu Lama
  Subject: globalization

Dave
  1993—United States
  Director: Ivan Reitman
  Cast: Kevin Kline, Sigourney Weaver, Frank Langella,
    Kevin Dunn, Ving Rhames
  Subjects: presidency, elections, political corruption
  Sensitivities: sexual situations

Day After, The
  1983—United States
  Director: Nicholas Meyer
  Cast: Jason Robards, JoBeth Williams, Steven Guttenberg,
    John Cullum, John Lithgow
  Subject: nuclear war
  Sensitivities: graphic violence

Dead Man Walking
  1995—United States / United Kingdom
  Director: Tim Robbins
  Cast: Susan Sarandon, Sean Penn, Robert Prosky,
    Raymond J. Barry, R. Lee Ermey
  Subject: death penalty
  Sensitivities: violence, sex, rape

Deep Impact
  1998—United States
  Director: Mimi Leder
  Cast: Robert Duvall, Tea Leoni, Elijah Wood,
    Vanessa Redgrave, Morgan Freeman
  Subjects: presidency, national security, military

The Deer Hunter
  1978—United States
  Director: Michael Cimino
  Cast: Robert De Niro, John Cazale, John Savage,
    Christopher Waken, Meryl Streep
  Subject: war
  Sensitivities: sex, violence

Dick
  1999—United States / France / Canada
  Director: Andrew Fleming
  Cast: Kirsten Dunst, Michelle Williams, Dan Hedaya,
    Will Ferrell, Bruce McCulloch
  Subjects: presidency, corruption, Watergate
  Sensitivities: sexual innuendo, language

Divided We Fall
Musíme si pomáhat
  2000—Czech Republic
  Director: Jan Hrebejk
  Cast: Bolek Polívka, Csongor Kassai, Jaroslav Dusek,
    Anna Sisková, Jirí Pecha
  Subjects: genocide, human rights
  Sensitivities: violence, sexual situations

Dr. Strangelove or, How I Learned to Stop Worrying and Love the Bomb
  1964—United Kingdom
  Director: Stanley Kubrick
  Cast: Peter Sellers, George C. Scott, Sterling Hayden,
    Keenan Wynn, Slim Pickens
  Subjects: war, nuclear weapons

Enemy of the State
  1998—United States
  Director: Tony Scott
  Cast: Will Smith, Gene Hackman, Jon Voight, Lisa Bonet,
    Regina King
  Subjects: presidency, national security, intelligence,
    civil liberties
  Sensitivities: violence

Erin Brockovich
  2000—United States
  Director: Steven Soderbergh
  Cast: Julia Roberts, David Brisbin, Albert Finney,
    Dawn Didawick, Valente Rodriguez
  Subject: environment
  Sensitivities: sexual innuendo

The Execution of Wanda Jean
  2002—United States
  Director: Liz Garbus
  Documentary
  Subjects: death penalty, legal system, civil rights, racism
  Sensitivities: language, violence

Fail Safe
  1964—United States
  Director: Sidney Lumet
  Cast: Dan O'Herlihy, Walter Matthau, Frank Overton,
    Ed Binns, Fritz Weaver
  Subjects: presidency, national security, war

Fall of the Romanoffs, The
  1917—United States
  Director: Herbert Brenon
  Cast: Peter Barbierre, W. Francis Chapin,
    Edward Connelly, Charles Craig, Pauline Curley
  Subject: communism
  Film is no longer extant

Fall of the Romanov Dynasty, The
Padeniye dinastij Romanovykh
  1927—Soviet Union
  Director: Esfir Shub
  Documentary
  Subjects: communism, war

Feed
  1992—United States
  Director: Kevin Rafferty and James Ridgeway

Documentary
Subjects: media, campaign, election, presidency

Fight Club
  1999—United States
  Director: David Fincher
  Cast: Edward Norton, Brad Pitt, Helena Bonham Carter,
    Meat Loaf, Zach Grenier
  Subject: capitalism
  Sensitivities: extreme violence, sexual situations, nudity

The Firemen's Ball
Horí má panenko
  1967—Czechoslovakia / Italy
  Director: Milos Forman
  Cast: Jan Vostrcil, Josef Sebanek, Josef Valnoha, Frantisek
    Debelka, Josef Kolb
  Subject: communism
  Sensitivities: sexual innuendo

The Front
  1976—United States
  Director: Martin Ritt
  Cast: Woody Allen, Zero Mostel, Herschel Bernardi,
    Michael Murphy, Andrea Marcovicci
  Subjects: communism, red scare, democracy, blacklist

Frontline (television)
  1996—*"Why Americans Hate the Press"*
  1996—United States
  Documentary
  Subjects: media, campaigns, elections

Gabriel Over the White House
  1933—United States
  Director: Gregory La Cava
  Cast: Walter Hutson, Karen Morley, Franchot Tone,
    Arthur Byron, Dickie Moore
  Subjects: democracy, fascism, presidency

The Genocide Factor
  2000—United States
  Director: Robert J. Emery
  Documentary
  Subject: genocide
  Sensitivities: genocidal violence

Gentleman's Agreement
  1947—United States
  Director: Elia Kazan
  Cast: Gregory Peck, Dorothy McGuire, John Garfield,
    Celeste Holm, Anne Revere
  Subjects: anti-Semitism, social justice

Ghosts of Mississippi
  1996—United States
  Director: Rob Reiner
  Cast: Alec Baldwin, James Woods, Virginia Madsen,
    Whoopi Goldberg, Susanna Thompson
  Subjects: civil rights, racism

Gods Must Be Crazy, The
  1980—Botswana
  Director: Jamie Uys
  Cast: Andrew Steyn, Sandra Prinsloo, N!xau, Louw Verwey
  Subjects: Africa, race relations

Godzilla
Gojira
  1956—Japan / United States
  Director: Ishirô Honda
  Cast: Raymond Burr, Takashi Shimura, Akira akarada,
    Momoko Kochi, Akihiko Hirata
  Subject: nuclear weapons

The Grand Illusion
La Grande Illusion
  1937—France
  Director: Jean Renior
  Cast: Jean Gabin, Dita Parlo, Pierre Fresnay,

Erich von Stroheim, Julien Carette
Subjects: war, nationalism, class relations

Great American Speeches Collection (video)
1997—United States
Documentary
Subjects: political parties, elections, media, rhetoric

Great Dictator, The
1940—United States
Director: Charles Chaplin
Cast: Charles Chaplin, Jack Oakie, Reginald Gardiner,
Henry Daniell, Billy Gilbert
Subjects: war, anti-Semitism

Guilty by Suspicion
1991—United States / France
Director: Irwin Winkler
Cast: Robert De Niro, Annette Bening, George Wendt,
Patricia Wettig, Same Wanamaker
Subjects: red scare, civil liberties, communism

Hair
1979—United States
Director: Milos Forman
Cast: John Savage, Treat Williams, Beverly D' Angelo,
Annie Golden, Dorsey Wright
Subject: individual freedom
Sensitivities: nudity

Harlan County, USA
1976—United States
Director: Barbara Kopple
Documentary
Subject: labor struggles
Sensitivities: mild violence

Hearts of the World
1918—United States
Director: D. W. Griffith
Cast: Valerie Germonprez
Subjects: war, human rights

Heir Conditioned
 1955—United States
 Director: Friz Freleng
 Cast: Mel Blanc
 Subject: capitalism

Herr Meets Hare
 1945—United States
 Director: Friz Freleng
 Cast: Mel Blanc
 Subject: fascism

Hitler's Children
 1942—United States
 Director: Edward Dmytryk and Irving Reis
 Cast: Tim Holt, Bonita Granville, Kent Smith, Otto Kruger,
  H.B. Warner
 Subject: fascism

Hollywood on Trial
 1976—United States
 Director: David Helpern
 Documentary
 Subjects: red scare, communism, freedom of speech

Holocaust (television)
 1978—United States
 Director: Marvin J. Chomsky
 Cast: Michael Moriarty, Meryl Streep, Deborah Norton
 Subjects: genocide, anti-Semitism
 Sensitivities: genocidal violence

I Married a Communist
 1949—United States
 Director: Robert Stevenson
 Cast: Laraine Day, Robert Ryan, John Agar,
  Thomas Gomez, Janis Carter
 Subject: communism

I Was a Captive of Nazi Germany
 1936—United States
 Cast: Isobel Lillian Steele
 Subject: fascism

I Was a Communist for the FBI
   1951—United States
   Director: Gordon Douglas
   Cast: Frank Lovejoy, Dorothy Hart, Philip Carey,
      James Millican, Richard Webb
   Subjects: red scare, communism

I'm on the Ballot
   2000—United States
   Director: Al Ward
   Documentary
   Subjects: third parties, campaigns, elections, media,
      presidency

In the Heat of the Night
   1967—United States
   Director: Norman Jewison
   Cast: Sidney Poitier, Rod Steiger, Warren Oates, Lee Grant,
      Larry Gates
   Subject: racism
   Sensitivities: mild violence

In the Line of Fire
   1993—United States
   Director: Wolfgang Petersen
   Cast: Clint Eastwood, John Malkovich, Rene Russo,
      Dylan McDermott, Gary Cole
   Subjects: presidency, assassination, campaigns, elections
   Sensitivities: violence language

Independence Day
   1996—United States
   Director: Roland Emmerich
   Cast: Bill Pullman, Mary McDonnell, Mae Whitman,
      Jeff Goldblum, Judd Hirsch
   Subjects: presidency, national security, conspiracy theory

Invasion of the Body Snatchers
   1956—United States
   Director: Don Siegel

Cast: Kevin McCarthy, Dana Wynter, Larry Gates, King
Donovan, Carolyn Jones
Subjects: red scare, communism, conformity

Invasion U.S.A.
1985—United States
Director: Joseph Zito
Cast: Chuck Norris, Richard Lynch, Melissa Prophet,
Alexander Zale, Alex Colon
Subject: terrorism
Sensitivities: violence

Iron Curtain, The
1948—United States
Director: William A. Wellman
Cast: Dana Andrews, Gene Tierney, Stefan Schabel,
Berry Kroeger, Frederic Tozere
Subject: communism

It Happened Here
1966—United Kingdom
Directors: Kevin Brownlow and Andrew Mollo
Cast: Pauline Murray, Sebastian Shaw, Bart Allison,
Reginald Marsh, Frank Bennett
Subject: fascism

It's a Mad Mad Mad Mad World
1963—United States
Director: Stanley Kramar
Cast: Spencer Tracy, Milton Berle, Sid Caesar,
Buddy Hackett, Ethel Merman
Subject: international relations

JFK
1991—United States / France
Director: Oliver Stone
Cast: Kevin Costner, Kevin Bacon, Tommy Lee Jones,
Laurie Metcalf, Gary Oldman
Subjects: presidency, conspiracy theories, military, foreign
policy, assassination
Sensitivities: language, sexual situations, violence

Journeys with George
  2002—United States
  Director: Aaron Lubarsky and Alexandra Pelosi
  Documentary
  Subjects: campaigns, elections, media, presidency

Judgment at Nuremberg
  1961—United States
  Director: Stanley Kramer
  Cast: Spencer Tracy, Burt Lancaster, Richard Widmark,
    Marlene Dietrich, Maximilian Schell
  Subjects: war crimes, genocide

Kaiser, Beast of Berlin
  1918—United States
  Director: Rupert Julian
  Cast: Rupert Julian, Elmo Lincoln, Nigel De Brulier,
    Lon Chaney
  Subjects: war, human rights
  This film is no longer extant

The Killing Fields
  1984—United Kingdom
  Director: Roland Joffe
  Cast: Sam Waterston, Haing S. Ngor, John Malkovich,
    Julian Sands, Craig T. Nelson
  Subject: genocide
  Sensitivities: genocidal violence

King Dinosaur
  1955—United States
  Director: Bert I. Gordon
  Cast: William Bryant, Wanda Curtis, Douglas Henderson,
    Patti Gallagher, Marvin Miller
  Subject: nuclear weapons

The Laramie Project
  2002—United States
  Director: Moises Kaufman
  Cast: Christina Ricci, Steve Buscemi, Laura Linney,
    Summer Phoenix, Dylan Baker, Amy Madigan

Subjects: homosexuality, hate crimes, social justice
Sensitivities: mild sexual content

The Last Hurrah
  1958—United States
  Director: John Ford
  Cast: Spencer Tracy, Jeffrey Hunter, Dianne Foster,
    Pat O'Brien, Basil Rathbone
  Subjects: elections, campaigns, political machines

Lenin in 1918
Lenin v 1918 godu
  1939—Soviet Union
  Director: E. Aron and Mikhail Romm
  Cast: Boris Shchukin, Nikolai Cherkasov, Mikheil Gelovani,
    Nikolai Bogolyubov, V. Markov
  Subject: commuinism

Lenin in October
Lenin v Oktyabre
  1937—Soviet Union
  Directors: Mikhail Romm and Dmitri Vasilyev
  Cast: Boris Shchukin, Bladimir Pokrovsky,
    Nikolai Okhlopkov, Vasili Vanin, Nikolai Sokolov
  Subject: communism

Life is Beautiful
La Vita è bella
  1997—Italy
  Director: Roberto Benigni
  Cast: Roberto Benigni, Nicoletta Braschi, Giustino Durano
  Subjects: genocide, anti-Semitism
  Sensitivities: genocidal violence

Lifeboat
  1944—United States
  Director: Alfred Hitchcock
  Cast: Tallulah Bankhead, William Bendix, Walter Slezak,
    Mary Anderson, John Hodiak
  Subjects: war, democracy

The Little American
  1917—United States
  Director: Cecil B. DeMille and Joseph Levering
  Cast: Mary Pickford, Jack Holt, Raymond Hatton
  Subjects: war, human rights
  Sensitivities: attempted rape

Loves of a Blonde
  1965—Czechoslovakia
  Director: Milos Forman
  Cast: Hana Brejchova, Vladimir Pucholt, Vladimi Mensik,
    Ivan Kheil, Jiri Hruby
  Subject: communism
  Sensitivities: sexual innuendo

Lumumba—Death of a Prophet
Lumumba: La mort du prophete
  1992—France
  Director: Raoul Peck
  Documentary
  Subjects: colonialism, race relations

Lumumba
Lumumba, retour au Congo
  2000—France
  Director: Raoul Peck
  Cast: Eriq Ebouaney, Alex Descas, Théophile Sowié,
    Maka Kotto
  Subjects: colonialism, race relations

*M*A*S*H* (television)
  1972–1983—United States
  Director: Alan Alda and Hy Averback
  Cast: Alan Alda, Wayne Rogers, Mike Farrell, Loretta Swit,
    McLean Stevenson
  Subject: war

The Man I Married, The
  1940—United States
  Director: Irving Pichel
  Cast: Joan Bennett, Francis Lederer, Lloyd Nolan,

Anna Sten, Otto Kruger
Subjects: communism, red scare

The Manchurian Candidate
1962—United States
Director: John Frankenheim
Cast: Frank Sinatra, Laurence Harvey, Janet Leigh,
   Angela Lansbury, Henry Silva
Subjects: fascism, red scare, political assassination,
   communism

Mars Attacks!
1996—United States
Director: Tim Burton
Cast: Jack Nicholson, Glenn Close, Annette Bening,
   Pierce Brosnan, Danny Devito
Subjects: presidency, national security, war
Sensitivities: drug innuendo

Matewan
1987—United States
Director: John Sayles
Cast: Chris Cooper, James Earl Jones, Mary McDonnell,
   Will Oldham, David Strathairn
Subjects: labor struggles, race relations, entrenched
   economic power

Metropolis
1927—Germany
Director: Fritz Lang
Cast: Alfred Abel, Gustav Frohlich, Brigitte Helm,
   Rudolf Klein-Rogge, Fritz Rasp
Subjects: democracy, labor relations
Sensitivities: sexual innuendo

Mighty Joe Young
1998—United States
Director: Ron Underwood
Cast: Bill Paxton, Charlize Theron, Rade Serbedzija,
   Regina King, Peter Firth
Subject: Africa

Minority Report
  2002—USA
  Director: Steven Spielberg
  Cast: Tom Cruise, Colin Farrell, Samantha Morton,
    Max von Sydow, Lois Smith
  Subjects: democracy, fascism, civil liberties
  Sensitivities: violence, medical procedure

The Missiles of October
  1974—United States
  Director: Anthony Page
  Cast: William Devane, Ralph Bellamy, Howard DaSilva,
    James Hong, Martin Sheen
  Subject: war

Missing
  1982—United States
  Director: Costa-Gavras
  Cast: Jack Lemmon, Sissy Spacek, Melanie Mayron,
    John Shea, Charles Cioffi
  Subjects: human rights, democracy
  Sensitivities: violence

Mission to Moscow
  1943—United States
  Director: Michael Curtiz
  Cast: Walter Huston, Ann Harding, Oskar Homolka,
    George Tobias, Gene Lockhart
  Subjects: fascism, communism

Mississippi Burning
  1988—United States
  Director: Alan Parker
  Cast: Gene Hackman, William Dafoe,
    Frances McDormand, Brad Dourif, R. Lee Ermey
  Subjects: racism, civil rights
  Sensitivities: violence, language

Monster's Ball
  2001—United States
  Director: Marc Forster

Cast: Billy Bob Thornton, Heath Ledger, Halle Berry,
 Peter Boyle, Sean 'P. Diddy'
Subjects: racism, death penalty
Sensitivities: explicit sex, language, violence

Monty Python and the Holy Grail (1975)
 1975—United Kingdom
 Director: Terry Gilliam and Terry Jones
 Cast: Graham Chapman, John Cleese, Eric Idle,
  Terry Gilliam, Terry Jones
 Subject: democracy
 Sensitivities: sexual innuendo

Mr. Death: The Rise and Fall of Fred A. Leuchter, Jr.
 1999—United States
 Director: Errol Morris
 Documentary
 Subjects: death penalty, holocaust denial

Mr. Smith Goes to Washington
 1939—United States
 Director: Frank Capra
 Cast: Jean Arthur, James Stewart, Claude Rains,
  Edward Arnold, Guy Kibbee
 Subjects: democracy, political machines, U.S. Senate

Murder at 1600
 1997—United States
 Director: Dwight H. Little
 Cast: Wesley Snipes, Diane Lane, Daniel Benzali,
  Dennis Miller, Alan Alda
 Subjects: presidency, national security, conspiracy
 Sensitivities: sex, violence, language

Murder on a Sunday Morning
Un Coupable Ideal
 2001—France / United States
 Director: Jean-Xavier de Lestrade
 Documentary
 Subjects: racial profiling, justice system, civil rights

My Fellow Americans
  1996—United States
  Director: Peter Segal
  Cast: Jack Lemmon, James Garner, Dan Aykroyd,
    John Heard, Wilford Brimley
  Subjects: presidency, corruption, conspiracy
  Sensitivities: language

Naked Gun 2 1/2:The Smell of Fear
  1991—United States
  Director: David Zucker
  Cast: Leslie Nielsen, Priscilla Presley, George Kennedy,
    O.J. Simpson, Robert Goulet
  Subjects: presidency, conspiracy
  Sensitivities: juvenile humor, sexuality

Network
  1976—United States
  Director: Sidney Lumet
  Cast: Faye Dunaway, William Holden, Peter Finch,
    Robert Duvall, Wesley Addy
  Subjects: globalization, media
  Sensitivities: nudity, sexual situation, language, violence

Nixon
  1995—United States
  Director: Oliver Stone
  Cast: Anthony Hopkins, Joan Allen, Powers Booth,
    Ed Haris, Bob Hoskins
  Subjects: presidency, Watergate, conspiracy, foreign
    policy, war
  Sensitivities: language

O Brother, Where Art Thou?
  2000—United States
  Director: Joel Coen
  Cast: George Clooney, John Turturro, Tim Blake Neison,
    John Goodman, Holly Hunter
  Subjects: racism, civil rights

On the Beach
  1959—United States
  Director: Stanley Kramer
  Cast: Gregory Peck, Ava Gardner, Fred Astaire,
    Anthony Perkins, Donna Anderson
  Subject: nuclear war

One Flew Over the Cuckoo's Nest
  1975—United States
  Director: Milos Forman
  Cast: Jack Nicholson, Louise Fletcher, William Redfield,
    Michael Berryman, Peter Brocco
  Subject: personal freedom
  Sensitivities language, nudity, suicide

The Pelican Brief
  1994—United States
  Director: Alan J. Pakula
  Cast: Julia Roberts, Denzel Washington, Sam Shepard,
    John Heard, Tony Goldwyn
  Subjects: presidency, political conspiracy, assassination
  Sensitivities: violence

The People vs. Larry Flynt
  1996—United States
  Director: Milos Forman
  Cast: Woody Harrelson, Courtney Love, Edward Norton,
    Brett Harrelson, Donna Hanover
  Subjects: free speech, pornography, civil liberties
  Sensitivities: nudity, language, sex, sexual situations

A Perfect Candidate
  1996—United States
  Directors: R.J. Cutler and David Van Taylor
  Documentary
  Subjects: campaigns, elections, media

Platoon
  1986—United States
  Director: Oliver Stone

Cast: Tom Berenger, Willem Dafoe, Charlie Sheen,
   Forest Whitaker, Francesco Quinn
Subject: war
Sensitivities: violence

Potemkin
Bronenosets Potyomkin
   1925—Soviet Union
   Director: Sergei Eisenstein and Grigori Aleksandrov
   Cast: Aleksandr Antonov, Vladimir Barsky,
      Grigori Aleksandrov, Mikhail Gomorov
   Subjects: war, communism
   Sensitivities: violence

Primary
   1960—United States
   Director: Robert Drew and Richard Leacock
   Documentary
   Subjects: campaigns, elections, presidency

Primary Colors
   1998—United States
   Director: Mike Nichols
   Cast: John Travolta, Emma Thompson,
      Billy Bob Thornton, Kathy Bates, Adrian Lester
   Subjects: presidency, campaigns, elections, corruption
   Sensitivities: language, sex

PT-109
   1963—United States
   Director: Leslie H. Martinson
   Cast: Cliff Robertson, Ty Hardin, James Gregory,
      Robert Culp
   Subject: presidency

The Rabbit of Seville
   1950—United States
   Director: Chuck Jones
   Cast: Mel Blanc
   Subject: war

The Red Menace
   1949—United States
   Director: R.G. Springsteen
   Cast: Robert Rockwell, Hannelore Axman,
      Betty Lou Gerson, Lester Luther, Bill Lally
   Subjects: red scare, communism

A Report on the Party and the Guest
O slavnosti a hostech
   1966—Czechoslovakia
   Director: Jan Nemec
   Cast: Ivan Vyskocil, Jan Klusák, Jiri Nemec, Pavel Bosek,
      Karel Mares
   Subject: communism

Roger & Me
   1989—United States
   Director: Michael Moore
   Documentary
   Subjects: capitalism, labor struggles
   Sensitivities: violence (rabbits are butchered; one man is
      shot)

The Rose of the Blood
   1917—United States
   Director: J. Gordon Edwards
   Cast: Theda Bara, Genevieve Blinn, Charles Clary,
      Marie Kiernan, Joe King
   Subjects: communism, terrorism
   This film is no longer extant

Rosewood
   1997—United States
   Director: John Singleton
   Cast: Jon Voight, Ving Rhames, John Readle, Loren Dean,
      Esther Rolle
   Subjects: racism, genocide, human rights
   Sensitivities: violence, sexuality

Schindler's List
  1993—United States
  Director: Steven Spielberg
  Cast: Liam Neeson, Ben Kingsley, Ralph Fiennes,
    Caroline Goodall, Jonathan Sagall
  Subjects: genocide, anti-Semitism
  Sensitivities: violence, sex, genocidal scenes

Seven Days in May
  1964—United States
  Director: John Frankenheimer
  Cast: Burt Lancaster, Kirk Douglas, Fredric March,
    Ava Gardner, Edmond O'Brien
  Subjects: presidency, conspiracy, military, national
    security, foreign policy

Shadow Conspiracy
  1997—United States
  Director: George P. Cosmatos
  Cast: Charlie Sheen, Donald Sutherland, Linda Hamilton,
    Stephen Lang, Ben Gazzara
  Subjects: presidency, conspiracy, political assassination
  Sensitivities: violence

Silent Running
  1972—United States
  Director: Douglas Trumbull
  Cast: Bruce Dern, Cliff Potts, Ron Rifkin, Jesse Vint,
    Steve Brown
  Subject: environment
  Sensitivities: mild violence

Simpsons, The (television):
"Two Cars in Every Garage, Three Eyes on Every Fish"
  (1990)
"Mr. Lisa Goes to Washington" (1991)
"Treehouse of Horror VII: Citizen Kang" (1996)
"Trash of the Titans" (1998)
  1989–2002—United States
  Created by: Matt Groening

Cast: Dan Castellaneta, Julie Kavner, Nancy Cartwright,
Yeardley Smith, Hank Azaria
Subjects: campaigns, elections, presidency, environment,
democracy

Soylent Green
1973—United States
Director: Richard Fleischer
Cast: Charlton Heston, Leigh Taylor-Young, Chuck Connors
Joseph Cotton, Brock Peters, Edward G. Robinson
Subjects: environment, corruption
Sensitivities: violence

The Spirit of '43
1943—United States
Director: Jack King
Cast: Donald Duck
Subjects: democracy, fascism, war

Star Wars
1977—United States
Director: George Lucas
Cast: Mark Hamill, Harrison Ford, Carrie Fisher,
Peter Cushing, Alec Guinness
Subjects: terrorism, war

Starship Troopers
1997—United States
Director: Paul Verhoeven
Cast: Casper Van Dien, Dina Meyer, Denise Richards,
Jake Busey, Neil Patrick Harris
Subjects: war, fascism
Sensitivities: graphic violence, nudity, sexual situations

State of the Union
1948—United States
Director: Frank Capra
Cast: Spencer Tracy, Katharine Hepburn, Van Johnson,
Angela Lansbury, Adolphe Menjou
Subjects: democracy, media, elections, campaigns,
presidency

Store Wars
  2001—United States
  Director: Micha X. Peled
  Documentary
  Subjects: capitalism, democracy

Stuff for Stuff
  1949—United States
  Documentary
  Subject: capitalism

The Sum of All Fears
  2002—United States
  Director: Phil Alden Robinson
  Cast: Morgan Freeman, Ben Affleck, Richard Marner,
    James Cromwell
  Subjects: terrorism, nuclear weapons, presidency
  Sensitivities: violence

Sunrise at Campobello
  1960—United States
  Director: Vincent J. Donehue
  Cast: Ralph Bellamy, Greer Garson, Hume Cronyn,
    Jean Hagen, Ann Shoemaker
  Subject: presidency

The Tempest
  1927—United States
  Director: Sam Taylor
  Cast: John Barrymore, Camilla Horn, Lewis Wolheim,
    Boris de Fas
  Subject: communism

Tender Comrade
  1943—United States
  Director: Edward Dmytryk
  Cast: Ginger Rogers, Robert Ryan, Ruth Hussey,
    Patricia Collinge, Mady Christians
  Subjects: communism, democracy

Them!
  1954—United States
  Director: Gordon Douglas
  Cast: James Whitmore, Edmund Gwenn, Joan Weldon,
    James Arness, Onslow Stevens
  Subject: nuclear weapons

The Thin Blue Line
  1988—United States
  Director: Errol Morris
  Cast: Randall Adams, David Harris, Gus Rose,
    Jackie Johnson, Marshall Touchton
  Subject: death penalty

Thirteen Days
  2000—United States
  Director: Roger Donaldson
  Cast: Kevin Costner, Shawn Driscoll, Bruce Greenwood,
    Drake Cook, Steven Culp
  Subjects: war, nuclear weapons

Threads
  1984—United Kingdom
  Director: Mick Jackson
  Cast: Karen Meagher, Reece Dinsdale, David Brierly,
    Rita May, Nicholas Lane
  Subject: nuclear war
  Sensitivities: violence

To Kill a Mockingbird
  1962—United States
  Director: Robert Mulligan
  Cast: Gregory Peck, John Megna, Frank Overton,
    Rosemary Murphy, Ruth White
  Subjects: racism, legal system, civil rights

Triumph of the Will
  Triumph des Willens
  1934—Germany

Director: Leni Riefenstahl
Documentary
Subject: fascism

Truman
  1995—United States
  Director: Frank Pierson
  Cast: Gary Sinise, Diana Scarwid, Richard A. Dysart,
    Colm Feore, James Gammon
  Subjects: presidency, foreign policy, campaigns, elections

Turning Point (television)
"Murder in Mississippi: The Price of Freedom" (1990)
  1990—United States
  Director: Roger Young
  Cast: Tom Hulce, Jennifer Grey, Blair Underwood,
    Andre Braugher
  Subjects: racism, civil rights

TV Nation (television)
  1993–94—United Kingdom / United States
  Director: Michael Moore
  Cast: Michael Moore, Rusty Cundieff, Karen Duffy,
    Jeneane Garofalo, Ben Hamper
  Subjects: civil rights, racism, labor struggle, media

The Twilight Zone (television)
"The Monsters Are Due on Maple Street" (1960)
  1959–1965—United States
  Director: Ron Winston
  Cast: Claude Akins, Jack Weston, Amzie Strickland,
    Barry Atwater, Anne Barton
  Subject: terrorism

Wag the Dog
  1997—United States
  Director: Barry Levinson
  Cast: Dustin Hoffman, Robert De Niro, Anne Heche,
    Denis Leary, Willie Nelson

Subjects: presidency, conspiracy, political corruption,
   national security, war
Sensitivities: sexual innuendo, language

War Game
   1965—United Kingdom
   Director: Peter Watkins
   Cast: Michael Aspel, Peter Graham
   Subject: nuclear war
   Sensitivities: violence

The War Room
   1993—United States
   Director: Chris Hegedus and D.A. Pennebaker
   Documentary
   Subjects: media, campaigns, elections, presidency,
      political parties

WarGames
   1983—United States
   Director: John Badham
   Cast: Matthew Broderick, Dabney Coleman, John Wood,
      Ally Sheedy, Barry Cordin
   Subject: nuclear war

Welcome to Sarajevo
   1997—United States / United Kingdom
   Director: Michael Winterbottom
   Cast: Stephen Dillane, Woody Harrelson, Marisa Tomei,
      Emira Nusevic, Kerry Fox
   Subjects: ethnic conflict, war
   Sensitivities: language, violence

The West Wing (television)
"College Kids" (2002)
"Two Cathedrals" (2001)
"Mr. Willis of Ohio" (1999)
"A Proportional Response" (1999)
"The Short List" (1999)
   1999–2002—United States

Director: Aaron Sorkin
Cast: Martin Sheen, Rob Lowe, Stockard Channing,
    Dule Hill, Allison Janney, Janal Moloney
Subjects: democracy, presidency, elections, civil liberties,
    civil rights, national security

When My Ship Comes In
  1934—United States
  Director: Dave Fleischer
  Cast: Betty Boop
  Subject: capitalism

When the Men Left Town
  1914—United States
  Director: C. Jay Williams
  Subjects: women's suffrage, democracy
  This film appears to be no longer extant

When the Wind Blows
  1986—United Kingdom
  Director: Jimmy I. Murakami
  Cast: Peggy Ashcroft, John Mills, Robin Houston,
    James Russell, David Dundas
  Subject: nuclear war

When We Were Soldiers
  2002—United States
  Director: Randall Wallace
  Cast: Mel Gibson, Madeleine Stowe, Greg Kinnear,
    Sam Elliott, Chris Klein
  Subject: war
  Sensitivities: violence

Why We Fight: The Nazis Strike
  1943—United States
  Director: Frank Capra
  Documentary
  Subjects: war, democracy, fascism

Wilson
  1944—United States

Director: Henry King
Cast: Charles Coburn, Alexander Knox,
    Geraldine Fitzgerald, Thomas Mitchell, Ruth Nelson
Subjects: presidency, foreign policy, war

Wings
1927—United States
Director: William A. Wellman
Cast: Clara Bow, Charles 'Buddy' Rogers, Richard Arlen,
    Jobyna Ralston, El Brendel
Subject: war

Xala
1975—Senegal
Director: Osumane Sembene
Cast: Makhouredia Gueye, Thierno Leye, Dieynaba Niang,
    Myriam Niang, Iliamane Sagna
Subject: colonialism

The X-Files (television)
1993–2002—United States
Director: Rob Bowman
Cast: David Duchovny, Gillian Anderson, John Neville,
    William B. Davis, Martin Landau
Subjects: conspiracy theory

Yankee Dood It
1956—United States
Director: Friz Freleng
Cast: Mel Blanc, Arthur Q. Bryan
Subject: capitalism

Yankee Doodle Dandy
1942—United States
Director: Michael Curtiz
Cast: James Cagney, Joan Leslie, Walter Huston,
    Richard Whorf, Irene Manning
Subjects: presidency, patriotism

You're a Sap Mr. Jap
1942—United States

Director: Dan Gordon
Cast: Jack Mercer
Subjects: war, fascism
Sensitivities: racial stereotypes

Young Mr. Lincoln
1939—United States
Director: John Ford
Cast: Henry Fonda, Alice Brady, Marjorie Weaver,
Arleen Whelan, Eddie Collins
Subject: presidency

Notes

Introduction

1. See our guide to video and DVD sources in the appendix.
2. Ernest Giglio, *Here's Looking at You* (New York: Peter Lang, 2000) and Michael Genovese, *Politics and the Cinema* (Lexington, MA: Ginn Press, 1986). Giglio discusses Dr. Genovese's groundbreaking efforts defining political film at length in his text, and then offers an alternative definition that includes studying the film's *intent* and *effect* to determine whether or not it is truly political. At the same time, Giglio advises that, despite all of the noble and systematic efforts to define political film, any one precise definition may be too elusive and doomed to failure. As Giglio suggests, "In the final analysis . . . the political character of a film may lie in the eye of the beholder rather than any textbook definition" (Giglio, 32–33).

3. Genovese's political taxonomy cited in Giglio, p. 23.

4. For a more complete definition and analysis of propaganda see Bruce L. Smith, "Propaganda," in *The International Encyclopedia of the Social Sciences* (New York: Macmillan, 1968). For further reading consult: Jacques Ellul, *Propaganda: The Formation of Men's Attitudes* (New York: Knopf, 1965); and, Garth S. Jowett and Victoria O'Donnell, *Propaganda and Persuasion* (Thousand Oaks, CA: Sage, 1999).

5. For an in-depth view of German propaganda, see Randall Bytwerk's collection of Nazi and East German propaganda: *http://www.calvin.edu/academic/cas/gpa/*.

6. One scene that is unsettling is near the beginning of the film where the Macedonian paramilitaries use a cat for target practice with their automatic weapons.

7. Francis Fukuyama, *The End of History and the Last Man* (New York: Free Press, 1992). Fukuyama argues that a liberal ideology is the final form of human government and that its last two significant universal challenges were fascism and communism in the twentieth century.

Chapter 2

1. Transcribed from the film.

2. The Senate itself has been an evolving institution. The 17th Amendment (1913) established the direct election of U.S. Senators. Prior to 1913, senators were selected by state legislators, as mandated by the U.S. Constitution.

3. The essay contest guidelines in *Reading Digest* stipulate that the essay entries be "fiercely patriotic."

4. "Mr. Lisa Goes to Washington": Nelson Muntz quote from *The Simpsons: A Complete Guide to Our Favorite Family,* Ray Richmond and Antonia Coffman, eds. (New York: HarperPerennial, 1997), 63.

5. ibid.

6. ibid.

7. Grant Matthews' (Tracy's) speech transcribed from the film.

8. Eric Schlosser, *Fast Food Nation* (New York: Perennial, 2002), 38.

9. ibid.

10. Transcribed from *The West Wing's* season four episode "College Kids" (original airdate: October 2, 2002).

11. Martin Sheen, "Foreword," in Aaron Sorkin, *The West Wing: The Official Companion* (New York: Pocket Books, 2002), viii.

12. Aaron Sorkin, *The West Wing: The Official Companion* (New York: Pocket Books, 2002), 46.

13. John Wells' quote from Aaron Sorkin, *The West Wing: The Official Companion* (New York: Pocket Books, 2002), 60.

14. Aaron Sorkin, *The West Wing: The Official Companion* (New York: Pocket Books, 2002), 47.

15. ibid, 62.

16. ibid, 67.

17. This aspect of the show is discussed in depth in Chapter Four, "The American Presidency."

18. For the quote, see *The West Wing* home page: http://www.nbc.com/The_West_Wing/index.html. For an index of "West Wing Hot Topics" see http://www.nbc.com/nbc/The_West_Wing/hot_topics/archive.shtml or http://www.nbc.com/nbc/The_West_Wing/hot_topics/index.shtml.

19. "Two Cathedrals" episode excerpt taken from Aaron Sorkin, *The West Wing Script Book* (New York: Newmarket Press), 396–97.

20. The United States proposed three institutions, the International Bank for Reconstruction and Development (or World Bank), the International Monetary Fund (IMF), and an International Trade Organization (ITO). The proposal for an international trade organization never got off the ground, and an on-going conference called the General Agreement on Tariffs and Trade (GATT) took its place instead. In the mid-1990s, GATT was, in turn, replaced by the World Trade Organization (WTO), which took on many of the functions of the originally proposed ITO.

21. Steven L. Spiegel and Fred L. Wheling, *World Politics in a New Era,* Second Edition (Fort Worth: Harcourt Brace College Publishers, 1999), pp. 260–61.

22. Warner Brothers cartoons also took on other issues as well. The 1936 cartoon *I Love to Singa* seemingly is a film about fitting into American culture.

23. See also *How They Got the Vote* (1913) and *When Men Wear Skirts* (1914).

24. Louis B. Mayer, a staunch Republican, held the film until President Herbert Hoover (1929–1933), also a Republican, was out of office. MGM released the film when Democrat Franklin Delano Roosevelt (1933–1945) took the reins of power, in large part because the movie is very critical of presidential inaction in the face of a deepening depression. In other words, Mayer and Hearst did not want the film—which advocates ultra-powerful executive action to combat joblessness and racketeering—to be seen as a direct attack on Hoover's performance and policies.

25. *Gabriel Over the White House* is also discussed in Chapter Four, "The American Presidency."

26. ibid.

27. David Edelstein, "Blame Runner," *Salon.com,* June 21, 2002: http://slate.msn.com/?id = 2067225.

28. The Patriot Act, legislation granting the Justice Department increased capacity, power and latitude to investigate and prosecute terrorism—including, among other items, expanded wiretapping authority—was passed overwhelmingly in the U.S. House and Senate. In the U.S. Senate, only one senator—Russ Feingold (D-WI)—opposed the hugely popular measure.

29. Associated Press, "Wal-Mart Now Pa.'s Biggest Private Employer," *Pittsburgh Post-Gazette,* Monday, October 21, 2002. Accessed online: http://www.post-gazette.com/breaking/20021021employp7.asp:

> Surpassing steel mills, coal mines, higher education and high technology, the world's largest retailer has taken over as Pennsylvania's largest private employer. . . . Wal-Mart has surged past the University of Pennsylvania, long the state's largest private employer with about 25,000 faculty and staff members, in a state Department of Labor and Industry ranking.

30. $63 million budget for *Fight Club*—see: http://us.imdb.com/Business?0137523.

31. "Shit they don't need"—quote attributed to Tyler Durden (Brad Pitt).

32. Roger Ebert's two-star review of *Fight Club* in the *Chicago Sun-Times* accessed online: http://www.suntimes.com/ebert/ebert_reviews/1999/10/101502.html.

33. http://www.suntimes.com/ebert/ebert_reviews/1999/10/101502.html.

34. http://www.the-numbers.com/movies/1999/FIGHT.html.

35. ibid.

36. David Crary, "'Jurassic Park' Fans U.S.-French Fight Over Films," *Chicago Sun-Times* (October 21, 1993), page 34. In a similar story, French farmers have also protested the effects of the United States and EuroDisney on French culture and politics. See Matthew Fraser, "EuroDisney has to cope with irate farmers, slack turnstiles," *The (Montreal) Gazette* (June 29, 1992), page B1.

37. See Benjamin R. Barber (1992) "Jihad vs. McWorld," *The Atlantic Monthly* 269 (3): 53–63 (March 1992); Thomas L. Friedman (1999) "Manifesto for a Fast World," *The New York Times Magazine* (28 March 1999), pages 40–44 ff.; Thomas L. Friedman, *Lexus and the Olive Tree* (New York: Farrar, Straus, Giroux, 1999); and, Thomas L. Friedman and Ignacio Ramonet (1999) "Dueling Globalizations: A Debate Between Thomas L. Friedman and Ignacio Ramonet," *Foreign Policy* 116: 110–127 (Fall 1999).

38. Michael Moore, *Downsize This! Random Threats from an Unarmed American* (New York: Crown Publishers, 1996).

39. Roger Ebert's review of *The Big One, Chicago Sun-Times* (April 4, 1998).

Chapter 3

1. Francis Fukuyama, "The End of History," *National Interest* 16: 1–31 (Summer 1989).
2. For further reading see Richard Taylor, *The Battleship Potemkin: The Film Companion* (New York: I. B. Tauris, 2000); and Herbert Marshall, *The Battleship Potemkin* (New York: Avon Books, 1978).
3. For a review of the work of Esther Shub, see Vlada Petric, "Esther Shub: Cinema is My Life" and "Esther Shub's Unreleased Project," *Quarterly Review of Film Studies* 3 (4): 429–56 (Fall 1978).
4. David Cook, *A History of Narrative Film* (New York: W. W. Norton and Company, 1981), p 314.
5. The Soviet Union officially became a nuclear power in 1949.
6. In fact, during the famous late-1940s hearings of the House Committee on Un-American Activities, 1943's *Mission to Moscow* was cited as an example of Hollywood's—and the Roosevelt Administration's—pro-Soviet subversion and tendency to sugarcoat, and even promote, communism. HUAC's criticism of the film, FDR, and former U.S. Ambassador to the U.S.S.R., Joseph E. Davies, led to the eventual blacklisting of *Mission to Moscow*'s screenwriter, Howard Koch. Koch later moved to England, and, along with his wife, found some success as a writer overseas. For Howard Koch's blacklist and subsequent move to the UK, see: http://us.imdb.com/Bio?Koch, + Howard.
7. Ron Briley, "John Wayne and *Big Jim McLain* (1952): The Duke's Cold War Legacy," *Film & History* 31:1 (2002), 28. Briley discusses Wayne's influence on the film, and his box-office drawing power, in detail.
8. Phillip A. Gianos, *Politics and Politicians in American Film* (Westport, CT: Praeger, 1998), 140.
9. Ernest Giglio, *Here's Looking at You* (New York: Peter Lang, 2000), 91.
10. ibid.
11. Phillip A. Gianos, *Politics and Politicians in American Film* (Westport, CT: Praeger, 1998), 140.
12. In the DVD version of the film, this scene is entitled "207 Commies, 1 Idiot"!
13. William H. Chafe, *The Unfinished Journey* (New York: Oxford University Press, 1991), 105.
14. ibid.

15. Rep. Dies had strong connections to the Ku Klux Klan, who welcomed (and cheered) the congressional committee's new focus on exposing and defeating left-wing "subversives."

16. "House Un-American Activities Committee (HUAC), 1934–77," National Archives and Records Administration, online: http://www.nara.gov/nara/legislative/house_guide/hgch25bw.html. Accessed 6/25/01.

17. Bruce Bl. Bustard, *A New Deal for the Arts* (Washington, DC: National Archives and Records Administration, and Seattle: The University of Washington Press, 1997), 94–95.

18. Bernstein was not the only blacklisted individual to earn kudos for his work on *The Front:* Zero Mostel garnered a nomination for Best Supporting Actor from The British Academy Film and Television Awards (BAFTA). The British Academy of Film and Television Awards, founded in 1947, are the major film awards held in Great Britain. In 1969 Mostel was nominated for Best Actor in a Musical/Comedy for his role in Mel Brooks' *The Producers.*

19. This account was taken from James Reid Paris, *Classic Foreign Films: From 1960 to Today* (New York: Citadel Press, 1993), p. 94.

20. Renata Adler, "The Firemen's Ball," *New York Times* (30 September 1968), p. 60.

21. For an excellent account of the events leading to the fall of the Novotny regime, the Soviet invasion and its aftermath from an American perspective see Alan Levy, *So Many Heroes* (Sagaponack, NY: Second Chance Press, 1980).

22. Vincent Canby "A Report on the Party and the Guests," *New York Times* (28 September 1968), p. 37.

23. Although there is some evidence to suggest that fascism attempted to link itself to a consistent theory. Theorist Giovanni Gentile sought to link fascism with Hegelian idealism. For a discussion of the non-theoretical aspects of fascism see Einaudi, "Fascism," in *The International Encyclopedia of the Social Sciences* (New York: Macmillan, 1968), p. 336.

24. For a discussion of German escapism in films during the Nazi period, see Richard Traubner, "The Sound and the Führer," *Film Comment* 14 (4): 17–23 (July–Aug 1978); and "Berlin II—The Retrospective," *American Film* 4 (7): 67–69 (May 1979).

25. David Cook, *A History of Narrative Film,* p. 312.

26. See Siegfried Kracauer, *From Caligari to Hitler: A Psychological History of the German Film* (Princeton: Princeton University Press, 1947), pp. 300–03.

27. David Cook, *A History of Narrative Film,* pp. 311–12.

28. See, for example, John Griffin, "Starship Troopers a Vulgar Shockfest of Teens vs. Bugs," *Montreal Gazette* (7 November 1997),

p. D2; and Ron Weiskind, "Brave New Bugs: 'Starship Troopers' Probes a Future of Fascism and Pest Problems" *Pittsburgh Post-Gazette* (7 November 1997), p. 4.

29. Of course this is an interesting idea that many people have played with in literature. Take for example the novel by Robert Harris, *Fatherland,* which tells the hypothetical story of Adolf Hitler's 75th birthday celebration in 1964. Even George Orwell's *1984* is based on the suspicion that the aftermath of the Second World War continues for some forty years. Those interested in such a genre might also want to consider Margaret Atwood's *Handmaid's Tale* as well.

Chapter 4

1. Most of the first half of this chapter—until *The West Wing* section—is taken directly from Kevan M. Yenerall and Christopher S. Kelley, "Shysters, Sycophants, and Sexual Deviants: The Hollywood Presidency in the 1990s," *White House Studies* volume 3, number 3, 2003. Earlier working versions of this section dealing with the depiction of the American presidency in the 1990s also appeared under the following titles at the two national conferences: "Shysters, Sycophants and Sexual Deviants: The Hollywood Presidency in the 1990s," paper presented at the Images of Presidents in Film and Television National Conference, Westlake Village, California, November 10–12, 2000; and "Shysters, Sycophants and Sexual Deviants: How Hollywood Depicts the Presidency in the 1990s," paper presented at the annual meeting of the American Political Science Association, Boston, MA, September 3–6, 1998.

2. Robert Brent Toplin, ed., *Hollywood as Mirror* (Westport, CT: Greenwood Press, 1993), p. vii.

3. Bruce Handy, "Acting Presidents." *Time* (April 14, 1997), p. 99.

4. Gore Vidal's play *The Best Man* staged yet another successful revival on Broadway in the fall of 2000. Charles Durning (President Hockstader) and Spalding Gray (William Russell), among others, led the star-studded cast. While the play ran during the heat of the 2000 presidential election, Vidal did not alter the script to critique Al Gore and George W. Bush or reflect the times.

5. The character Groeteschele, a professor of international relations, hardcore realist and Pentagon adviser, was based on Henry Kissinger.

6. George Clooney reprised Fonda's role in a made-for-television version of *Fail Safe* in 2000.

7. John H. Lenihan, "Hollywood Laughs at the Cold War, 1947–61," in Robert Brent Toplin, ed., *Hollywood as Mirror* (Westport, CT: Greenwood Press, 1993), 141.

8. See: Lenihan, "Hollywood Laughs at the Cold War, 1947–61," p. 141; Lacayo, pp. 72–3.

9. Lenihan, "Hollywood Laughs at the Cold War, 1947–61," p. 140.

10. In *Gabriel Over the White House* (1933), a playboy bachelor president (Walter Huston) is transformed (with the aid of some divine intervention—in this case, the angel Gabriel) into an energetic crusader, albeit one who declares martial law and suspends crucial civil liberties, engineers a massive government employment plan, decisively and violently rids the country of bootleggers, and brings all of the nations together for a peace treaty. In essence, the film advocates a benevolent dictatorship in times of great national turmoil, such as the Great Depression.

11. Howard Fineman, "Last Action President," *Newsweek* (July 21, 1997) p. 66.

12. Stryker McGuire and David Ansen, "Stone Nixon," *Newsweek* (December 11, 1995), p. 66.

13. Oliver Stone, "A Filmmaker's Credo," *The Humanist* (September/October, 1996), p. 5.

14. Tom Junod, "Our Man in the White House," *Esquire* (April 1998), p. 70.

15. Richard Lacayo. "All the Presidents' Movies," *Time* (March 16, 1998), p. 73.

16. Dee Dee Myers quoted in "Primary Reaction," *U.S. News & World Report* (March 9, 1998), p. 15. For a positive appraisal of the film and Travolta's performance in particular, see Eric Pooley, "Tale of Two Bills," *Time* (March 16, 1998), pp. 62–3.

17. James Kaplan, "True Colors?" *New Yorker* (March 2, 1998), p. 24.

18. Senator-actor-lawyer Fred Thompson has extensive Hollywood-Washington connections, serving as U.S. Senator from Tennessee (1995–2003), appearing in several major films in the 1980s and 1990s, and serving as a lawyer on the Senate Watergate Committee.

19. It should be noted, however, that the moral center of *Primary Colors* is Stanton scandal-cover-upper extraordinaire Libby Holden (a brilliant Kathy Bates), who ultimately rejects the politics of innuendo and scandal-mongering, and takes her life when the Stantons reveal their willingness to acquiesce to sheer gutter politics.

20. Howard Fineman, "Last Action President," *Newsweek* (July 21, 1997), p. 67.

21. George Stephanopoulos, "White House Confidential," *Newsweek* (May 5, 1997), p. 34.

22. Stephanopoulos, "White House Confidential," p. 34.

23. Michael Sragow, "Gross Projections," *Mother Jones* (January 1990), p. 24.

24. Christopher Sharrett, "Cinema's Social Conscience," *USA Today* (January 1991), p. 31.

25. Thomas Patterson, *Out of Order* (New York: Vintage, 1993), p. 194.

26. See, for example, Joseph N. Cappella and Kathleen Hall Jamieson. *The Spiral of Cynicism: The Press and the Public Good* (New York: Oxford University Press, 1997).

27. Gallup Poll. "Clinton's Personal Characteristics." January 1, 1999. http://www.gallup.com/poll/trends/ptimage.asp. Accessed 9/11/2000.

28. Christopher Ruddy, *The Strange Death of Vincent Foster: An Investigation* (New York: Free Press, 1997).

29. For a detailed discussion of this "cottage industry" from a former insider, see David Brock, *Blinded by the Right: The Conscience of an Ex-Conservative* (New York: Crown, 2002). According to Brock, *The American Spectator,* The Federalist Society, and Richard Mellon Scaife were among the seminal movers and shakers funding politically-motivated investigations of the Clintons' sexual, political, and financial relationships.

30. Lacayo, "All the Presidents' Movies," p. 72.

31. Patterson, *Out of Order,* 196.

32. Ibid.

33. Stephanopoulos, "White House Confidential," p. 34.

34. See the scathing attack of the press in Richard Harwood, *Citizens and Politics: A View from Main Street America* (Dayton: The Kettering Foundation, 1991).

35. For example, note the believability not just of the average person but also of legitimate news outlets of the boorish behavior of the Clinton administration as it left office in January 2001. News stories were rampant of the pilfering of Air Force One, lewd photos left in the copying machines, computers damaged and phone lines cut. These wild allegations never were confirmed.

36. Richard Harwood, "The Alienated American Voter: Are the News Media to Blame?" *Brookings Review* (September 22, 1996), No. 4, Vol. 14, p. 32.

37. Bruce Handy, "Acting Presidents," *Time* (April 14, 1997), p. 99.

38. Handy, p. 99. Joe Eszterhas' book, *American Rhapsody* (New York: Knopf, 2000) contains passages speaking from President Clinton's private part.

39. An earlier version of the *West Wing* section of this chapter was presented at the 2001 meetings of the American Political Science Association. See: Kevan M. Yenerall, "The West Wing, the Presidency, and the Classroom: Left Wing or Right for the

Times?" Paper presented at the annual meeting of the American Political Science Association, San Francisco, California, August 30–September 2, 2001.

40. See for example: Tom DeLay's speech at the National Press Club on May 4, 2000; several NPR segments (from *Fresh Air* to *Weekend Edition*); lengthy coverage in *Brill's Content, Salon.com, Washington Post,* CNBC's *Headliners and Legends* television program, and even editorial pages of major newspapers. Members of the cast have visited the Clinton and Bush White Houses, lobbied members of Congress, and were even the topic of outgoing press secretary Joe Lockhart's satirical video sketch at the 2000 White House Correspondent's Dinner.

In terms of treatment by academics, see especially Peter C. Rollins and John E. O'Connor, eds. *The West Wing: The American Presidency as Television Drama* (Syracuse University Press, 2003); and *Hollywood's White House: The American Presidency in Film and History* (Lexington: The University Press of Kentucky, 2003). These books are the end product of several scholarly panels devoted entirely to *The West Wing* at the national "Presidents in Movies and Television" conference, sponsored by the Film & History League, held in Westlake, California, November 10–12, 2000.

Terence Smith of PBS' *NewsHour with Jim Lehrer* has devoted significant on-air time to *The West Wing,* including revealing interviews with Sorkin, Marlin Fitzwater, and Thomas Schlamme.

In terms of its "prime-time family friendliness," *The West Wing* was praised by the "Family Friendly Forum" for its lack of explicit sex and violence. The "Family Friendly Forum" is "a collaboration of 48 major advertisers created to encourage networks, studios, and production companies to create and air more programs during prime time that are relevant and interesting to parents and children." See: "'Gilmore Girls,' 'Malcolm' Win Family Nods," *Atlanta Journal-Constitution* (August 3, 2001).

Aaron Sorkin's *The West Wing Script Book,* featuring eight full-length scripts, was published by Newmarket Press.

41. Peter Ames Carlin, "'West Wing' Gives New Meaning to Link Between TV and Politics," *Portland Oregonian* (July 24, 2001).

42. Matthew Miller, "The Real White House," *Brill's Content* (March 2000), p. 90.

43. Donnalyn Pomper, "On *The West Wing:* White House Narratives That Journalism Cannot Tell," Paper presented at the "Images of American Presidents in Film and Television" Conference, November 10–12, 2000, Westlake Village, California.

44. Matthew Miller, "The Real White House," *Brill's Content* (March 2000), 88–95 + .

45. Matthew Miller, "The Real White House," *Brill's Content* (March 2000), p. 113.

46. Donnalyn Pomper, "On The West Wing: White House Narratives That Journalism Cannot Tell," Paper presented at the "Images of American Presidents in Film and Television" Conference, November 10–12, 2000, Westlake Village, California.

47. Terence Smith Interview with Marlin Fitzwater, *The NewsHour with Jim Lehrer,* September 8, 2000. PBS online: http://www.pbs.org/newshour/media/west_wing/fitzwater.html.

48. Sam Seaborn (played by Rob Lowe) left the Bartlet White House to run for Congress in the 4th season (2002–03). Seaborn was replaced by Will Bailey (Joshua Malina).

49. The numbers of viewers vary from week to week, obviously. Season two's two-part premiere, "In the Shadow of Two Gunmen," drew well over 20 million viewers. Summer reruns—especially season two reruns in the summer of 2001—have fared poorly, as have all summer 2001 reruns from the major networks.

50. John Carman, "Absurdity Dominates Fall Lineup," *San Francisco Chronicle* (August 1, 2001).

51. For example, Caryn James, the chief television critic of the *New York Times,* and John Carman of the *San Francisco Chronicle.*

52. Tom DeLay, "The Challenge of Cultural Renewal," speech delivered at the National Press Club, May 4, 2000. Accessed online via Rep. DeLay's web page: http://www.majoritywhip.gov/news.asp?formmode = SingleSpeech&id = 176.

    Tom DeLay (R-TX) represents the 22nd district of Texas. His homepage is http://tomdelay.house.gov/.

53. Ibid.

54. In a 2000 episode of Matt Lauer's *Headliners and Legends* devoted to *The West Wing,* Republic strategist and chief McCain 2000 aide Mike Murphy (also a part-time guest host of CNN's *Crossfire*) criticized and mocked the show for being overly simplistic by portraying Republicans as ghouls and Democrats as unimpeachable and squeaky-clean. For Pinkerton's criticism of the show on ideological grounds, see: Matthew Miller, "The Real White House," *Brill's Content* (March 2000), pp. 90, 113.

55. Matthew Miller, "The Real White House," *Brill's Content* (March 2000), 88–95 + .

56. Matthew Miller, "The Real White House," *Brill's Content* (March 2000), p. 113.

57. John Matviko, "Organization's First Conference—A Major Success," *Rewind: The Newsletter of the Film and History League* 1:1 (March 2001); Jennifer Ruark, "Hot Type," *Chronicle of Higher Education* (January 5, 2001), A18.

Chapter 5

1. "Faithful servant" in *The Birth of a Nation* was the title given to African Americans who remained in some degree of servitude to, or performed household duties for, white families in the South after the Civil War. The film depicts "faithful servants" as loyal, loving, caring, bighearted souls who despise the freed blacks and their Northern "carpetbagger" friends. In fact, in the film they fight the evil, agitating, and often sex-crazed emancipated African Americans.

2. As membership in the Klan increased steadily in the 1920s, many would cite the heroic portrayal of the Klan in *The Birth of The Nation* as a contributing factor.

3. Leon F. Litwak, "The Birth of a Nation," in Michael C. Carnes, ed., *Past Imperfect: History According to the Movies* (New York: Owl Books, 1996), 136.

4. In fact, the NAACP would publish a pamphlet entitled, "Fighting A Vicious Film: Protest Against The Birth of a Nation." In the pamphlet the film is referred to as "three hours of filth." Available at the Library of Congress website: http://lcweb2.loc.gov/service/rbc/rbc0001/2001/20010102001fi/20010102001fi.pdf

5. For the Wilson quote see Litwak, 136–141.

6. Litwak, 136.

7. ibid.

8. "Tommy Johnson": a composite of legendary blues artist Robert Johnson (1911–1938). The mythology surrounding Johnson's stellar guitar playing is that he sold his soul to the devil in return for amazing guitar skills. For more on this matter, see Robert Johnson's classic blues rumination, "Cross Road Blues." Johnson, a native of Hazelhurst, Mississippi, died under mysterious circumstances near Greenwood, Mississippi. For more information on Robert Johnson, as well as other American blues legends, see: http://www.thebluehighway.com/tbh1.html.

9. Ethan and Joel Coen, *O Brother, Where Art Thou?* (London: Faber and Faber, 2000), 84.

10. For a fascinating recounting of the wide-ranging political influence wielded by the White Citizens Councils throughout the South in the 1950s–1960s, see President Jimmy Carter's *Turning Point: A Candidate, a State, and a Nation Come of Age* (Times Books, 1992), which chronicles Carter's first major campaign in Georgia.

11. On December 5, 2002, at a 100th birthday celebration on Capitol Hill honoring outgoing Senator Strom Thurmond (R-SC), Trent

Lott said the following: *"I want to say this about my state: when Strom Thurmond ran for president, we voted for him. We're proud of it. And if the rest of the country had followed our lead, we wouldn't have had all these problems over all these years, either."* Bipartisan criticism of Lott's statement followed, and, by the end of the year, Sen. Bill Frist (R-TN), became the White House's choice for Senate Majority Leader.

12. Also of note is the overwhelming success of *O Brother's* soundtrack, a tribute to vintage Appalachian, folk, country, and gospel music. The Coens and producer T-Bone Burnett introduced millions to the work of the Stanley Brothers (especially Dr. Ralph Stanley) Gillian Welch, and Alison Krauss and Union Station, among many others, and captured the Album of the Year Grammy in February 2002. Two highly successful nationwide concert tours—dubbed "Down from the Mountain"—commenced in the winter and summer of 2002. To date, the *O Brother* soundtrack has sold well over six million copies.

13. This is the official "tagline" of the film. See the Internet Movie Database: http://us.imdb.com/Title?0285742.

14. Desson Howe, "The 'Monster's' Within," *Washington Post* (February 8, 2002).

15. Hackman, who portrayed FBI agent Joseph Sullivan, lost out to friend Dustin Hoffman, who won the Best Actor Oscar for his role in Barry Levinson's *Rain Man.*

16. Concerning the portrayal of African Americans and other criticisms of the film, see Chafe, William H. (1996) "Mississippi Burning," in *Past Imperfect: History According to the Movies,* Mark C. Carnes, ed. (New York: Owl Books).

17. A good companion piece to the two provocative television segments would be Moore's book chapters "Why O. J. is Innocent" in *Downsize This!* (1996) and "Kill Whitey" in *Stupid White Men* (2001).

18. See the excellent Wallace timeline provided by PBS's American Experience *George Wallace: Settin' the Woods on Fire* web site: http://www.pbs.org/wgbh/amex/wallace/timeline/index_3.html.

19. Eric Foner, "Matewan," in Mark C. Carnes, ed., *Past Imperfect* (New York: Owl Books, 1996), 204.

20. Hesson Dowe, *Washington Post* (October 16, 1987).

21. Foner, 204.

22. See the back cover of the official VHS copy of *American Dream,* Prestige Films and HBO Video, 1992.

23. Peter Rachleff, *Hard-Pressed in the Heartland* (Boston: South End Press, 1993), 5.

24. ibid.

25. "Cradle to grave" is Tom Kay's characterization of Moore's view that corporations have a responsibility to the communities and the workers beyond the company's bottom line.
26. Ernest Giglio, *Here's Looking at You* (New York: Peter Lang, 2000), 43.
27. Moore's response to allegations of inflated or false unemployment numbers—see CNN's *People in the News* profile of Moore, October 2002.
28. "Gun Exposé Voted Top Factual Film," *The BBC News World Edition,* December 13, 2002: http://news.bbc.co.uk/2/hi/entertainment/2571735.stm

Chapter 6

1. Five to ten percent estimate: see Ernest Giglio, *Here's Looking at You* (New York: Peter Lang, 2000).
2. For further discussion of *Primary Colors,* see Chapter Four, "The American Presidency."
3. Ernest Giglio, *Here's Looking at You* (New York: Peter Lang, 2000), 98.
4. Giglio, 94.
5. Bob Roberts' album titles are all stolen from legendary Bob Dylan works. Bob Roberts rips off the classic Dylan albums *The Freewheelin' Bob Dylan* (1963), *The Times They Are A-Changin'* (1964), and *Blonde on Blonde* (1966).
6. In the 1988 presidential campaign, George Bush's campaign attacked Democratic nominee Michael Dukakis for his record on crime as Governor of Massachusetts. One famous ad that attacked a Massachusetts parole program featured a revolving door prison with hardened criminals being let out for parole. Willie Horton was a man who, while on parole for murder, raped a woman. A group of Bush supporters aired ads featuring Horton's face and attacked Dukakis as soft on crime.
7. Ray Richmond and Antonia Coffman, ed., *The Simpsons: A Complete Guide to Our Favorite Family* (New York: HarperPerennial, 1997), 38.
8. ibid.
9. ibid.
10. Marge is not the only Simpson to support incumbent Governor Mary Bailey: Lisa Simpson, the intellectual, agitating 2nd grade daughter of Marge and Homer, sports a shirt that reads: "If I were old enough to vote, I'd vote for Mary Bailey."
11. Richmond and Coffman, 38.
12. The official "tagline" for *Bulworth.*

13. Edward Guthmann, "Beatty's Rap: Hilarious `Bulworth'—the Truth Sets a Senator Free," *San Francisco Chronicle* (May 22, 1998). Accessed online: http://www.sfgate.com/cgi-bin/article.cgi?f = /c/ a/1998/05/22/DD19624.DTL.

14. ibid.

15. ibid.

16. Tim Robbins announced the plot-line of the Bob Roberts sequel in an interview on ABC's talk show *The View* in the fall of 2002.

17. Desson Howe, "A Winning 'Candidate,'" *Washington Post* (July 13, 1996). Accessed online: http://www.washingtonpost.com/wp-srv/ style/longterm/review96/perfectcandidatehowe.htm.

18. In 2000, Chuck Robb lost his bid for another term to George Allen.

19. ibid.

20. The official "tagline" for *The War Room*.

21. *The War Room* was also nominated for, but did not win, the Academy Award for Best Documentary.

22. http://www.pbs.org/weta/voteforme/about.htm.

23. Their credits include installments in the landmark *Eyes on the Prize* civil rights series.

24. http://www.pbs.org/weta/voteforme.

25. From the official "Vote for Me" home page: http://www.pbs.org/ weta/voteforme/about.htm.

26. It was a good night for President Bush and the Republican Party: Republicans regained control of the closely divided Senate and picked up seats in the House of Representatives. It was only the third time since the Lincoln presidency that the president's party gained House seats in midterm elections, and the first time for Republicans. Nationwide, the country was nearly split down the middle: roughly 40,000 votes would have tipped the balance of power to the Democratic Party. Survey research suggests that a stunning 25% of the voters made their choices in the final weekend before the midterm elections or on Election Day itself.

27. Pennebaker's credits include such classics as *Don't Look Back, Monterey Pop, The War Room,* and *Primary.*

28. *New York Times* content cited in Eric Boehlert, "The Press vs. Al Gore," *Rolling Stone* (December 6–13, 2001). For further evidence of the press' characterization of Gore, see media critic Howard Kurtz's insightful "Media Notes" columns throughout the fall of 2000 in *The Washington Post.* Alexandra Pelosi discussed her film and reporters' perception of Gore (as distant) and Bush (as chummy) on Comedy Central's *The Daily Show with Jon Stewart* on November 12, 2002.

29. For the press's increasingly hostile treatment of Gore, see: Jane

Hall, "Gore Media Coverage—Playing Hardball," *Columbia Journalism Review* (September/October 2000). Hall's original research and review of the Pew Charitable Trusts and Project for Excellence in Journalism study can be accessed online at http://www.cjr.org/year/00/3/hall.asp.

30. Results of the Project for Excellence in Journalism media study cited in Jane Hall, "Gore Media Coverage—Playing Hardball," *Columbia Journalism Review* (September/October 2000).

31. The media's tendency to cover campaigns using a game schema rather than a governing framework, as well as the focus on "character," is covered extensively in Thomas Patterson, *Out of Order* (New York: Vintage, 1994). The focus on strategy, process, and tactics is also revealed in the fall 2000 study by the Project for Excellence in Journalism. See also Harvard University professor Thomas Patterson's web site "The Vanishing Voter Project" (http://www.vanishingvoter.org) and his book, *The Vanishing Voter* (New York: Knopf, 2002).

32. Alexandra Pelosi is no stranger to the most serious side of politics. In addition to her work with NBC covering George W. Bush in the 2000 campaign, politics is a Pelosi family tradition: her grandfather was mayor of Baltimore and her mother, Nancy Pelosi became the highest-ranking woman in the history of the U.S. House of Representatives. Shortly after the 2002 midterm elections, Nancy Pelosi, then the Democratic Party's Minority Whip, became Minority Leader for the House Democrats, replacing Missouri congressman Richard Gephardt.

33. For further in-depth discussion of these issues and the role of third parties in the United States, see Steven J. Rosenstone, Roy L. Behr, and Edward Lazarus, *Third Parties in America,* 2nd ed. (Princeton: Princeton University Press), 1996.

34. Maine and Nebraska do not use the "winner take all" system employed by the other 48 states and the District of Columbia.

35. When he can't recall his name, Homer refers to Bob Dole as "Mumbly Joe."

36. Richmond and Coffman, ed., 211.

37. ibid.

38. ibid.

Chapter 7

1. For a discussion of why Mearsheimer thinks that the end of the Cold War might mean more instability and war, see his articles: John J. Mearsheimer (1990) "Why We'll Soon Miss the Cold War,"

Atlantic Monthly (August 1990), pp. 35–50; and John J. Mearsheimer (1990) "Back to the Future: Instability in Europe After the Cold War" *International Security* 15 (1): 5–56 (Summer 1990). For an example of devising a foreign policy based on which states are powerful and might become powerful see John J. Mearsheimer (2001) "America the Great Pacifier," *Foreign Affairs* 80 (5) 46–61 (September/October 2001).

2. Samuel P. Huntington (1996) *The Clash of Civilizations and the Remaking of World Order* (New York: Simon and Schuster).

3. Bruce Russet (1993) *Grasping the Democratic Peace: Principles for a Post–Cold War World* (Princeton: Princeton University Press); and Michael W. Doyle (1986) "Liberalism and World Politics," *American Political Science Review* 80 (4): 1151–1169 (December 1986).

4. Francis Fukuyama (1989) "The End of History," *The National Interest* (Summer 1989); and Francis Fukuyama (1992).

5. Catherine Lovatt (1999) "Europe: What are East and West?" *Central European Review* 23, available at: http://www.ce-review.rg/99/23/lovatt23.html.

6. Jay Leyda, *A History of the Russian and Soviet Film* (New York: Macmillan, 1960), 350.

7. William K. Everson, *American Silent Film* (New York: Oxford University Press, 1978), 292.

8. Carl von Clausewitz, *On War* (edited and translated by Michael Howard and Peter Paret). (Princeton: Princeton University Press, 1976).

9. Roger Ebert's three-star review of *Thirteen Days, Chicago Sun-Times,* January 12, 2001.

10. Paul Boyer, "Dr. Strangelove," in *Past Imperfect: History According to the Movies,* Mark C. Carnes, ed. (New York: Owl Books, 1996), 266–269.

11. Carnes, 267.

12. Carnes, 266.

13. Carnes, 269.

14. Carnes, 266.

15. See Nils Petter Gleditsch, Håvard Strand, Mikael Eriksson, Margareta Sollenberg, and Peter Wallensteen (2001) "Armed Conflict 1946–99: A New Dataset," presented at the 42nd Annual Convention of the International Studies Association, Chicago, IL, February 20–24, 2001. Available at: http://www.isanet.org/achive/ngp.html.

16. The official website for the inquiry into the events of Bloody Sunday can be found at *http://www.bloody-sunday-inquiry.org.uk*.

17. Sean Anderson and Stephen Sloan, *Historical Dictionary of Terrorism* (London: Scarecrow Press, 1995).

18. Barry James, "International Terrorism Expected to Worsen in the 1980s," *United Press International,* August 12, 1981.

19. See, for example, the vote at the United Nations to postpone work on the Comprehensive Convention Against Terrorism following the September 11th attacks when diplomats found it difficult to find common ground on how to define terrorism. News reports can be found at "Terrorism convention: Fresh talks in January," *The Hindu* (November 23, 2001); and, "U.N. Deadlocked on Anti-Terrorism Treaty," available at: Inter Press Service World News, http://www.oneworld.net/ips2/oct01/01_13_005.html.

20. George Rosie, *Directory of International Terrorism* (Edinburgh: Mainstream Publishing, 1996).

21. See Chris Cobb "A Tragedy Coming to the Western World," *Ottawa Citizen* (June 2, 2002), page A9.

Chapter 8

1. Paddy Chayefsky, *The Collected Works of Paddy Chayefsky: The Screenplays* (New York: Applause Books, 1995), 125–126.

2. *Network's* prophetic commentary on globalization is discussed in chapter two, Liberal Ideologies: Democracy and Capitalism.

3. Chayefsky, 183.

4. For more on the light (press) vs. dark (politicians and government) aspect of *All the President's Men,* as well as criticism of the film, see: William E. Leuchtenburg, "All the President's Men," in Mark C. Carnes, ed., *Past Imperfect* (New York: Owl Books, 1996), pp. 292–295.

5. See *The Simpsons* episode, "The Trash of the Titans": original airdate, April 26, 1998.

6. Harry Harrison, *Make Room! Make Room!* (New York: Berkley Publishing Company, 1967).

7. Wesley Morris' review from the *San Francisco Examiner* (March 17, 2000): http://www.sfgate.com/cgi-bin/article.cgi?f = /e/a/2000/03/17/WEEKEND6120.dtl.

8. From Roger Ebert's review of *Erin Brockovich:* http://www.suntimes.com/ebert/ebert_reviews/2000/03/031703.html.

9. http://www.the-numbers.com/movies/2000/ERINB.html.

10. The Illinois case sparked a great deal of controversy and debate. For a review of the events leading up to the suspension see Maureen O'Donnell, "Illinois to Stop Executions: Ryan Panel to Study 13 Wrongful Convictions," *Chicago Sun-Times* (January 31, 2000), p. 3; and, Dirk Johnson, "Illinois, Citing Faulty Verdicts, Bars Executions," *New York Times* (February 1, 2000), p. A1. While some argued that this evidence was a call for fundamentally reconsid-

ering the death penalty others argued that this was not the case—see David Frum, "The Justice Americans Demand," *New York Times* (February 4, 2000), p. A29.

11. Mary Dejevsky, "US Implicated in 'Missing' Death," *The Independent* (October 9, 1999), p. 6; Ben Macintyre, "Papers suggest CIA role in Chile killings," *The Times* (February 14, 2000); and, Diana Jean Schemo, "F.B.I. Watched an American Who Was Killed in Chile Coup," *New York Times* (July 1, 2000), p. A6.

12. For an examination of the impact of "Holocaust" on television history see the Museum of Broadcast History website page on the mini-series at: http://www.museum.tv/archives/etv/H/htmlH/holocaust/holocaust.htm.

13. See James Lardner, "Making History." *New Republic* (May 13, 1978) and Lance Morrow, "Television and the Holocaust." *Time* (New York) (1 May 1978).

14. Elie Wiesel, "Trivializing the Holocaust: Semi-Fact and Semi-Fiction," *New York Times* (16 April 1978).

15. For the film's official website, see http://www.genocidefactor.com/.

16. Stephen D. Krasner, *Structural Conflict: The Third World Against Global Liberalism.* (Berkeley: University of California Press, 1985). p. 267.

17. Rhonda Howard, *Colonialism and Underdevelopment in Ghana* (New York: Africana Publishing Company, 1978), p. 19.

18. Robert S. Brown, "Conditionality: a new form of colonialism? With the African continent in economic crisis, more and more countries are finding that they have no other option but to strike a deal with the IMF; but at what cost to their political and economic sovereignty?" *Africa Report* 29: 14–18 (1984).

19. One of the preeminent histories of this period and the events in Congo is contained in Adam Hochschild, *King Leopold's Ghost: A Story of Greed, Terror, and Heroism in Colonial Africa* (Boston: Houghton Mifflin, 1998).

20. The film *Lumumba* is the second project that director Raoul Peck has taken on concerning the life of Patrice Lumumba. In 1991 he directed the film, *Lumumba—Death of a Prophet.*

Politics
Media &
Popular Culture

David A. Schultz, *General Editor*

This series is devoted to both scholarly and teaching materials that examine the ways politics, the media, and popular culture interact and influence social and political behavior. Subject matters to be addressed in this series include, but will not be limited to: media and politics; political communication; television, politics, and mass culture; mass media and political behavior; and politics and alternative media and telecommunications such as computers. Submission of single-author and collaborative studies, as well as collections of essays are invited.

Authors wishing to have works considered for this series should contact:

Peter Lang Publishing
Acquisitions Department
275 Seventh Avenue, 28th floor
New York, New York 10001

To order other books in this series, please contact our Customer Service Department at:

800-770-LANG (within the U.S.)
(212) 647-7706 (outside the U.S.)
(212) 647-7707 FAX

or browse online by series at:

WWW.PETERLANGUSA.COM